Distance Manipulation

Northwestern University Press
Studies in Russian Literature and Theory

Founding Editor
  Gary Saul Morson

General Editor
  Caryl Emerson

Consulting Editors
  Carol Avins
  Robert Belknap
  Robert Louis Jackson
  Elliott Mossman
  Alfred Rieber
  William Mills Todd III
  Alexander Zholkovsky

Distance Manipulation

THE RUSSIAN MODERNIST SEARCH
FOR A NEW DRAMA

Joanna Kot

NORTHWESTERN UNIVERSITY PRESS / EVANSTON, ILLINOIS

Northwestern University Press
Evanston, Illinois 60208-4210

Copyright © 1999 by Northwestern University Press. Published 1999.
All rights reserved.

Printed in the United States of America

ISBN 0-8101-1654-5

Library of Congress Cataloging-in-Publication Data

Kot, Joanna, 1959–
    Distance manipulation : the Russian modernist search for a new drama / Joanna Kot.
       p. cm. — (Studies in Russian literature and theory)
    Includes bibliographical references.
    ISBN 0-8101-1654-5
    1. Russian drama—20th century—History and criticism.
2. Aesthetic distance. 3. Modernism (Literature)—Russia.
I. Title. II. Series.
PG3086.K68   1999
891.72'309—dc21   99-27761
                                                            CIP

The paper used in this publication meets the minimum requirements of the American National Standard for Information Sciences—Permanence of Paper for Printed Library Materials, ANSI Z39.48-1984.

Contents

Introduction   1

Chapter One   Anton Chekhov's *The Cherry Orchard*   23

Chapter Two   Zinaida Gippius's *Holy Blood*   49

Chapter Three   Fedor Sologub's *The Triumph of Death*   63

Chapter Four   Aleksandr Blok's *The Puppet Show*   83

Chapter Five   Viacheslav Ivanov's *Tantalus*   107

Conclusion   123

Notes   131

Works Cited   141

Index   163

Introduction

THE FOLLOWING STUDY analyzes distance manipulation in a number of Russian modernist plays that estrange most audiences. It begins with Anton Chekhov's *The Cherry Orchard* (1904), which is used as a springboard to discuss more experimental dramas. These plays include Zinaida Gippius's *Holy Blood* (1900), Fedor Sologub's *The Triumph of Death* (1906, 1907), Aleksandr Blok's *The Puppet Show* (1906), and Viacheslav Ivanov's *Tantalus* (1906).

The study shows the various techniques through which distance is manipulated in each play. Both elements that increase the distance (distancing) and those that decrease distance (emotive) are described. This analysis further defines the proportion between the two directions of movement, revealing that in some of the works distance dominates, in others emotiveness controls the movement, and in still others there exists a balance between the two. In addition, the study proves that in these experimental dramas the relationship between distance and genre—traditionally a close one—continues to be safeguarded. However, as will be shown, though the relationship between distance and genre persists, its nature is very often changed, sometimes drastically. This analysis reveals that a straightforward and direct connection between the "size" of the distancing and a canonical genre, as sanctioned by tradition and recipient expectations, is disrupted in these works. This disruption is due to the fact that each mixes several genres or utilizes only parts of one, rather than being written in the puristic mode of a single genre. Nevertheless, the continued existence of a link between distance and genre—even if in a changed form—allows for the occurrence of at least a minimal emotional identification (one of several types) between the recipient and some aspect of the play. Despite the difficulties created for the recipient by radical distance manipulation, the aesthetic reception of the most successful of these texts includes more than an intellectual reaction. Their reception involves an emotional component through which the work can continue to fulfill an ethical function. Finally, this volume explains how in terms of distance manipulation different elements in a play carry different weights. For example, the stylistic usage of language continues to be of overwhelming importance, despite the emphasis on nonverbal communication in modernist drama.

Distance Manipulation

The analyzed plays illustrate the great diversity of paths that modernist playwrights chose in their search for new dramatic forms. Some of the works appeal to the popular tastes and imagination of the recipient, yet, as will be demonstrated, this does not guarantee their dramatic success. Others choose more esoteric and less visible means of transforming tradition, with varying results.

At this juncture, a brief definition of distance should be helpful.[1] Every recipient when confronting an artistic creation brings with him his own cultural norms that he engages in the confrontation. In addition, the work offers its own conventions, which may be called "expectations." Together, the norms and expectations serve as one of the principal elements stimulating in the recipient an "awareness of fictionality," that is, the realization that he personally is distanced from and not involved in the object or events appearing before him. In turn, this awareness gives the recipient the freedom to engage emotionally in the experience of artistic reception and yet retain the distance of fictionality. The actual nature and degree of engagement will be dictated mostly by the inner conventions of the work, which should stimulate expectations desired by the playwright. However, the background and state of mind of the recipient do play a certain role here as well. Furthermore, traditionally, the distance—in other words the position of the work vis-à-vis the recipient—and the type of identification that results from it are more or less fixed in any given work and are closely connected to its genre. For example, one expects greater distance, and thus lesser identification, in traditional comedy than in traditional tragedy. Modern drama, on the other hand, very often introduces a shifting distance—continuously drawing in and pushing away the recipient and thus undercutting the genre expectations which he may have. Nevertheless, differences notwithstanding, depending on either the "size" of the set distance or the balance of the shifting distances, the end result is always a greater or lesser emotional identification with some aspect of the work, even when shifting occurs.[2] Thus, there exist two types of distance in the process of aesthetic reception. The first type comes with the awareness of fictionality—and stays throughout the duration of the play. The second kind is a positioning that takes place on the macro-level of the play when the work's inner conventions begin shaping the type of identification that will occur. The distance manipulation discussed in this study refers to the second type, as the first is a given in all cases.

Distance then plays an essential role in all aesthetic reception of art. It is, therefore, present in all aesthetically valid art, including drama. Something new, however, happens in the twentieth century. An unprecedentedly large number of artistic creations—in fact the majority of what critics, scholars, reviewers, and audiences consider to be contemporary, serious, innovative, and great works—manipulate distance in such a way as to estrange the recipient. In terms of theater it is enough to consider the reception of such by no means very recent plays as those of Bertolt Brecht, Eugène Ionesco, or Samuel Beckett. To this day, theater managers still prefer to stage Tennessee Williams's gritty realism or William Shakespeare's classics, not to mention lighter fare with even more mass appeal, than so-called experimental works. This predilection is based on economic factors which show that, though the audience may be intellectually intrigued by a performance of *Waiting for Godot* or *Mother Courage,* it will prefer and respond more emotionally to *The Glass Menagerie* or *Much Ado about Nothing.* Today's dramatic critics often do sense the fact that they are intentionally being pushed away and confused in the innovative works, that as recipients they are purposefully being made very uncomfortable. Nevertheless, discussions on this subject are most often limited to a single technique that does not do justice to the complexity of the phenomenon. At times the critics' sensations are translated into statements about "alienation" and "experimentation."[3] However, the term "alienation" is discussed for the most part as a theme in literature and not as a formal element of the structure.[4] Of course, Bertolt Brecht's "techniques of alienation" (what are called "distancing techniques" in the present study) have received scholarly attention, but they are only a small part of a much larger picture.

For this reason, a thorough analysis that could answer some important questions arising out of distance manipulation would lead to a better understanding of the development of all of twentieth-century drama. Such questions include the following: Through what techniques and elements is distance manipulated? Are strong distancing effects balanced with emotive elements or are the former allowed to dominate texts? How does innovative distance manipulation in modern works affect the perception and function of genres? Why are so many of these plays rejected by recipients? How is the process of reception and recipient involvement changed?

Distance is not the only distinguishing feature of modern drama. However, the importance of this element—a normal aspect of all reception of art throughout history—manifestly increases in contemporary dramatic works. Frequently, distance is manipulated in modern plays in ways that are unexpected to the recipient, often greatly so. Furthermore, what is most unusual is the fact that shifting distance can be observed in twentieth-century plays, not in conjunction with the demands of different genres, but within one individual work.[5]

Such profound estrangement as that witnessed toward many twentieth-century plays is an unusual phenomenon in theatrical history. In earlier periods, the innovative works that estranged recipients to such a degree that they went unrecognized—or, though recognized were persistently avoided during the lifetime of their creator—were few and far between. The first inklings of a major change to come, at least in theoretical terms, date back to the end of the eighteenth and beginning of the nineteenth centuries, when the sci-

Distance Manipulation

entific revolution was slowly but surely undermining the idea of a religious *theatrum mundi*. It is during this transitional period between neoclassicism and romanticism that Friedrich Schiller, as well as the Schlegel brothers, Friedrich and August, make theoretical statements in which they warn about the dangers of too much identification. In other words, they see some form of distance as a necessary component of the process of aesthetic reception.[6] The Schlegels even seem to suggest the need of something akin to a shifting distance—the distinguishing feature of twentieth-century literature and, more important, drama. Similarly, one can observe how neoclassical comedy combines with elements of sentimentalism and preromanticism to produce innovative effects which can be labeled "distancing." For example, genres, styles, and conventions are mixed in surprising ways in such plays as Pierre Beaumarchais's *The Marriage of Figaro* and in Gotthold Lessing's *Mirra von Barnhelm*.[7]

Romanticism furthers the seeds of change in the realm of distance manipulation. The subjectivity and individualism of romantic art adds to a rift between "serious art" and "popular art," which emerges during the nineteenth century and continues to grow. Nevertheless, formal, as opposed to thematic, estranging tendencies still appear in a rather embryonic form during this period. This is due to the fact that, for all the romantic artist's subjectivity and loneliness, he still stresses his ties to his people, his nation; he is above them, but he is also a representative of their aspirations. In other words, the modern artist's spiritual crisis has not yet reached acute proportions and he has not yet begun to reject all existing philosophies and paradigms. Therefore, most often estrangement is limited to the thematic level—concerning protagonists but not the recipient. Examples of such thematic treatment include Alfred de Vigny's *Chatterton* and Friedrich Schiller's *Maria Stuart*. On the other hand, formal experimentation with distance manipulation exists as an isolated phenomenon only in a handful of romantic plays, most often in those that were influenced by Shakespearean drama. Examples include such works as Alfred de Musset's *Lorenzaccio* and Georg Büchner's *Woyzeck*. The only actual group of Romantic plays that radically experiments with formal aspects of distancing is to be found in Polish literature, namely in Adam Mickiewicz's *Forefathers' Eve, Part III*, Juliusz Słowacki's *Salomea's Silver Dream*, Zygmunt Krasiński's *Un-Divine Comedy,* and later the "white tragedies" of Cypriot Kamil Norwid. The diversity of style and methods of distancing within this group foreshadows the variety of modernistic experiments.

Thus, the theoretical groundwork for experimenting with distance manipulation had already been laid almost a century earlier. However, it is only around 1880 with the beginning of modernism that one can observe the sudden appearance of an unprecedented stream of works that might be called "estranging." They are radically new in form; they distance and confuse the recipient. By now it has been well established that the weltanschauung of modernism is the result of far-reaching social, political, economic, and cul-

Introduction

tural changes, which date from the end of the eighteenth century. These changes finally develop and coalesce to such a degree that the majority of modernist intellectuals and artists begins to experience an acute sense of estrangement from the world around them. It is important to note that this phenomenon of alienation occurs against the background of a majority that is energetically and optimistically participating in the booming capitalism that most of Europe and America enjoyed in the nineteenth century.[8] This majority, in other words, the principal consumers of art, will, as the twentieth century progresses, come to share, at least to some degree, in the same spiritual crisis. Therefore, over time these consumers will become a bit more receptive to experimental works. However, at the beginning of the century that is rarely the case. Nevertheless, what does happen, often despite the absence of a significant audience, is that the creative minority actualizes its sensation of estrangement in artistic works. It does so, first of all, by introducing estrangement (often then called "alienation" or simply "loneliness") as one of the major themes of modernist literature, especially in those works that are classified as fin-de-siècle.[9] The theme has continued to dominate art till our own day. Much more important for this study is the fact that the artists' spiritual crisis also brings about radical experimentation with the form of literary and dramatic works. Thus, there appears at the turn of the century a body of literature, and more particularly of plays, that contains elements greatly estranging the average recipient from the fictional worlds presented in them and making an emotional response to them more difficult, if not impossible, to achieve. This occurs quite some time before more recent theories such as Bertolt Brecht's "theater of alienation." It is also contrary to the theoretical declarations of most of the authors involved. Furthermore, the phenomenon is very widespread and playwrights who produce such dramas can be found in practically every European modernist literature. They range from William Butler Yeats and John Synge in Ireland to Aleksandr Blok and Nikolai Evreinov in Russia, from August Strindberg in Sweden to Alfred Jarry and Paul Claudel in France, from Gabriele D'Annunzio in Italy to Hugo von Hofmannsthal and Franz Wedekind in Germany, from Tadeusz Miciński and Stanisław Wyspiański in Poland to Maurice Maeterlinck in Belgium. A similar situation can also, of course, be observed in poetry and prose.

Modernism then serves as an acute turning point both in terms of experimentation with distance manipulation and in terms of the spiritual crisis that brings about such experimentation. The importance of this period for the development of modern drama cannot be overstated. Chronologically within modernism, symbolism was the first movement that engaged in these experiments. Both the practice and theory of the symbolists influenced subsequent modernist groups, such as, for example, the futurists—even if they denied the influence. Often these later avant-gardists actualized the most extreme of the symbolist ideas. It is thus definitely worth considering the source, as it were, of modern dramatic experiments. Chekhov, of course, was not a symbolist and cannot really be pigeonholed by such a designation. Nevertheless, his work does contain elements of symbolism. Above all, he serves as a rare example of a brilliant kind of experimentation that succeeded. For that reason, the following study focuses on a Chekhov play and on a number of symbolist dramas that clearly demonstrate a radical approach toward distance. However, before beginning the actual analysis of specific works, some theoretical aspects need to be discussed. Therefore, the rest of this chapter considers the following matters: a more precise definition of distance and drama; why the choice of drama over other literary forms; what problems with reception arise when distance is no longer connected so clearly to genre; what is meant by the term "traditional" that is so often juxtaposed with the "estranging" works, but which is rarely defined by critics; and, finally, why these particular works were chosen for scrutiny.

Distance as a normal aspect of all aesthetic reception has been, in theory at least, widely recognized throughout the twentieth century. Though the characteristics ascribed to the phenomenon do vary, its existence has been generally accepted since Edward Bullough's 1912 groundbreaking article "'Psychical Distance' as a Factor in Art and an Aesthetic Principle." Distance has been discussed in the writings of many practitioners of drama, as well as in the works of major dramatic theorists. It has also been acknowledged in the statements of semioticians and in sociological discussions of reception.[10] Even Jerzy Grotowski—who in his experimentation with the so-called Poor Theater desires to abolish distance—is forced to admit that once distance is abolished he no longer has theater or art, but a religious ritual.[11] Implicitly the concept has been intimated as far back as Samuel Johnson and Samuel Taylor Coleridge. Furthermore, as has been mentioned, the concept of distance is discussed by Friedrich Schiller and the Schlegels. It is also recognized by Immanuel Kant and Gotthold Lessing. However, as has been explained, for the most part the possibilities of distance manipulation are not practically applied in actual plays until modernism.

As stated earlier, the first moment of distance in the process of aesthetic reception is the appearance of a tacit awareness in the recipient. This is a recognition of the fact that the images of a work or performance that he is confronting are fictitious.[12] This awareness of fictionality occurs in the recipient as a result of stimulation by what are usually called "norms." Most of these norms evolve naturally over time within a particular culture or community. Thus, there may be difficulties in reacting to a work whose conventions develop in a culture very different from that of the recipient.[13] Moreover, these conventions exist on two levels. On the broader level any recipient approaches an aesthetic experience with the background of everything that he has learned, everything that is a part of his culture. The very act of intending to go to a theatrical performance, of sitting in a plush chair alongside

Introduction

other spectators, activates the recipient's communal memory. The act awakens within him certain cultural conventions and literary traditions and thus leads to an awareness of fictionality. Furthermore, a number of basic elements, such as symmetry and rhythm, are also activated at such a moment. These elements, even if they "have no pronounced aesthetic value; nevertheless, [. . .] function as a regulating criterion of aesthetic value."[14] On the more specific level, there exist the conventions activated by the given work. More accurately known as "expectations," they are created in the recipient from the very first word, sound, or image that confronts him. These expectations are an amorphous, shifting cultural web of conventions, partially dependent on the historical period and the country, but, overall functioning homogeneously to create a particular "traditional" image. Thus, in Western art the conventions appearing in a given work set the recipient up to expect a particular type of fictitious world. For example, in literature this may mean the expectation of a definite genre, style, character, story, or experience. This first moment of distance is a given in all cases.

Once the fictionality of a work is tacitly accepted, the recipient feels emotionally cushioned and safe. He knows that the matter does not concern him personally. This gives him the freedom to engage in the work "with seriousness," in other words, to become deeply emotionally involved, as if the fiction were a reality, though all the while retaining the distance of "fictional awareness."[15] Volition, agreeing to respond as if dealing with fact and not fiction is, therefore, an important part of aesthetic reception. The recipient must be willing to engage freely in the process, for if he refuses to do that—perhaps "not being in the mood" or being preoccupied with his personal problems—he will not "experience" the aesthetic reception. On the other hand, once he has willed to become involved he can then react emotionally, can experience fear, hope, envy, love, etc. He can permit himself to feel pseudovicarious emotions that may actually be stronger than "real" emotions, since he feels safe enough to "let go," knowing that there won't be any personal consequences.

The precise nature of this engagement is determined primarily by the work. Undoubtedly, however, the personal cultural and emotional baggage of the recipient plays a part in the engagement. The latter is made clear in Bullough's example in which the recipient of a production of Othello is a jealous husband betrayed by his wife. The husband does not "experience" a real aesthetic process because he becomes too personally involved in the events occurring on stage. Nevertheless, personal elements not withstanding, the more important factors determining the nature of the recipient's engagement are the conventions and structure of the work itself. It is at the moment of the recipient's initial engagement—and after the moment of his awareness of fictionality—that the artist manipulates distance in such a fashion as to establish the type of relationship between the recipient and the work that he desires. The artist then continues to maintain the chosen distance throughout the duration of the play, or, as in modern drama, to shift it continuously in unexpected ways.

The difficulty of discussing distance in relation to twentieth-century art is that all great art in one way or another breaks the recipient's expectations and surprises him. And yet twentieth-century theoreticians and artists often talk about distance as if they were the first to discover it. Actually, what really seems to change in modern times is, first of all, the degree or strength of the distance as experienced by the recipient. In an unprecedentedly large number of modern creations, the distance seems to be so great that recipients experience above all confusion, incomprehension, and, as a result of these, a loss of any desire for interaction and identification with the work.

This unusually strong sense of estrangement may be, at least in part, the result of the playwrights' attempt to redefine the nature of identification. Modernist writers often begin to see identification within the reception process as a strictly intellectual phenomenon. Starting with the nineteenth century, the Horatian principle *dulce et utile* is often rejected, seen as equivocal, or separated into two distinct parts. Sometimes, the second part is retained, while the idea of "entertainment," depending on the artists' approach, is consciously overlooked or depreciated. Yet on occasion the reverse has occurred and emotion/entertainment becomes the focal point. Examples of such emphasis are the "art for art's sake" and the "theatricalizing" movements in drama. As an example of the first approach one can consider the ideas of Bertolt Brecht. During the greater part of his life he sees the notion of "alienation" as requiring the rejection of emotion, especially in the sense of empathy. Instead, he aims for intellectual identification. This intellectual response would in the end involve the recipient's emotions. However, the involvement would not occur within the process of reception, where the emotions are classified as "pure pleasure." Instead, emotional involvement in the political message would take place. The result should be the political activizing of the recipient. A similar "intellectualizing" effect is observed in numerous modernist plays and throughout the twentieth century.

The second change that becomes noticeable in recent times is the manipulation of form in order to create an ever shifting sense of distance within a single work. This phenomenon contrasts greatly with the more or less fixed distance that one finds in traditional drama and that helps determine the genre of the particular piece.[16] For example, comedy traditionally increases distance, making the recipient feel superior to the characters and not threatened by them. However, it does not obliterate the recipient's feeling of sympathy with the plight of the characters. Tragedy, on the other hand, diminishes that distance, leading to greater identification on the recipient's part, usually with the protagonist of the play. It should not "under-distance" the recipient, however, as this may reduce the stature of the work to that of melodrama.

Introduction

The latter is a popular "low form" that elicits from the recipient extremely intense emotions of fear and suspense. However, such intensity can eradicate the aesthetic response, which requires some degree of artistic distance. Furthermore, the melodrama's emotional and ideational range is very limited, whereas complexity of thought and feeling are often a positive element in terms of aesthetic reception. At the same time complexity of thought can also be a problem in many modern plays and is often due to the increased "citationality" of the text, as well as the stronger reliance on nonverbal elements, such as objects or gesture. The average recipient is not prepared for this way of presenting material. However, the greatest difficulty with many modern plays is the fact that they constantly shift distance, thus undercutting the recipient's expectations and making him feel lost, uncertain, sometimes irritated. In the plays under discussion in this study, all of the authors do precisely that. They alternately push away and draw in the recipient. Nevertheless, as will be shown, some of these works are actually "dramatically successful." Usually the success can be linked to a careful balance between the two directions of movement, that is, distancing and emotiveness. Furthermore, these successes show the playwrights' understanding of the fact that elements in a work may be of varying significance and strength. For example, a major element such as the stylistic usage of language can tip the scale, depending on how it is used, in one or another direction. In order to achieve a balance it must be juxtaposed by equally strong components that pull the work in the opposite direction. Finally, the successful plays reveal a realization on the playwrights' part that oversimplification and the resultant underdistancing may not lead to success; that a complex range of emotions combined with interesting ideas will be more successful than a single, blazing sensation such as is often offered in popular forms of drama.

Regardless of the degree and nature of distancing, at the end of the process of aesthetic reception, at its heart, lies an emotional identification. It is premised upon distance and it may or may not be preceded, followed, or accompanied by a more reasoned and analytical response. In fact, the most successful plays seems to consist of an intricate combination and a wide spectrum of ideas and emotions. Attempts have been made to describe and classify in some way this identification. Most, however, have tended to be too restrictive. As important a work as Peter Szondi's *Theory of the Modern Drama* limits the understanding of drama by assuming that basically it is a mimetic art.

Distance, then, is a normal aspect of the aesthetic reception of any work of art. Therefore, one may ask why readers should focus on drama in a scholarly study. There are two reasons. First, if one goes back to the roots of this phenomenon in modernism, one will soon notice that the modernists themselves, mainly, though not exclusively, under the influence of Nietzschean philosophy, consider drama the most important of literary genres because of its supposedly religious origins in Dionysian ritual. This is to some degree a fallacious assumption and, as stated earlier, the inability to distinguish between ritual and the conventions of art leads to many dramatic failures. Be that as it may, the assumption elevates the significance of the genre. Equally important, drama is valued by modernists because of its ability to elicit a response from a mass audience.[17]

Second, beginning with modernism and throughout the twentieth century, drama has been part of an ongoing search for a new autonomous art form: the theatrical performance—a form that would be composite in nature and that would express the problems and needs of modern man.[18] For example, Richard Wagner calls for a *Gesamtkunstwerk* (total art work) "in which all the arts are synthesized through the sensibilities of a single master artist." Adolphe Appia describes the performance as an integration of the three-dimensional actor into a hierarchical three-dimensional stage design. The connection between the two parts is to be achieved primarily with the help of lighting. Gordon Craig offers the concept of a "superpuppet" playing against a single mobile setting. Stanisław Wyspiański suggests a synthetic theatrical art that will unite different cultural layers—from the ancient Greek Acropolis through medieval Kraków to modern day political reality. In addition, his dramas mix real persons with embodied dreams and personified symbols. Vsevolod Meierhold continues a search that will last a lifetime, moving gradually from the concept of *uslovnyi teatr* ("conventional" theater) to biomechanics. Of note in the aforementioned list is the fact that it is directors who are in the forefront of trying to forge new dramatic art forms. The early, turn-of-the-century modernist writers do not produce a large body of dramatic masterpieces. Yet, in all of their literary production, though especially poetry, one senses a persistent need to break out of the single voice of the lyric into a plurality of voices, in other words, a need for at least the rudiments of drama.[19]

Thus the manipulation of distance in drama carries special historical significance. It is in some ways at the very center of the modern artist's search for new forms. Unfortunately, the study of distance in a literary work is not an easy task. Difficulties arise both because of the complicated nature of the literary text, as well as because of the enormous number of variables that are involved in the creation of distance. The analysis of distance manipulation in a dramatic text is further confounded by the fact that drama itself poses very special questions and problems. Some of these difficulties must now be briefly addressed.

One can begin by noting the complicated nature of an artistic text. On the one hand, it is a completed, closed, and stable entity, an artifact that exists in a more or less fixed form in print. On the other hand, it is a fluid, unstable phenomenon or experience that stimulates each individual cultural memory in a different way and at the same time is continuously changed by its surroundings, thus allowing for numerous interpretations.[20]

Introduction

Even more important for this study, the enormous complexity of distance needs to be emphasized. First of all, as part of the phenomenon of aesthetic reception, distance manipulation automatically includes a recipient, a macrolevel form of communication between work and recipient, as well as the whole cultural sphere of conventions and expectations. Unfortunately, these are all extremely complicated and slippery phenomena and our understanding of them is far from complete.[21] Yet the writing of every dramatic theorist tacitly assumes their existence without trying to explain them. For example, when Eric Bentley or Martin Esslin describes the differences between comedy, tragedy, melodrama, farce, and so on, their descriptions and definitions are clearly premised on popularly accepted cultural conventions. These conventions go back to the ancient Greeks, have been reinterpreted by neoclassicism, and then have been entrenched by nineteenth-century theatrical practices. That fact is never made clear in their books. Moreover, there is the question of who is the recipient; how do we define him? Does one carry out a sociological study of readers and audiences, despite the difficulties and limitations inherent in such an undertaking? Does one posit a model of some abstract recipient, though such models tend to idealize him and make him much more intelligent than the average person? It seems that the only way open at present, if one wants to move beyond an endless theoretical discussion of terms and analyze actual works, is to make two assumptions. First, one needs to assume a "virtual recipient" whom the author encodes into his text, expecting that this recipient can rely on the same codes that the author himself is using.[22] The virtual recipient can be more broadly understood than a historically defined recipient, equal to him, or narrower if the author decides to write for a particular localized audience, such as his friends. For the purposes of this study, the term "recipient" will carry one of three definitions and in each case this will be clearly indicated. Thus, it can refer to: (1) the virtual recipient; (2) the contemporary recipient of the second half of the twentieth century; and (3) the modernist recipient of the turn of the century. The last two will be referred to when a diachronic comparison is especially called for, but most of the time it will be either the virtual recipient who is signified or every recipient who confronts the work.

Second, in order to proceed with the actual analysis, one must adopt Bentley's and Esslin's approach: a tacit and rather informal acknowledgment of the existence of certain cultural conventions, without offering specific definitions. Though sociological studies of these phenomena certainly have great value, they remain too far removed from actual works and the manner in which they function.[23] Thus, the analysis of distance in this study will focus on the formal structural elements (see below) of Chekhov's *The Cherry Orchard*, Gippius's *Holy Blood*, Blok's *The Puppet Show*, Sologub's *Triumph of Death*, and Ivanov's *Tantalus*. Moreover, the study will show how these elements differ from or are similar to the structural elements of traditional drama. Such

Distance Manipulation

a comparison will of course be premised on the tacit acknowledgment that there indisputably exists "a something" which we have come to call "traditional Western drama." This phenomenon is a complex web of structural elements, conventions, expectations, norms, and the interrelationships between them. The validity of such an acknowledgment will, hopefully, be shown in the value of what is revealed through the following analysis of actual plays.

One final fact that should be kept in mind is that the average theater audience (not necessarily the virtual recipient encoded in the text or the elite intellectual) that comes to see a play, both at the beginning of the twentieth century and now, has been brought up on popular fare. At the beginning of the century, "popular" meant melodrama, realistic *pièces bien faites*, farce.[24] Today, popular genre more and more often means television. Whatever the popular medium, it builds very traditional, stereotypical expectations in the recipient.

Returning to the complexity of distance, the second reason for it comes from the fact that on each level it is created through a multitude of elements. Therefore, it is frequently very difficult to try to separate out a few "distancing techniques." Nevertheless, a few examples of particular nontraditional distancing techniques and strategies may be enumerated. These examples include discarding traditional compositional parts, such as the exposition and denouement; juxtaposing elements of farce/comedy with a lack of farcical "energy"; moving the play in the direction of discontinuity with the real world, as usually happens in absurdist drama; or creating a deictic orientation toward an off-stage there, rather than the more usual eternal present. In addition, among examples of traditional distancing techniques may be listed that of distorting and foregrounding linguistic elements, as well as that of using parody and caricature. Overall, the phenomenon should be traced on every level of structure, in the interrelationships between the levels, within a specific context, and always in reference to content and themes. However, each play must be treated as an individual case, where not every level may be affected equally. The study of structure means that one begins by briefly considering the subject matter of the given drama, since obviously form exists not in and of itself, but as an intrinsic part and reflection of content. Next, an examination of the larger parts of composition is called for, as, for example, the arrangements of acts and scenes vis-à-vis each other. There are traditionally established patterns and tendencies of arrangement that form part of the readers' expectations, like the use of the first act for the exposition, the placement of the climax—in a four-act play—in the third act. Following that, the way the plot and action are presented must be examined. Traditionally, for example, a farce will be much more action oriented than a tragedy, and plot tends to develop in an ascending line toward a climax, to be followed by a resolution. Then, characters and methods of characterization need to be considered. Here again, every recipient has certain definite expectations as

Introduction

to presentation, behavior, and type, which, for example, in Western culture leads him to identify "comically" with a Falstaff and "tragically" with a Hamlet. Next, the use of scenic space, as designated by stage directions and spatiotemporal markers within the primary text, must be analyzed. In terms of stage directions, it is not really surprising that they begin to grow extensively during the modernist era, a time when the playwright is trying to keep control over his work against the growing creativity and authority of a new breed of great directors. Furthermore, the use of language in the broadest sense must be studied: from deictic markers, through stylistics, word choice, and rhythm, to the absence of language and communication, as well as the increasing role of silence during the period. In each case it can be shown what is traditional and what is a new and innovative aspect of the given layer.

In many ways this definition of structure seems obvious. In practice it should show its effectiveness, especially when the various layers are juxtaposed against each other in concrete examples. In brief, a web must be spun. It will, hopefully, contain all of those elements that relate to and are involved in distance manipulation, though that does not mean that in any given work some elements will not be omitted for being unrelated to the phenomenon. Finally, it must be kept in mind that distance in itself is never a definitive goal for any artist. It is simply an intermediate step along the path toward a final engagement of the virtual recipient. Distance is increased because the playwright feels that he must first estrange so as to present matters in a new light, from a new, surprising angle. Only after a fresh perspective has been achieved can the recipient become emotionally involved.

Despite all of these difficulties, however, an attempt to understand the phenomenon and to trace it in particular works would be helpful. So far, for the most part, we sense distance in twentieth-century drama; we feel that it is different than its usage in more traditional forms. We see an intuitive, often unfocused preoccupation with it in theoretical writing. It makes itself felt in actual plays and in theatrical productions. While responding to the all-pervasive presence of distance, it has been an interesting challenge to explore this uncharted territory and to reach a number of theoretical conclusions that should be of help to audiences, directors, and scholars alike.

Complex though the phenomena of distance and text may be, they are further complicated when the exploration occurs in a dramatic text. First of all, due to its symbiotic interaction with the stage, drama has always been a highly ambiguous genre. Discussions of its nature have been particularly lively in the last twenty years or so. Moving away from the traditional attitude that the dramatic text is just another literary genre and that the theatrical performance is an illustration of the work, the discussions have of late focused almost exclusively on the performance. The text has been treated simply as one of many constitutive elements of the former. In addition, the debate has often used linguistic and philosophic theories to define drama.[25]

Distance Manipulation

For the purposes of this study, it has proven most useful to treat drama as an autonomous text, separate from other literary texts and one that contains inscribed information on the "virtual performance" that any recipient experiences.[26] On the one hand, it is a written art form because, like any fictional text, it presents a closed textual world that is accessible only by reading the text and that is not part of the real world. On the other hand, drama has a special ontological status, because its written text establishes a relationship not only to every other literary text (which is also true of poetry and prose), but also to every performance—be it actual or potential. Thus drama is characterized by two major elements that are not present in other kinds of literary texts. First, every dramatic text contains a "semantic figure of the performance" that is created from a myriad of minute particles carrying theatrical information.[27] Second, the language of drama has its own rather unique character. It is not the elliptical language of everyday communication. Yet, when compared to other literary genres, it is characterized by a high degree of "incompleteness" or "indexicality" that can be completed only by being objectified in performance.[28] Put another way, the language of drama is neither completely functional and transparent as everyday conversation, nor completely opaque and directed toward itself as poetry.

The dramatic text then is different from other literary texts because of its indexical language and the virtual performance inscribed in it. Furthermore, traditionally there has existed a special and close relationship between distance and the genre of a dramatic work. However, if one analyzes distance in some of the highly experimental plays of the twentieth century, one notices that modern drama affects a definite change in this relationship between distance and genre. To begin with, the concept of genre has become problematic for quite some time—namely, ever since the romantics increasingly began to mix various genres and to create such hybrid genres as "romantic drama." For the purposes of this study, one can consider genre as both a set of rules and ideological forces that define the structure of different types of works.[29] They may be compared, though only to some extent, to the grammar of a language. This "grammar" contains the codes common to all speakers of the given language, but is then individually realized in the actualization of single "speakers," that is, playwrights. In some historical periods (neoclassicism, the Renaissance), genres have been rigorously applied as a prescription for writing. In others (romanticism), they function more like a set of customs that need to be remembered. In either case, genres are the strongest link between aesthetic reception and literary tradition. They have the power to evoke very definite expectations from the recipient, to awaken communal, cultural memory.

Traditionally, distance has been more or less stable within the confines of a given work and has been tied to the latter's genre. Tragedy is presumed to keep the smallest distance, with every recipient identifying the most strongly

Introduction

with the protagonist(s). In comedy the distance is greater. Therefore, this genre has, as a consequence, developed many traditional techniques for increasing distance (incongruity, parody, stereotyping, and so on). However, in traditional comedy every recipient is still expected to retain some measure of sympathy for at least some of the characters. It is satirical comedy in the pure sense (Juvenal, Petronius) that is designed to make the recipient the most uncomfortable. This is so because, while criticizing the state of matters, it attacks the recipient himself and offers no solutions.

As stated, the situation begins to change with romanticism. Authors, mainly under the influence of Shakespeare, begin to avoid the three unities in drama; to introduce a loose, scene-oriented composition; and to combine dramatic elements with epic and lyric ones. Examples of such changes include Victor Hugo's *Hernani,* Alfred de Musset's *Lorenzaccio,* and Zygmunt Krasiński's *Un-Divine Comedy.* The tendency is continued much more radically during modernism and throughout the twentieth century. The result of such practices is that genres stop being injunctions for creating and yardsticks for determining quality and success. However, their function by no means disappears. Greco-Roman norms—as redefined by neoclassicism—continue to determine dramatic practice throughout the nineteenth century. More important, they have to this day remained the standard against which drama is, for the most part, analyzed, judged, and interpreted. It is enough to consider such classics of twentieth-century drama theory as the works of Eric Bentley and Martin Esslin to see the validity of this assertion. Furthermore, the cultural memory and literary traditions that are constituent parts of genres continue to shape and strongly influence every recipient's expectations whenever he comes in contact with a work of art.

At this juncture, it may be useful to question the innovative qualities of the modern mixing of genres, particularly in comparison to Shakespeare's practices. Were the modernists and their successors simply returning to the earlier practices of a master? This fallacious assertion is borne out by the fact that one would never mistake the plays of Shakespeare for those of Anton Chekhov, Stanisław Wyspiański, or Bertolt Brecht. This disparity of impression lies in the differing aims of the periods, as well as in their different philosophical stances. On the one hand, before modernism, for all of the cultural variety, all of the differences between historical periods, all of the doubts and questions, a belief in some underlying sense in existence persists. It may be called God or fate or world spirit.[30] William Shakespeare is undoubtedly the product of a skeptical, probing Renaissance philosophy. Yet his era, as evinced by his works, retains a belief in certain inherent social structures, in a natural order of the universe. Even the romantics, for all of their vision of life as an antinomic phenomenon, still hold certain absolute values such as Freedom, Nation, the Individual—all with capital letters. Furthermore, they still tend to find all-embracing philosophical solutions to problems, be it

Georg Hegel's World Spirit or Adam Mickiewicz's Messianism. Thus, when these earlier writers do mix genres, it is for a different reason than their successors. Shakespeare's combinations of the lyrical, epic, and dramatic underscore an artistic attempt to write for an intended audience that corresponds to society as a whole.

On the other hand, the modernists' combining of genres has at its core a very different intellectual situation. The disparity of the elements that they use is most often a sign of the complete collapse of absolute values and all-embracing philosophies.[31] The fact that no single perspective predominates, that characters belonging to different theatrical codes are placed together on the stage, that different styles of language are used, reflects the underlying uncertainty, even emptiness of the modern consciousness. These authors do not give answers because they cannot give them. They can only, as Anton Chekhov remarked about his own work, ask questions.

Therefore, one can posit a fundamental break between modernism and all earlier periods, even if the ground had been prepared since at least the end of the eighteenth century. Thus, in this study, the term "traditional" will refer to premodernist drama—not that "traditional" drama was not written throughout the twentieth century, nor that one cannot find examples of "nontraditional" drama before Henrik Ibsen. However, overall, one can generalize and state that "traditional" refers to all of those literary practices, norms, traditions, and cultural expectations that arise out of the philosophical coherence persisting in the Western world until modernism. As disparate as Sophocles, Shakespeare, and Racine may be, their work grows out of a sense of underlying stability that is no longer available as a solution to the modern artist or recipient. However, it must be strongly emphasized that this stability continues to persist in the modern artist and in every recipient as a stratum of cultural memory and fulfills a very important role in all aesthetic reception.

If one now goes back to the relationship between distance and genre, one sees that something very fundamental changes when authors begin manipulating distance and releasing it from its direct ties to genre. On the one hand, for the artist, this seems to offer a "heady freedom" during the creative process. On the other hand, for the recipient, even if he is privy to the author's immediate milieu and belongs to the intellectual elite of the time, it creates serious problems. It requires that he be much more conscious, aware, involved, and intelligent than the recipient of premodernist drama. This is so because in plays with shifting distance, the author dangles bits and pieces of genre conventions in front of every recipient. By doing so he awakens the recipient's expectations for a certain genre, "whets his appetite" so to speak, and then hides the dangling piece behind other, different pieces suggesting different genres. Something familiar is offered to the recipient in such works, but the familiarity does not last long enough to create certainties. Instead, unexpected shifts keep teasing him, appearing only to disappear. Of course,

Introduction

every masterpiece is full of surprises for the recipient, but in the case of "modern" works the sense of ambiguity, uncertainty, unfamiliarity, and confusion is much greater and requires a much more complicated and active sorting out and interpreting.

Three more points need to be considered in relation to this new usage of genres for distance manipulation. First, how does one differentiate between the usage of genre as something momentarily dangled before the recipient and the whole concept of intertextuality? Here is where the definition of genre becomes so important. Intertextuality, though it too awakens common cultural memory, is a more individualized tool of the author and a less forceful one. Genre is stronger and even more violent.[32] The term "violence" is used here with positive connotations to emphasize the strength of genre. For all of the historical permutations that genres have undergone, for all of the disavowals of traditional genres that have occurred in modern times, they are still a powerful force in aesthetic reception. They automatically channel, direct, and control a recipient's reactions, helping him to safeguard the historicity of a work, while not interfering with its aesthetics.

The second question that must be raised is why employ genres at all, why present their broken bits and pieces? The answer is that they are used because they are absolutely necessary in the reception of innovative works. In deciphering a work, every recipient can only apply those codes that he knows. With innovative works the recipient attempts to apply what he knows but discovers that he needs, at the very least, to begin creating new codes for himself—with the help of the known ones. In other words, if the codes of the sender and recipient do not overlap at least minimally, there will be no communication. Within these common codes, genres have always played and continue to play a vital role. Though torn apart through shifting distance, genres are still important in this new and difficult kind of reception.[33]

Third, the incompleteness of genres in the new approach to distance raises the question of the openness and closure of drama. Studies have been done that define the difference between the new and old types of drama primarily on the basis of the concept of openness versus closure. Openness here can of course refer to perspective, resolution, and characterization. It is usually the first two of these that are brought to mind in reference to modern drama. Openness of perspective and resolution means simply that the author offers several perspectives of seemingly equal value, that he does not choose one over the other, and that he leaves the choice and resolution of the problems raised by his work to each individual recipient. Bertolt Brecht's *The Good Woman of Setzuan,* Tom Stoppard's *Jumpers,* and drama of the absurd can serve as examples of open plays. Anton Chekhov's *The Cherry Orchard* is another case in point.

However, though there is undoubtedly a strong tendency toward aesthetic openness in modern works, that is not the only possible solution when

Distance Manipulation

distance is manipulated. It is true that if a shifting distance is used, then very often perspective and ending will be open, though not necessarily characterization (see Aleksandr Blok's *The Puppet Show*). Nevertheless, as will be shown, Zinaida Gippius's *Holy Blood* is a play in which shifting distance does not lead to openness, but rather to closure—through a single-minded focus on one set of ideas. Furthermore, in modern drama, distance is sometimes simply greatly increased without really shifting. Such experiments are certainly known both in modernism, as well as in later periods (see Viacheslav Ivanov's *Tantalus*). In terms of perspective, then, the play will tend to be closed. Therefore, the concept of openness versus closure, though often useful in revealing the overall tendencies of modern drama, is not always a defining factor in terms of the changing approach to distance in drama.

Closure presupposes a definite philosophical and ethical stance on the part of the playwright. The absence of such a stance in open drama is connected to yet another problem that arises out of the innovative manipulation of distance. It has been stated in the discussion on the definition of distance that regardless of every recipient's background, he approaches a text or performance with a certain set of expectations. It is due to the full or at least partial fulfillment of these expectations that to this day the standard aesthetic reception of a given work includes an act of identification on the part of every recipient with some aspect of the textual world. Furthermore, due to the nature of drama (its lack of a narrator, its realization through concrete actors, its immediacy, its mass reception), this identification often seems to be stronger for plays than for other literary genres. The problem lies in the fact that if reception means identification, then one can no longer speak of a strictly aesthetic phenomenon, and aesthetics is linked to ethics. Unfortunately, in the second half of the twentieth century, ethics has become an uncomfortable subject in literary theory and criticism, one that is skirted, presented as extremely complex and in need of great circumspection, or even rejected outright.[34] Nevertheless, the implication is unavoidable and with it comes a further question: how does the fact that certain plays purposefully distance the virtual recipient in nontraditional ways reflect upon the relationship between the ethics and aesthetics of these works? This is a vital question for Bertolt Brecht, but it is also of importance for Russian drama and theater where the arts always carried a social, moral, and political burden. The Russian modernists, though they all show great interest in form, overall have less of a "form for form's sake" approach to art than do their Western counterparts. Certainly Zinaida Gippius sees drama as a vehicle for spreading her religious ideas. Viacheslav Ivanov, as the theoretician of the second generation of Russian symbolists, describes it as a "communal religious rite" that substitutes for orthodox religions and offers participants a spiritual experience. Even Anton Chekhov, the supreme antimoralist who insists that the author's subjective point of view must be cleansed from a play, actually

Introduction

presents a certain vague moralistic subtext to the events of his plays. Thus, if identification is made more difficult or even impossible, and if every recipient is forced to rely more on his intellect during the reception process, what happens to the ethical "weightiness" that a work of art may exert upon him? Can that function of art be safeguarded in the new circumstances? This is a question that will be answered in the actual drama analyses of chapters 2 through 6.

The theoretical groundwork having been established, one needs to consider briefly the specific historical situation of Russian modernist drama and theater, especially of the symbolist period. In many respects the situation parallels that of western Europe. First, as in the West, drama is the last literary form to respond to modernistic impulses, and it does so only after the appearance of symbolist poetry and prose. Second, when changes do begin, they do so in the theater, rather than among playwrights. Just as in France where André Antoine's Théâtre Libre brings about changes in French dramaturgy, so Konstantin Stanislavsky's and Vladimir Nemirovich-Danchenko's Moscow Art Theater helps change the face of Russian drama. Modernism, for the most part, is the era of great visionary theater directors, and even stage designers, rather than playwrights. It is names such as Gordon Craig, Adolphe Appia, André Antoine, Georg Fuchs, Jacques Copeau, Max Reinhardt, Konstantin Stanislavsky, and Vsevolod Meierhold that are remembered to this day and that have influenced later generations. Only a handful of modernist playwrights (Anton Chekhov, Stanisław Wyspiański) have continued to be a staple of the theatrical repertoire. Third, it is important to remember that both in western Europe and in Russia the developments of modernist drama and theater are often for a long time overshadowed by popular realist playwrights. In England, for example, the works of George Bernard Shaw are much more popular than those of William Butler Yeats. In Poland the dramas of Stanisław Wyspiański appeal less to the average audience than do the naturalistic plays of Gabriela Zapolska. In Russia Maksim Gorky was for a long time considered a much better playwright than Anton Chekhov.

Furthermore, in Russia, as in the West, once modernist drama makes its appearance, it creates a motley scene with writers experimenting in many different directions. Within each current there are numerous variations. Thus, Valerii Briusov's *The Earth* (*Земля*, 1904) might be called a symbolist play. Aleksandr Blok's *The Rose and the Cross* (*Роза и крест*, 1912) and Mixail Kuz'min's *Alexis Man of God* (*О Алексее человеке божьем*, 1908) are examples of medieval neomysteries. In *The Devil Play* (*Бесовское дело*, 1907), Aleksei Remizov employs folk elements. However, Kuz'min in *The Venetian Madcaps* (*Венецианские безумцы*, 1912) chooses to stylize the eighteenth century in a very art-for-art's sake fashion. Then there are numerous attempts at neoclassical plays, ranging from great faithfulness to the original models, such as in Innokentii Annenskii's *Laodamia* (*Лаодамия*, 1907), to the mixing of classicism and decadent aesthetics, as in his *Thamyras the Cythara Player* (*Фамира Кифаред*, 1906). Another important current is the "theatricalizing" movement, emphasizing ludic elements and including such plays as Nikolai Evreinov's *Happy Death* (*Веселая смертъ*, 1908). Allegory is amply represented in the oeuvre of Leonid Andreev. Finally, there is a current known as "romantic escapist," with such varied works as Nikolai Gumilev's *Don Juan in Egypt* (*Дон Жуан в Египте*, 1912) and Marina Cvetaeva's *Casanova's End* (*Конец Казановы*, 1922).

This variegated dramatic scene is further complemented and complicated by a colorful theatrical scene. Besides the well-established theaters such as the Moscow Art Theater, there are numerous theater-studios that often exist for only a short period of time, but that must be remembered for one groundbreaking performance. These are supplemented by theatrical experiments in private homes, such as the Tower Theater (Башенный Театр) that puts on a single memorable presentation in Viacheslav Ivanov's apartment—Calderón de la Barca's *Devotion to the Cross*. By the second decade of the twentieth century, cabarets become an important fertilizing ground for theater. Though it is very hard to reconstruct the performances that took place in such cabarets as the Wandering Dog (Бродячая Собака) or the Crooked Mirror (Кривое Зеркало), they undoubtedly function as creative sources of inspiration for more permanent institutions.

Finally, it needs to be noted that Russian modernism, like its Western counterparts, is a very international movement. Even personal contacts between directors span the length of the European continent, as when the British stage designer Gordon Craig stages *Hamlet* in Moscow. More often the cross-fertilization is not direct but passes through numerous hands. Nevertheless, the influence of other cultures on Russian theater is significant. Simply in terms of performances of foreign works, the range is very broad. Russian theaters frequently stage the works of Maurice Maeterlinck, Henrik Ibsen, Gerhart Hauptmann, and Stanisław Przybyszewski. Major events include the staging of the Indian classic *Sakantula* and Calderón de la Barca's *Devotion to the Cross*. Right at their doorstep, Russian modernists have the Habimah Theater, which both borrows from the Russians and inspires them with its own experiments within Yiddish culture.

The period, then, from which these analyzed plays is taken is one of tremendous ferment, creativity, and eclecticism. It is, therefore, not surprising that the five works differ greatly from each other, and, except for Chekhov, represent several currents within symbolist drama. For a number of reasons Anton Chekhov's *The Cherry Orchard* appears as the most useful starting point. Revolutionary at the time it was written, it has acquired lasting fame and is frequently staged to this day, yet it continues to fascinate and trouble and even irritate both recipients and directors. Very few European

Introduction

modernist playwrights achieved such permanent success as did Chekhov. He wrote plays that were, and are, extremely complex and often ambiguous. His works are simultaneously thoroughly universal, and, contrary to appearances, deeply involved in the very specific changes occurring in Russian society at the turn of the century. The author's dramas cannot be pigeonholed as either comedies or tragedies, since they contain elements of many dramatic genres. He has created very memorable characters, and yet analysis shows that these characters are in certain respects de-psychologized as compared, for example, to realistic ones, and that their status as protagonists is usually diminished. In addition, he experiments extensively with language. Finally, he is keenly aware of the possibilities and limitations of the stage, and he puts the former to some spectacular use. In terms of Chekhov's oeuvre, critics acknowledge that *The Cherry Orchard* represents a supreme kind of balance of opposites. Taking into consideration its success, complexity, and innovativeness, the play can be employed as an important starting point and springboard for an analysis of the remaining works.[35] Each of these plays represents a different current within modernism and reveals features typical of that current as well as its own unique characteristics.

Zinaida Gippius's *Holy Blood* was actually written before *The Cherry Orchard* (in 1900). It appears as a response to the philosophical and religious quest of the Merezhkovskii circle, to the literary experiments and ideas of the symbolists, and to the period's heated discussions on the status of women. As will be shown, the play is a complex, interesting, and in many ways successful presentation of these diverse issues in an experimental form. It is the first Russian modernist play written in folkloric style, and perhaps the earliest Russian play to manipulate distance—successfully. Though not of the same depth as *The Cherry Orchard*, artistically it is immeasurably better than such early experiments as Nikolai Minskii's *The Sun* or Dmitrii Merezhkovskii's *Return to Nature*.

Fedor Sologub's *The Triumph of Death* was written in 1906 and 1907. The work was the result of Sologub's closeness at the time to Vsevolod Meierhold's concept of *uslovnyi teatr*. Both artists included the idea of "play" in theater, but also emphasized anti-illusionism as a means of creating quasi ritual. These works often stylize the conventions of previous ages in order to underscore the universalism of the themes being presented, with stylization often leading to borrowing from folklore. This play belongs, first of all, to the medievalist current, a modernist trend that appeals to a wide variety of writers in many countries. Second, *The Triumph of Death* utilizes a popular, but not folkloric, genre, namely, melodrama, in order to increase its dramatic impact. The romantics had done something similar in such works as Victor Hugo's *Hernani* or Percy Bysshe Shelley's *Cenci,* and that is why Sologub's play is often placed within yet another frequently seen current of modernism, namely, the neoromantic one.

Written in 1906 at the instigation of the short-lived Fakely movement, Aleksandr Blok's *The Puppet Show* is undoubtedly the single best-known and most influential dramatic experiment of the time. Like *The Triumph of Death*, it too utilizes elements of a "low genre" in order to produce a radically new experience. In this case the playwright turns toward commedia dell'arte. However, he employs not so much the historically pure Italian form as a kind of essence of commedia filtered through a long international tradition and extremely popular in Russia at the beginning of the twentieth century. Commedia, in turn, leads to the use of the grotesque—an aesthetic category and way of perceiving reality that becomes increasingly popular in the twentieth century.

Finally, Viacheslav Ivanov's *Tantalus* can be considered. Inspired by Friedrich Nietzsche's notions of an ecstatic Dionysian art, the playwright seeks to create a new kind of mystery play that would allow recipients to unite emotionally in a quasi-religious rite that substitutes for *sobornost'* (church unity in Christ). Ivanov is not alone in turning to antiquity in drama; numerous European writers do so. However, in form his works are much more radical than most, especially in terms of the use of a chorus and a highly unique language style. The playwright's experiment would serve as a source of inspiration for later, even postrevolutionary proletarian experiments that at first glance differ greatly from his symbolist Neoplatonism.[36]

The following five chapters each analyze one of the aforementioned plays and include discussions on which elements of the given work distance in traditional ways and which are emotive in a traditional manner, which elements distance in new nontraditional ways and which function emotively in new nontraditional substitutive ways. Much of what has been presented has already been suggested by other critics, and that debt is acknowledged in the course of the analysis. However, the point of view, the focus, the emphasis, and the highlighting are certainly the author's own. In each case the aim is to produce a thorough study of distance manipulation and its consequences on reception. Furthermore, the discussion of the deictic and communicative structures of these works is original, since, as far as this author has ascertained, they have not been studied in these particular plays.

The final chapter brings the various threads together. It shows which distancing elements are strongest, and thus, must be balanced with equally strong emotive elements. It discusses which approaches to distance appear to be most successful dramatically. It also critiques the use of various genres and what happens when only fragments of genres are offered to the recipient. In short, this chapter shows how a play can be radically new and experimental and yet still elicit identification on the part of the recipient by not forgetting the essence of drama, namely, emotion—often raw and violent in the greatest of masterpieces.

Chapter One

Anton Chekhov's *The Cherry Orchard*

THOUGH "RAW" AND "VIOLENT" do not seem at first glance like apt descriptions of Anton Chekhov's drama *The Cherry Orchard* (Вишневый сад), emotion is undoubtedly a major component of this work. Moreover, the play is a useful starting point for an analysis of distance manipulation for three reasons. First, it is a masterpiece that has influenced generations of writers throughout the twentieth century. Second, it is an example of radically innovative, yet successful, distance manipulation. Third, in *The Cherry Orchard,* more than in any other play, Chekhov considers the receptive limitations of the audience and therefore creates a work that carefully balances distancing with emotive effects, both traditional and nontraditional in character.

Before showing in detail the nature of this balance, a few words must be said about the position of the play within Chekhov's oeuvre and how it relates to his earlier dramatic experiments. The author's flirtation with drama has a long history and goes back to his days as a medical student. However, neither those early short attempts, nor his first full-length play, *Ivanov* (1888), show any of the genius that would appear in his later works. After *Ivanov* and until 1896, Chekhov's dramatic experiments are really limited to short, one-act farces, such as *The Bear* (1888) and *The Wedding* (1890). Though not helpful to the writer in terms of constructing a longer play, they do help him to sharpen his comedic skills and to develop an understanding of the stage. Chekhov's first real dramatic success comes when the Moscow Art Theater stages *The Sea Gull* in 1898. Only three more plays follow: *Uncle Vanya*—a remake of an earlier work—*The Three Sisters* (1901), and *The Cherry Orchard. The Sea Gull, Uncle Vanya,* and *The Three Sisters* show the maturation of the writer's dramatic style, as well as much experimenting with recipient expectations and distance manipulation. However, all three are a bit uneven, tending at moments to be overburdened by "philosophizing." That perfect merger of tragedy and comedy, of the emotive and the distancing, is only achieved in Chekhov's final dramatic work, *The Cherry Orchard.*

The Cherry Orchard may be recognized as a masterpiece of world literature, and yet the history of its reception has been one of ongoing and well-documented misunderstandings.[1] In general, Chekhov's plays, which were initially labeled by many critics as undramatic and badly structured, were really accepted by audiences only after Konstantin Stanislavsky began to produce them.[2] However, for the author this theatrical success did not end the misinterpretations and conflicts, since he often strongly disagreed with Stanislavsky's staging. The director saw the plays as realistic dramas of the everyday (*bytovaia* drama), as nostalgic farewells written in a tragic key to a way of life that was fast disappearing. Chekhov, on the other hand, insisted that he was writing comedies, and this was especially true of *The Cherry Orchard*—his final attempt to create the kind of comedic drama that he had desired all along. In the case of this work the author partly departs from and partly improves on his previous models in the hope that he will at last be understood. In fact, he states that he is writing not just a comedy, but a farce. Unfortunately, Stanislavsky's reaction is the same as it has been to all of the other dramas and he again concludes that he has been handed a work that is at most tragicomic, if not fully a tragedy. Therefore, he proceeds to stage the play in a manner that the playwright finds both too drawn out and too lachrymose.[3] Similarly, in later periods, Chekhov's works, for all their popularity, are frequently interpreted in ways that more than likely would have seemed incorrect to the author. For example, Soviet directors tend to present *The Cherry Orchard* as a sharp satire on the old order and the exploiting classes. On the other hand, English and American directors often stage his dramas as rather sentimental and nostalgic scenes from upper-class life on country estates.

    A similar ambiguity can be observed if one shifts attention to present-day literary criticism. Contemporary critics have come to recognize the complexity of *The Cherry Orchard*. Many of the critical statements indirectly acknowledge that the form of this play constitutes a supreme balance of opposites. Yet scholars often do not formulate clearly or agree upon the nature of that balance. Some speak of "continuity versus change," others of "dialecticism," still others of "private versus public spheres."[4] Furthermore, seldom do scholars try to explain the reason for this new form: why does Chekhov continue to risk misunderstanding and to struggle with a form of drama that so many recipients so often misinterpret? As A. Skaftymov points out, Chekhov is not the type of writer to experiment with new form for the sake of new form. Skaftymov discusses the playwright's belief that dramatic conflict lies in situational forces beyond the control of the individual, in the monotony of everyday life. Moreover, in Chekhov's worldview it is these forces that bring about change and serve as catalysts for developments in the lives of the characters, as well as for their behavior. It is this belief, writes Skaftymov, that leads the playwright to introduce the numerous nondramatic and seemingly superfluous details of everyday life, including the pauses and silences that make the recipient so uncomfortable.[5]

    Skaftymov is certainly correct in his presentation of Chekhov's outlook on existence. Throughout the author's ouevre, it is not the characters who will change and act upon the possibilities. Rather, the dramatic conflict lies in the situation. Such an interpretation of reality is in itself a distancing factor. By tradition, every recipient is accustomed to an active hero, even if, Hamlet-like, he has moments of inactivity. Sooner or later, the protagonist is supposed to take the situation into his own hands and act upon it. This kind of an attitude is all the more expected in traditional comedy where philosophical content is often slight and attention is focused on an action-packed plot. That is not to say that in many traditional dramas fate does not play a role, for it does. However, in these traditional works the presence of fate never denies the protagonist a will, the possibility of acting, or the responsibility for his actions. In *The Cherry Orchard,* as in all of Chekhov's plays, the characters are diminished in size and the psychological motivation is reduced because the characters do not act. Forces beyond their control manipulate them and their behavior, leaving the characters with hypertrophied consciousness (the traditional Russian superfluous man). The confusing and thus distancing aspect of this presentation is that Chekhov offers in his textual world neither a fully deterministic universe, nor the simple, ironic, and stereotyped characters typical of many traditional comedies.[6] The playwright does not wish to dehumanize his characters, seeing dehumanization as an unfortunate tendency already present in society due to the occurring social and economic changes. Instead, he always defends individual human dignity and rights. Furthermore, he does not absolve his characters of responsibility. Unable to act, they nevertheless carry the burden of their behavior with them.

Yet overall, a strictly realistic analysis of Chekhov's plays is reductive in that it ignores the nonrealistic aspects of the playwright's technique. One must not overlook such elements as leitmotivs, plays on words, and hints at another reality, elements that were immediately noticed by the symbolists, as well as by other modernist artists.[7] Furthermore, the author himself, besides making statements seemingly favoring realism, at times suggests an approach to literature reminiscent of the modernists. For example, he states that "the whole meaning, the whole drama of a person's life are contained within, not in outward manifestations" and he pens the subversive sounding phrase: "пошл[ый] язык . . . и пошл[ые] мелки[е] движени[я], коими должны изобиловать современные драма и комедия" (petty language and petty, trifling movements with which contemporary drama and comedy should overflow).[8]

Similarly, Iurii Annenkov, in his memoirs, attributes to Chekhov the following words that seem to echo the modernists' calls for an *uslovnyi teatr:* "Сцена требует известной условности. У нас нет четвертой стены . . . сцена—искусство, сцена отражает в себе квинтэссенцию жизни" (The stage requires a known conventionality. We do not have a fourth wall . . . the stage is art, the stage reflects the quintessence of life).[9] Furthermore, a study of the playwright's *Notebooks* (*Zapisnye knizhki*) reveals an amazing awareness of linguistic possibilities, with the author considering neologisms, puns, and unusual phrases in a way that is definitely close to the modernist playfulness and experimentation with literary language. Vladimir Mayakovsky, who of course never saw these notebooks, considered Chekhov a kindred spirit precisely because of the way he treated language.[10] In fact, though a realistic interpretation has validity, it is in the modernist aspects of Chekhov's plays that one finds the best explanation for the sensation of balancing on the edge that any recipient experiences when he confronts the author's dramas. Modernist elements also account for the continuing frustration and simultaneous fascination with these plays and particularly with this, Chekhov's last.

To begin, all of Chekhov's works, including *The Cherry Orchard,* present characters and society in a state of imbalance, alienation, and self-alienation. This existential situation lies at the basis of the whole modernist spiritual crisis.[11] Perhaps in Russia this image is strengthened by the tradition of the superfluous man that already had its own rich history before the period began. Be that as it may, in all of Chekhov's dramas most of the central characters belong to what might be called "the old noble-intellectual order" that cannot adapt to the new social conditions. Simultaneously, the position of this order in the familiar and traditional past is fast dissolving. Its members feel estranged from the world around them, from others in their milieu, as well as from their individual selves. In *The Cherry Orchard* this group is represented by Liubov' Ranevskaia and her brother, Leonid Gaev, who fritter away their estate on a life of triviality and leisure. Even in the face of a complete loss of their property, they show no change. To them the new order remains so incomprehensible that at times they literally do not and cannot understand the words and ideas of the new bourgeoisie. The group of characters that constitutes their spiritual opposite is made up of those persons who have adjusted and have made good in the new order. They too are almost never depicted simply as villains, and among this group the most complicated and interesting psychologically is undoubtedly the self-made man, Ermolai Lopakhin. Though successful in the new order of things, he too experiences alienation.

The need to present this existential estrangement, strengthened by Chekhov's desire only to pose but not answer questions, leads him to create a dramatic form that performs a balancing act with regard to the manipulation of distance. It is this modern phenomenon of manipulating distance that allows one to gather together many of Chekhov's innovative elements, techniques, and tendencies, and that perhaps constitutes the essence of his dramatic art. Distance underlies the whole concept of form and in some sense determines it. It allows one to avoid such generalizations as "continuity versus change" or "dialecticism" that really refer to thematic matters, rather than to form. It is broader and more basic than such terms as "tragicomedy" or "poetic drama," both of which have been applied to Chekhov's works. The former term has a long history and cannot be employed usefully to pinpoint the innovative aspects of *The Cherry Orchard*. The latter also has existed at least since romanticism, as, for example, in Aleksandr Pushkin's *Little Tragedies* or in Adam Mickiewicz's *Forefathers' Eve*. In general, it excludes comedic elements. Distance as the essence of *The Cherry Orchard* is what William Grubber is referring to when he writes that this play "is a theater about comedy [and] the playwright creates meaning by innovative play with the given of his age and its attitude toward the theater."[12] In other words, Chekhov introduces a whole series of elements that distance the recipient in new and unexpected ways, and not simply in the manner of traditional comedies. Simultaneously, he uses both traditional distancing and emotive elements, as well as new substitutive emotive elements. The author pushes his virtual recipient away as far as he thinks it possible without losing him, forcing the recipient to feel discomfort and disorientation. Then he leads him back, soothes him for a while, and engages his emotions, for he instinctively knows that he must keep a balance, that he cannot introduce only new and unfamiliar elements. All audiences have their limitations, and in his final play Chekhov is able to maintain an almost miraculous high-wire act between the traditional and the innovative, to give his audiences "a lesson in funambulism."[13] It should be noted that even traditional comedy tends to be characterized by a much greater ambivalence and balancing of opposites than does tragedy. However, Chekhov's ambivalence and balancing is of a new order in its consistent and constant shifting of distance. Previously, there were very few comedies that functioned in this fashion. The playwright's balancing provides every recipient a better experience of the ambiguous lives of characters who live during a transitional period of history. These characters are alienated by many of the new phenomena that are appearing around them. Simultaneously, they are all creatures with ties to the past. Their thoughts and emotions are conditioned by two thousand years of western European history. Thus, they too, like both the modernist and the contemporary recipient, live in a world where they are continuously pulled toward some things and pushed away from others.

    The difficulty of describing this balancing act lies, first of all, in the fact that distance in this work is constantly shifting, so that a synchronous description of one scene says nothing about the diachronic effect of the play. The second problem arises from the dual functioning of certain elements. As will be shown, a number of Chekhov's techniques at first distance every recipient because they overturn his expectations. Eventually, as the play progresses, they begin to function emotively, though they may engage the recipient differently than traditional drama. As an example of this duality, one can consider the weaving of leitmotivs and images. If these are very pronounced, as is the case with the orchard in *The Cherry Orchard*, they will initially distance. Though leitmotivs and images create a feeling of the familiar and offer a sense of comfort by creating "anchoring points" in a complex reception process, they are not the element that traditionally moves the play forward. Therefore, at first any recipient will wonder why the given image is repeated so often in so many contexts, and he will devote his efforts to searching out the action and through it the plot. He will also try to define the image's meaning without being able to do so precisely. Over time such an element will begin to elicit an emotional response from the recipient. However, it will be an abstract emotionalism, rather than the personalized emotional identification characteristic of traditional drama. Nevertheless, difficulties of analysis notwithstanding, it is possible to achieve a better understanding of the nature of distance manipulation.

One can begin by looking at the overall structure of the work. A first glance reveals that there is no clear-cut division into the traditional dramatic parts of exposition, development, climax, and denouement.[14] Thus, the recipient is not carried through the play according to his expectations. Traditional drama offers a familiar path. The exposition draws the recipient into the story. This is followed by a sweeping movement toward a climax that takes the recipient's breath away and offers him the pleasure of a vicarious emotional frisson. Then there is a conclusion that unravels the knots and allows both characters and recipient to experience a cathartic relief. Instead, in this play, as studies have shown, the composition "is accomplished according to the principle of unorganized articulation, of a kind of disintegration of composition in which the devices of interruption, severance and recurrence of themes stand out."[15] Such a composition distances any recipient.

However, Chekhov counters the distancing effect by doing a number of things. First, he leaves the remnants of an exposition to minimally guide the recipient into the story. For example, Ania's description of her experiences in Paris (p. 321), and even more dramatically her memories of the death of her brother (p. 323), are needed only on the macrolevel of communication, since Varia presumably must know all of the information stated in these passages.[16] Second, the entire fourth act in this play can be treated as an extended, though untraditional, denouement. Knots are not untangled and the characters do not change after undergoing profound revelations; neither is social stability restored, as is the case in comedy. The characters, however, do spend their time parting from each other and from their former lives, as symbolized by the orchard. Third, though the overall composition is one of disintegration, there is in each act one predominating theme.[17] This theme, weaving itself through numerous variations, lends cohesion to the whole act. For example, in act 1 the theme of Ranevskaia predominates, act 2 is devoted to Lopakhin, and act 3 focuses upon the sale of the estate.

The weaving of themes is similar to the way that scenes function in this play. Here, scenes do not evolve one from another by cause and effect as in traditional drama, where the actions of one scene logically lead to the actions of the next one. Yet, it has been demonstrated that scenes do play an important part in *The Cherry Orchard*. Their contrasting flow creates a montagelike effect and it is the relationship between them that produces the poetry of this work.[18] One can, for example, consider the first few scenes of act 1. The play opens with Lopakhin and Duniasha. It is a quiet, reflective scene that catches the stillness and boredom of life on a country estate—a definite contrast to any recipient's expectations for the beginning of a comedy, where a burst of energetic bustle is expected. Lopakhin reminisces about himself and about Ranevskaia, almost immediately introducing the undercurrent of his strong affection for her, an undercurrent that will resurface on a number of occasions. Duniasha talks about her nerves and about the proposal of marriage that she has received. This secondary character adds a slight comical touch to the scene—a smile, though certainly not a loud comedic laugh. Her behavior starts another thematic thread that will be woven throughout the text, for she is a parodic version of a "lady," of Ranevskaia herself. On the other hand, Lopakhin's memories and his anger at Duniasha's pretentiousness initiate yet another thematic thread. This thread concerns the inner uncertainty of this self-made man. As is eventually revealed, Lopakhin suffers from an inferiority complex because of his origins. At the same time, he is able to appreciate the beauty, gentility, and poetry of the old order that is crumbling and that he is helping to destroy. The stage then empties completely. Suddenly, an excited, nervous crowd bursts forth onto it. It is a very brief scene: a few short remarks that in an instant give the recipient a minimal introduction to Ranevskaia's emotionalism, Gaev's immaturity, and Sharlotta's absurd behavior. Nevertheless, the scene leaves the recipient with a sense of confusion because there are too many as yet unknown characters on the stage and the contact is too brief to sort out who is who. Next, the recipient is given an exchange between Ania and Duniasha that is a complete opposite to that bustle and that relieves the feverish tension of the previous scene. The tempo is slow and even wilting. Ania reminisces, but not feverishly; what comes across above all is her exhaustion. Duniasha returns to her marriage proposal, keeping alive the recipient's gentle smile. She also introduces the theme of Trofimov. In the next scene between Ania and Varia, the mood is still subdued, but also much more serious. Ania relates her experiences in Paris, thus revealing the depth of her difficulties with her mother's behavior. The theme of the estate is introduced. Finally, the theme of Varia's spinsterhood—a more serious problem than Duniasha's marriage complications—makes its appearance. Thus, one sees that fragments of exchanges that can be classified as scenes are an essential aspect of composition in this play, with the author constantly changing the mood, starting thematic threads that are then picked up in later scenes and developed with variations. The juxtaposition of scenes that appear like incongruous building blocks, though not traditional, eventually contributes to an emotional response in every recipient—of a more undefined, abstract kind.

With scenes juxtaposed by mood, and not linked through cause and effect, it is not surprising to note that on yet another structural level, namely plot, Chekhov distances each recipient by not offering him a traditional type of plot. Due to certain peculiarities of drama—the lack of a narrator, the limitation in time and space, the filtering through actors—traditional drama tends to have a simply and clearly defined plot and a lot of action and symmetry in comparison to prose fiction. The modernists began breaking down these traditions, with Maurice Maeterlinck paving the way. Chekhov, however, goes much further in undermining the recipient's expectations and "he puts a radical end . . . more radical than is generally assumed, to the traditional Aristotelian action drama."[19] Traditionally, of course, plot is the sequence of events and actions in the order in which they are presented in a given work. This play has no plot because it has no action, at least not in the traditional sense; almost nothing occurs, and certainly not on stage. In this work, it would be more precise to speak of "events" occurring, rather than actions.

To better understand what happens, one can take C. Brémond's very useful definition of traditional action. Brémond defines action as follows: "1. There is an initial situation which allows for change; 2. This possibility is acknowledged and actualized; 3. The result of this actualization is a new situation."[20] Thus, one sees that it is the second half of step two of Brémond's definition that is missing in *The Cherry Orchard*. Even when change occurs in this play, it is not brought about by the willed behavior of the characters, but by the situation itself, by forces beyond the characters' control. The characters are usually highly aware of the possibility for change—the first half of Brémond's step two—but awareness is, for the most part, the only thing of which they are capable.

One way in which Chekhov formally expresses his interpretation of reality is through the absence of a traditional kind of plot. In its place the author substitutes not so much events as movement. Movement refers, first of all, to the most basic physical movement on stage where Chekhov contrasts large groups of characters with small ones—slow, reflective gestures with noisy, confusing ones. For example, consider the contrast between the opening scene of act 1 with its quiet reflective mood and the appearance of just two characters, and the nervous bustle of a whole group of characters in scene two. Similarly, all of act 3 functions as a counterpoint of appearing and disappearing dancers. Here, Chekhov uses the visual possibilities of the stage both to convey messages by juxtaposing changing images, as well as to create the illusion of something occurring in the absence of the expected traditional type of action.

Furthermore, movement also refers to the intricate "patterning of characters."[21] The play offers every recipient a complicated system of checks and balances, where one individual is compared with another, where groups are juxtaposed to each other, and where individuals are contrasted over time with themselves. Each character represents more than one aspect of society, and thus twelve characters seem to make ten times that number. The cast can be grouped by social background (i.e., the landowning class versus former peasants), by sex, and by age. Moreover, within each of these groups the characters are contrasted with each other. This patterning includes the different ideologies and attitudes of the characters. Equally significantly, it reveals their emotional relationships and states. In fact, the two—ideas and emotions—really cannot be separated and both together decide what the characters' attitude is toward others, as well as toward themselves. The intricacy of this patterning can be partially illustrated by studying a single scene. For example, consider in act 1 the scene between Ranevskaia, Gaev, and Lopakhin, with Firs adding additional overtones. Simply by listing in sequential order the ideas and emotions that are expressed here, it is possible to see how the author paints, as it were, his scene with ever-changing flicks of the brush. He begins with Firs putting a pillow under Ranevskaia's feet. This elicits her thanks and emphasizes the delicacy and generosity of her character. She then gushes joy at her return home (a strong display of emotions being an essential part of her character), brings herself back to the present moment, and once again thanks Firs. Lopakhin then interjects with a statement about time—emphasizing his entrepreneurial side. Next, he proceeds to reveal how much he likes Ranevskaia and how much he wishes to talk to her. He then moves to the theme of his origins and then back again to his feelings for Ranevskaia. She intrudes with her own emotions and memories that focus on the old cupboard. This brings out in her brother, Gaev, the memory of their old nurse's death—a fact that his sister notes briefly and dismisses, thus underlining her flightiness. Gaev then mentions the departure of another servant. The seeming depth of his emotions is undercut by the single gesture of his taking a fruit drop. Next, Lopakhin goes back to his feelings for Ranevskaia, and then immediately—without a break—he explains his plan to save the estate. Gaev rejects the idea as nonsense, while his sister expresses total bewilderment: she literally cannot understand such a proposal. One can stop here. Sixteen different emotions or ideas have just flickered before the recipient in the space of one and a half pages. Moreover, that is not the end of the matter, since all of the emotions and themes brought up in this scene will recur with variations at different times and with different combinations of characters. One sees that the basic compositional principle of *The Cherry Orchard* consists of showing ever-changing emotions and thoughts, and that these in turn create moods which are an important part of the poetry of Chekhov's scenes, as discussed above. It is in this ballet-like movement across the stage of gestures and relationships that the meaning of the play is to be found, not, as in traditional works, in action and plot development. This is the "undercurrent" that Konstantin Stanislavsky felt, but wasn't always able to grasp. For each recipient such a technique of composition initially distances, but eventually draws him in emotionally, though, as mentioned earlier, he may experience a more abstract type of emotionalism.[22] At first, he watches the patterning expecting action and plot. In his focus on and search for the traditional he may miss the fact that the patterning is what matters, since that is where the significance of the play lies. Furthermore, the fact that what every recipient receives is a variety of subjective, contrasting, and ephemeral points of view about events or situations leads to ambiguity and openness of construction. Chekhov's method of presenting a collection of very subjective voices whose words are never qualified by any actions complicates matters for each recipient even more than would be the case in traditional works. He is left with a multidimensionality, inconclusiveness, and openness to which he is not accustomed and which he may find confusing. Over time, however, the patterning of characters will begin to affect the recipient, just like "the poetry of scenes" does. Eventually, the ever-changing emotions and ideas will form a kind of rhythm. The recipient will intuitively hear this rhythm, take pleasure in it, and, most important, with its help, he will somehow come to understand something about the characters and about the content of this play.

The complex rhythm of Chekhov's play is also created by a further nontraditional substitutive emotive technique that also helps give overall unity to the work. This is accomplished through the use of recurring images. Much discussion has focused on trying to define the nature of these images, their relation to symbols and to the techniques of the symbolists.[23] They have been labeled "symbols," "leitmotivs," "correspondences," and "key words." For the purpose of this study it would be useless to enter into this debate. Suffice it to say that the author employs recurring images that are reminiscent of symbols. These images serve to provide guiding threads in the text and to expand the horizons of the work by hinting at other worlds, though not transcendental ones. They also offer intuitive knowledge to all recipients, knowledge that cannot be easily expressed in analytical terms. In many ways they function in a fashion similar to the "patterning of characters." In *The Cherry Orchard,* it is of course the orchard itself that is the primary recurring image. It fulfills a large number of functions and yet in many ways remains elusive and a major difficulty in staging. Patrice Pavis writes that the orchard has been internalized by every character in the work and that each uses it to express his or her relation to the world. Its uselessness and fading beauty, as well as its chill, suggest the passing of the old social order. The overall impression of white from the blossoms suggests living among desires rather than accepting reality. At the same time, the whiteness carries associations of virginity, sterility, and death in reference to some of the characters. Furthermore, by being a creation of man within nature it mediates between the latter and civilization. The list of functions continues.[24] However, by forcing upon every recipient an element that will initially appear confusing, and even unnecessarily importunate, the playwright will eventually increase the emotiveness of his work. This occurs because the image offers glimpses and hints of complex psychological and social phenomena that can be grasped only intuitively.

Finally, Chekhov introduces a structural element that works emotively because it represents one of the most familiar aspects of all human lives, namely, the holiday social occasion. Here, the holiday functions as an axis around which the whole play is organized. The license of the ritual, of the holiday, was often seen in Greek New Comedy, but there the orgiastic momentary freedom led to a reassertion of stability in society. In *The Cherry Orchard,* Chekhov distorts the New Comedy element and does not reestablish social norms, thus coming close both to the worldview and to the dramatic techniques of the symbolists. Like Maurice Maeterlinck, for example, Chekhov takes an archetypal approach to the holiday. He suggests, at least in all of his mature plays, that the holiday is a reactivation of an ancient, familiar, ceremonial situation. The holiday functions as a liberating moment for its participants, precisely because of the security of common memory that it offers. It is during the holiday that the individual becomes a part of community, "that he is least enclosed in his private rationalization and most open to disinterested insights."[25] The symbolists very clearly saw the holiday, the ritual, as an extension of or alternative to theater, and this in turn was based on their belief in a direct correspondence between life and art. In Chekhov, there are a number of examples where a failed work of art (Treplev's play in *The Sea Gull*) or a failed holiday (the names-day party in *The Three Sisters*) seems to indicate a failed life. Similarly, in *The Cherry Orchard,* the social occasion, namely, the ball in act 3, appears malapropos both in terms of when it takes place, as well as because of its character. Occurring at the same time as the sale of the estate, it brings together an incongruous assortment of people: Ranevskaia, the clerk Epikhodov, the stationmaster, the eternal student Trofimov, the spinster Varia, and the like. All of these diverse characters attempt to dance a stately grand-rond as executed by a Jewish orchestra. As the ball progresses a number of them step forward in order to express those truths that previously they had avoided stating. Ranevskaia, for example, admits to being cognizant of the fact that her lover will eventually destroy her. The ball collapses sadly when the news of the estate's sale reaches her.

In terms of distance manipulation, the use of the holiday as an archetype functions emotively, since like all archetypes it appeals to some of the most basic and instinctive elements of every recipient's life. The recipient can identify with a holiday, even if it is a failed one and the characters involved in it seem strange or distant. The familiarity of the event to some degree brings the protagonists closer to the recipient.

In short, an analysis of the major compositional parts of the play reveals how carefully Chekhov balances nontraditional distancing elements with various types of emotive elements. A lack of a traditional division into parts and of a traditional development is countered by the predominance of one theme in each act and by remnants of an exposition and a denouement. The absence of a typically nineteenth-century division into scenes turns out to be illusive, since in actual fact there exist fragments of exchange that could be classified as scenes and that play an important part in the weaving of mood. The absence of a traditional plot and action is balanced by an innovative use of movement. Finally, additional unity is achieved by using leitmotivs and an archetypal approach to the holiday.

Though not structural, there is one more element in *The Cherry Orchard* that helps determine the work's overall shape, and that element has been carefully and ultimately ambiguously balanced. This is the question of continuity versus discontinuity, or, in other words, the relationship between the textual world and the real world. In realistic plays a continuity is suggested between events in the fictional world and those in the real one. Each recipient feels that the characters could freely exit and enter from offstage and move between the two worlds. In absurd drama, on the other hand, no such continuity exists. The stage is all that there is and the recipient is presented with a metaphor of the existential and metaphysical isolation of the characters. In this respect, *The Cherry Orchard* seems to move in two directions at once.[26]

On the one hand, the characters, as in a Maeterlinckian play, are a group of misfits who seem cut off from the real world. They do not fit accepted behavioral norms and it is very difficult to imagine them functioning in the real world. The lovers Trofimov and Lopakhin, for example, are hindered only by their own impotence, which lays imaginary problems and impediments on their path to personal fulfillment. The servants, especially Jasha, are arrogant and useless and talk back to their employers in a way that is completely incompatible with their position. Ranevskaia's and Gaev's behavior is irresponsible in a tragic situation. The ball scene in act 3 is a complete example of incongruity and parody: a Jewish orchestra playing the stately grand-rond, the young heroine Ania dancing with the postal official, Sharlotta demonstrating ventriloquy, and so on. In other words, all of the characters seem to be drifting out of their assigned social stations and norms, and in the end it seems that the step between Chekhov's misfits and the lost souls of the Theater of the Absurd is not so very large. The Theater of the Absurd either leaves reality completely behind and moves into a hallucinatory world of its own, or transforms that reality by endowing it with an absurd character. Chekhov, of course, is not an absurdist playwright, but he goes much further in terms of questioning reality than any other preabsurdist writer.[27] His textual world becomes relative and ambiguous and thus every recipient's grasp of the real world becomes more tenuous.

This discontinuity is further strengthened by the space that Chekhov creates for his misfits. The collapse of social structure can be perceived by the fact that the boundary between the public and the private sphere is abolished.[28] Certainly, it seems so when one compares Chekhov's plays to those of Henrik Ibsen, though Chekhov does not go as far in blurring boundaries as would August Strindberg in *A Dream Play.* Nevertheless, in his mature works, including *The Cherry Orchard,* the playwright situates many of his very private and personal exchanges in public places, especially places conceived of as passageways or thoroughfares. The first and last acts of the play take place in a nursery that is now a hallway and that during the course of the play is stripped of its furniture. The second act is situated next to a row of telegraph poles, with the juxtaposition of the poles and an old shrine emphasizing the flux that exists in society. Traditional norms, standards, and patterns of behavior that have existed for hundreds of years are fast disappearing. Many of the characters feel lost and as a result their actions become incongruous. The new order has not fully taken shape. Therefore, the protagonists hover in "their places in between," trapped in a kind of limbo that is not only spiritual, but often material, and even economic.

Concurrently, the play contains elements that move it in the direction of an obvious continuity between the textual world and the real world. First of all, there is a clear sociohistorical context to the work. The play is set in a definite historical time frame, between 1890 and 1910, when enormous economic and social changes were taking place in Russia. Despite their odd behavior, each character in the play simultaneously in some way typifies the response of his or her social group to the play's contemporary changes. Firs, by far the oldest, represents that generation of peasants who still remember serfdom and who yearn for the safety that it offered. Lopakhin belongs to the younger generation of peasants. They have experienced serfdom only as children or as stories from their elders. They have done very well in this time of change, but nevertheless cannot rid themselves of feelings of spiritual inadequacy vis-à-vis the landowners. Ranevskaia and Gaev are both part of the landowning class. This class is tumbling from its position and is so unprepared for the changes occurring around it that it can only respond inadequately with bewilderment or the antiquated gestures of a bygone era. Similarly, one can place Varia, Trofimov, and Jasha in their particular sociohistorical milieus.[29]

Moreover, the historically and socially precise aspects of the characters are strengthened by the myriad of seemingly insignificant details, objects, and incidents of everyday life in which the work abounds. Interspersed among the more serious statements are the umbrellas, galoshes, hatboxes, sugar drops,

Distance Manipulation

brooches, and herring that take up so much of life in the real world, but that previously had not appeared on the stage. Of course, the details have only the "appearance of randomness," as true randomness would be unintelligible.[30] Such careful crafting of images and objects has something in common with symbolist technique. However, in Chekhov, it does not carry the transcendental associations that it did in symbolism and, therefore, in some way it harks back to Lev Tolstoy's technique of the "superfluous detail." Socially precise characters are actually part of a wider phenomenon known by many critics as a "broadening of horizons." This "broadening" is constantly taking place throughout the play. Chekhov achieves this expansion through a number of elements. First, he creates links between his characters and offstage by introducing a large number of unseen characters who are mentioned, but never appear. In *The Cherry Orchard,* there are close to fifty such unseen characters: mothers, fathers, other relatives, friends, servants, gardeners, and so on. Creating links to the outside world through unseen characters is not unique to Chekhov, but he makes much greater use of this technique than many other playwrights.[31]

A more complex element with respect to the "broadening of horizons" is the organization of space in act 2. The telegraph poles and shrine, on the one hand, form a public setting for private discussions, and on the other hand, they bridge the gap between the characters and the outside world. Their problems are directly connected to the props appearing on stage, the shrine and the telegraph poles, the latter of which also happens to connect the estate with other sites. In addition, a passing stranger becomes mixed up in the discussions of the characters, emphasizing that their problems cannot be separated from those of the rest of the world. Finally, further interaction between the real and the textual worlds occurs in the last act. This act, with its combination of mundane affairs and lyrical mood, with no denouement or catharsis, shows that the characters' problems have not been neatly resolved. In everyday life, of course, this is often the case.

All of these elements are linked together and strengthened by Chekhov's use of time. Chekhov's plays are filled with references to the future.[32] In the work *The Three Sisters,* the sisters dream of going back to Moscow, Astrov speaks of what will happen in two hundred years, and Vershinin speaks of working for future generations. In *The Cherry Orchard,* Gaev dreams of getting the money for the estate from a rich relative, Trofimov spouts about gardens of the future, and Lopakhin explains how he will capitalize on the estate. What is important is that all of these glances into the future expand the background against which the characters are presented and thus they serve to make them more comic, to cut them down to size, and as a result to diminish the level of tragedy. Therefore, what to the characters seem like earth-shattering crises, are seen by the recipient for what they are, the everyday problems of everyday people. This element gives their problems "their true dimension, placing them in a wide temporal context in which they become what they really are— . . . a shudder of microscopic proportions which will be forgotten and disappear in the vast darkness of time."[33] Thus, in yet another way, the connection between the presented world and the universe outside it is established. This time it is done through a comedic effect, which is not really that surprising considering that comedy in general deals with ordinary people, rather than unique heroes.

Finally, there is one more all-encompassing element that in a rather unusual way strengthens the continuity, namely, the play's rhythm. This is something that will be discussed in greater detail later. Here, it is sufficient to note that the continuous mistiming, missteps, incongruity, and inappropriate moments undermine the expected effect of the play and thus let in the real world. These uncomfortable moments are "realistic" because they reflect what often happens in the real world when real people are faced with insurmountable problems. They also break the recipient's expectations as to the "behavior" of a play, where traditionally such inconsistencies would have been eliminated. In constant danger of dissolving into reality, *The Cherry Orchard* "explores the relationship between stage and society in an elliptical and highly ironic manner."[34] The play forces every recipient to rethink both his expectations of theatrical reality, as well as his method of organizing reality outside of the theater.

It may seem that there are more techniques for creating the effect of continuity in *The Cherry Orchard* than of discontinuity. However, one must take not only a qualitative, but also a quantitative approach and analyze the number of times the two different sets of techniques make an appearance. Then, overall, the two tendencies of continuity and discontinuity become balanced. Once again, it turns out that the recipient is continuously being drawn into the illusion of a realistic play, then being pushed away as in a more anti-illusionistic work.

Besides the structural, another major level of the work on which distance can be manipulated is that of language.[35] The difficulty of discussing this level, as has been shown, lies in the fact that all comic discourse tends to be "disturbed" in some way. This is partly what Daniel Gerould means when he writes of incongruity, though he discusses the phenomenon in a broader sense that includes various levels of structure. A more language-specific study has been offered by Michael Issacharoff. He describes how in comedy the semiotic triad of signifier, signified, and referent is "[s]omehow unbalanced or distorted in at least one of its components."[36] As a result, one of the components is always foregrounded. Certainly, the language of *The Cherry Orchard* fits this definition in many ways. The play, for example, contains numerous non sequiturs between two characters which show that they are not listening to each other, with the second utterance undercutting the first, as in the following:

Distance Manipulation

Епиходов . . . никак не могу понять направления, . . . жить мне или застрелиться, собственно говоря, но тем не менее я всегда ношу при себе пистолет. Вот он . . . . (*Показывает револьвер.*)
Шарлотта. Кончила. Теперь пойду.

Epikhodov. . . . I can't understand the direction in any way, . . . should I live or shoot myself, speaking for myself, though none the less I always carry a pistol with me. Here it is. . . . (*Shows a revolver.*)
Sharlotta. I'm finished. Now I'll go. (p. 335)

Similarly, a single character may suddenly shift direction, either verbally or visually: "Гаев . . . Проценты мы заплатим, я убежден. . . . (Кладет в рот леденец)" (Gaev. . . . We'll pay the interest, I'm sure. . . . [*Puts a drop into his mouth*] [p. 333]). Here the gesture of swallowing a fruit drop breaks the force of the statement. One can also find examples of verbal repetition, both lexical and syntactic: "и я уехала за границу, совсем уехала, чтобы никогда не возвращаться, не видеть этой реки . . ." (and I went abroad, went away completely, so as to never return, never to see that river . . . [p. 339]). In *The Cherry Orchard,* in contrast to earlier plays, repetition is usually not exact. Rather, the author offers variants that still echo each other without being identical. In previous works, Chekhov more frequently used exact repetition of sounds and grammatical forms, like a string of verbs in the same person and tense. Furthermore, here repetition may also consist of a combination of words and visual images, a characteristic typical of farce. An example of the latter occurs when Epikhodov enters for the first time, his shoes squeaking, upon which reference is made verbally to the shoes (pp. 318–19). In addition, incongruity is represented by lexical oddities and mistakes, such as by the "какого?" in place of "что" that Gaev often utters. Then there are syntactical incongruities as when Epikhodov loses himself in a convoluted sentence that reveals his pretentious attempts at education: "Собственно говоря, не касаясь других предметов, я должен выразиться о себе, между прочим, что судьба относится ко мне без сожаления, как буря к небольшому кораблю" (Speaking for myself, not touching upon other subjects, I must express myself about myself, by the way, that fate treats me without compassion, like a storm, a small ship [p. 336]). Here, the humor is derived from a combination of redundant interjections and a misplaced attempt at poetic comparison. Such examples of disturbed discourse are numerous in this work, and in this respect, at least, its language upholds traditional comedic expectations and retains the traditional distance of this genre.

Another measurement of the language's "normalcy" in terms of any recipient's expectations is its deixis. The usage of this term here follows the theoretical work of Keir Elam and Alessandro Serpieri. Due to the fact that the dramatic world is always, regardless of the type of play, much less fully stipulated than the world of narrative prose, the role of what is called "the context of utterance" becomes much more important. This "context" helps the recipient to orient himself and to interpret the presented world. "The context of utterance" may be defined as the network of references within the dramatic discourse made by the speakers about or to themselves and their listeners, as well as about the direct spatiotemporal coordinates of the interlocutors. These references are known as deictic markers. It is important to note that studies have revealed that the foremost orientation of almost all traditional plays throughout their duration is toward an *I* addressing a *you* in the *here* and *now*. In other words, an orientation toward an eternal and yet continually changing present.[37] With a few adjustments for the language of the text, Elam's and Serpieri's theories can be applied to any dramatic text. For example, personal pronouns are less important in Russian texts, while verb endings play a significant role. Furthermore, in practice it has also proven useful to combine deictic segmentation with Roman Jakobson's model of communication.[38] By simultaneously studying the deixis and the actual communicative function of each segment, it becomes possible to define more precisely the direction of each speaker's orientation and the function of each utterance.

A detailed segmentation of the text of *The Cherry Orchard* has shown that the deictic orientation of this play is traditional, and thus, in this respect, not undercutting recipient expectations. In fact, it is more traditional than that of *The Three Sisters*, where the characters are given to "philosophizing." In this work the only break from the here and now occurs via reminiscences. The distancing effect of the reminiscences is also softened by the fact that they tend to be tied to concrete objects present on stage, such as the cupboard about which Gaev waxes poetical. In opposition to Chekhov's deictic traditionalism, some of the other plays examined in the following chapters will experiment with deixis in surprising ways.

At the same time, applying Roman Jakobson's model of communication shows some anomalies. Expressives are used much more frequently than is normal in traditional works. Expressives are emotive elements that constantly emphasize the emotional states of the characters and eventually heighten the involvement of all recipients. They are also perhaps the strongest source of the feverishness that is often associated with Chekhov's works.

On the other hand, the appellative, another primary Jakobsonian function, appears much less frequently than expected. It is said that the speech event in plays is an actual dramatic action, and studies have been done that show dramatic dialogue as a series of moves between characters with a strong "perlocutionary" effect. Keir Elam defines the "perlocutionary act" as an act "performed by means of saying something, such as persuading someone to do something, convincing one's interlocutor, moving him to anger, and so on." Thus, a "perlocutionary effect" is the attribute of an utterance that successfully fulfills the perlocutionary act and elicits a definite action and response from the interlocutor.[39] In *The Cherry Orchard,* the perlocutionary effect is minimal, and utterances rarely evince a response in action from the listener. This is one of the reasons behind Jenny Stelleman's insistence that the characters in Chekhov's plays, though unhappy with the situation, actually retain the status quo through their manipulation of language.[40] A lot of words are poured forth in *The Cherry Orchard*—as in all of the playwright's works: the characters speak incessantly.

In addition, Chekhov's language distances by undermining every recipient's understanding of the relationship between language and communication.[41] The playwright weakens the bond between signifier and signified when he creates language that does not communicate. His dialogue is filled with cross-purpose utterances, unfinished thoughts, thematic shifts, repetition, questions without answers, nonsense words, streams of words, and negations. All of these elements produce silence, noncommunication that is used to present the characters' alienation from the world around them, as well as from themselves. Such a negative usage of language makes a very strong and radical statement. It serves not only to present a state of chaos and the randomness of reality, for that could be achieved by other methods. In a very modernistic fashion, Chekhov moves further to query the whole structure of drama and of all literary art. Language previously had been the unquestioned medium of both, the one element that was most taken at face value as being a means of communication. Instead, like many of his contemporaries, the playwright brings out the possibilities of nonverbal communication: silence, gesture, movement, and the weaving of images.

Finally, language functions as a key feature in the creation of this play's rhythm, a topic about which numerous critics have written.[42] They present it as a complex orchestration of the whole work and one that involves several elements. These include the by now famous pauses, as well as silent moments, intonation as choreographed through numerous stage directions and punctuation marks, various types of repetition, seemingly useless remarks, nonverbal sounds, interruptions, and nonsense words or phrases. In addition, all of these must be analyzed in conjunction with the movement and gestures both of individuals and groups. Overall, the rhythm of *The Cherry Orchard* is unexpected and nontraditional, and thus it increases distance by breaking recipient expectations.[43] It is a broken, "syncopated rhythm" reminiscent of modern music. Its "brokenness" is a product of several factors. First, pauses are much more numerous in this play than in traditional ones. Second, the majority of stage directions refers to emotions rather than to physical actions and the actors are constantly asked to vary these emotions. Third, there appear very few long utterances by a single character on one topic, or exchanges between various individuals of any significant length. Instead, even utterances of three or four lines will often treat several subjects, each of which elicits a very different emotional state in the speaker.

The importance of rhythm is enormous. In Chekhov, it is often more important than the actual words. Whereas silence may function expressively in his work, words often become trite, are ignored by listeners, or appear as "markers charting the territory of silence" or figures of noncommunication. The rhythm, however, is always finely tuned and carries information, even if the content does not. Reliance on a musiclike element, rather than on speech itself, reflects the modernist age, and is very apparent in many symbolist and avant-garde works. Though modernism sees a great revitalization of the literary language, it also witnesses a marked devaluation of the word. The word is deemed incapable of fully expressing many emotional, intuitive, and subconscious states. It is also considered to be powerless and even untruthful due to overconventionalization and overuse. Chekhov is among the first Russian writers to move away from an almost exclusive reliance on words to the use of an overall rhythm produced by means of many elements, certainly not just verbal ones.

Thus, though incongruity is in many respects a normal aspect of disturbed comic discourse, the incongruity found in *The Cherry Orchard* combines traditional elements with untraditional ones. The primary innovative feature is an amazing orchestration creating a syncopated, irregular rhythm that will initially distance and frustrate the recipient, but eventually draws him into a complex web of emotional states.

Both structure and language are part of a broader level of distance manipulation that has thus far been continuously touched upon but not openly explored. This is the whole area of genre expectations. Genre expectations are linked not only to structure and language, but also to characterization and a number of other elements that need to be discussed.

First, one can begin by noting that initially when encountering *The Cherry Orchard*, every recipient will be led to expect a comedy. As has been mentioned, Chekhov informed Konstantin Stanislavsky that he had written not just a comedy, but almost a farce. He subtitled the play "Комедия в четырех действиях" ("Comedy in Four Acts"). Furthermore, for today's recipient the assumption that this is a traditional comedy is strengthened in the first moment of contact because Chekhov retains the proscenium arch. That would not have been the case for the modernist or the virtual recipient. However, in the present, where various avant-garde performances have dispensed with the traditional type of stage, a proscenium arch suggests to the recipient, at least for a while, that he may assume the traditional role of an "unseen watcher."[44]

In terms of building up the more specific expectations for a traditional farce in *The Cherry Orchard*, one can begin by considering characterization. Many of the secondary characters such as Epikhodov, Pishchik, and to some degree, Sharlotta, are farcical figures. They are drawn very broadly, greatly exaggerated, and characterized by a limited number of repeated and ridiculous features, many of which are visual and auditory. Epikhodov is marked by his clumsiness and his unhappy love for Duniasha. Pishchik is remembered for his equine traits, his tendency of putting himself to sleep, and his obsession with money. Even more important, the protagonists themselves exhibit certain traits typical of the genre. Chekhov overturns many of the conventions of melodrama, but instead of moving the characters toward "real life," "he enhances their 'staginess' by caricaturing each according to a particular affective outline.... Most of the changes shift the roles decisively toward farce: buffoon, senex [senile old man], virgin."[45] Consider, as an example of the stereotypical virgin, the standoffishness of the earnest Varia: bustling with her big chain of keys, complaining about her work and desirous of marriage but unable to relax and deal with her only suitor. Similarly, the senility of the aged Firs, in the role of senex, is constantly emphasized.

Farce is also suggested by the fact that the play contains quite a bit of stage business. Stage business is a characteristic of traditional farce, though not necessarily of comedy. This is so because farce is always very visually oriented, while comedy may be confined to verbal humor. Chekhov clearly suggests farce when he fills his work with squeaking shoes, dropped and squashed things, tumbles down the stairs, half-eaten cucumbers, conjuring tricks, and other such similarly physical effects.

In support of more general comedic expectations, the work contains a large amount of incongruity. Incongruity between situation and response is a basic source of humor in all forms of traditional comedy. In *The Cherry Orchard,* "the actions of the characters are inappropriate, inadequate, and irrelevant to the situation in which they find themselves and to the problem they face."[46] Since incongruities in comedy are of different kinds, it can be determined that in this case we have an example of "the comedy of the spendthrift or the wastrel." Ranevskaia continues to scatter money and in the most absurd way ignores or deflects the proposals made by Lopakhin to parcel out the land to prospective buyers. Gaev escapes from this problem through his billiards and his food. Thus, in terms of the relationship between situation and solution, incongruity reigns and the comedic expectations of the recipient are upheld.

Chekhov also employs the old comedic technique of parodying the major characters through the secondary ones.[47] The overwrought and fainting Duniasha caricatures a lady. Jasha has become an arrogant and dandified fop whose impertinence toward his masters should be unacceptable to them. Epikhodov is a provincial clerk with great intellectual pretensions, and so on. It must be noted that the presentation of the servants is not a sign of elitism in Chekhov. Their behavior simply mirrors the degradation and disintegration of the landowning class. Though overall the use of this technique by the playwright agrees with its traditional application, Chekhov introduces a twist of his own. In traditional comedy, both the protagonists and the secondary characters are rather stereotypical and not complex. Simply put, the latter group is drawn more broadly and with more exaggeration. Chekhov, on the other hand, constructs the reflection of primary characters in secondary ones in an innovative fashion that in some way prefigures the metatheatricalism of later works, such as Aleksandr Blok's *The Puppet Show*. In *The Cherry Orchard,* there is an "inherent tension between the *emploi,* . . . that is to say the stock roles that Chekhov's main characters perform, and their inner life."[48] It is true that as the play progresses, the protagonists keep falling back on the "theatrical patterns" of stock characters, thus revealing their "inability . . . to become autonomous personalities."[49] However, these protagonists also have a more serious side that lurks underneath the surface and that from time to time makes its appearance.

While they may be serious on occasion, the characters' comedic aspect is further strengthened by their unchangeability. Unchangeability is typical of comedy where characters do not undergo a revelation and catharsis. Until the very end of the play, the protagonist's actions—or attempts at action—to save the orchard continue to be inadequate. For all of their talking and self-exploration, Chekhov's characters are unable or unwilling to transform themselves.

Simultaneously, distance in *The Cherry Orchard* is increased by the fact that comedy and farce are frustrated in a number of ways. First, the farce is frustrated at every step by a lack of "energy."[50] Farce is a genre characterized as visual, but not only in regard to stage business. It is also visual in that the recipient actually sees before him the action-packed plot: the conniving, dueling, courting, and rescuing that are part of the story. As has been demonstrated earlier, that is not at all the case with *The Cherry Orchard*. Here, there is very little action in the traditional sense, and what there is does not seem to fit the mold of comedy. Ranevskaia's husband dies of drink, her son drowns, her lover robs her, and finally she loses the one thing that she values, namely, the estate. Furthermore, the plot and tempo constantly appear to falter, to be retarded. Chekhov achieves this effect through a number of techniques. First, he breaks up the tightly knit chain of action typical of farce. Second, he inserts serious exchanges of dialogue into comic ones. Third, he adds pauses and mistiming that are pathetic in nature rather than funny. Already the very first scene of *The Cherry Orchard* begins to destroy every recipient's expectations. It is true that the expository information conveyed in it is usual for a traditional work. In addition, Lopakhin, who delivers the message, is funny in many respects. He even characterizes himself as a misfit: the rich man who has not become comfortable with his new situation, as when he says of himself: "Со свинным рылом в калашный ряд" (You cannot make a silk purse out of a sow's ear [p. 318]). Nevertheless, the overall effect of the scene is confusing to all recipients because of the manner in which the character delivers his speech. The presentation is filled with a lazy waiting, with introspective pauses, and with uncertain and disjointed phrases, all of which are associated much more with the psychologically developed characters of tragedy than with figures of comedy. Content fulfills the recipient's expectations and thus diminishes distance, while form undercuts that comfortable feeling and pushes him away.

The other example illustrating how farce is undermined, and one that has been much discussed, is the description of the sound of a string breaking. Sound is certainly an important part of traditional comedy. However, in this case, the breaking of the string creates a serious mood. The sound is described in the text as "замирающий, печальный" (dying, sad). Despite Chekhov's insistence that it should be shorter and lighter than what Konstantin Stanislavsky was proposing in his production, it definitely introduces a somber tone, and, depending on the staging, even a menacing one.[51]

A much more complex issue in terms of distance manipulation is the area of characterization. Though some aspects of characterization point toward farce (exaggeration, unchangeability), some of its elements force the recipient in the opposite direction. First, there is the complexity of the characters, more typical of serious drama than of comedy. Behind the stock masks, there lurk and appear, from time to time at irregular and unexpected intervals, genuinely more serious and complex personalities. Ranevskaia, for example, admits on occasion that her lover will be the source of her destruction. Such is the case in her conversation with Trofimov in act 3, in which, cognizant of the fact that she may receive censure, she asks for mercy. Also, Gaev, in a moment of lucidity, will realize that he and his kind have become dispensable. Of all the characters, it is Lopakhin who is perhaps the most interesting, and we know that the author intended for him to be the center of the play.[52] Seemingly drawn as a comic character, a nouveau riche, clumsy and undiplomatic, he shows a complex interior, a poetic soul, and a depth of feeling and intelligence, all of which are intended to confuse the virtual recipient. Furthermore, it is not just Lopakhin who is so interesting, for even a minor character like Sharlotta appears to have a mixture of traits. Generally a comic figure who chews on cucumbers and does conjuring tricks, she has moments of a very real and pathetic loneliness that undercut her origins in farce. In turn, the psychological complexity increases the depth of feeling experienced by the characters; this is further emphasized, as will be discussed later, by an abundant use of expressives. Overall, characterization in *The Cherry Orchard* functions simultaneously in a distancing and an emotive fashion. On the one hand, complexity and depth of feeling are emotive because they create the illusion of three-dimensional figures and this elicits identification on the part of today's recipient with certain of the characters.[53] On the other hand, the tension between stock and "realistic" characters discussed above creates distancing.[54] The two directions of development allow Chekhov's characters to hark back to an earlier, Golden Age of comedy.

Whether the actual emotion elicited from the recipient is sympathy, as in comedy, or compassion, as in tragedy, is a debatable matter, one left up to the actor or theater director to decide. In either case, Chekhov's characterization is surprising and distancing as it moves allegedly comedic characters toward the tragic mode. Simultaneously, that very movement creates characters that are easier to identify with and more emotive. There is, of course, room for maneuvering in a dramatic text due to the "incompleteness" of its language, and, for this reason, much of the interpretation might depend on the actual production.

The manipulation of distance on the level of characterization is summarized well by Herta Schmid when she describes the two most famous styles of staging Chekhov's plays, that of Konstantin Stanislavsky and that of Vsevolod Meierhold.[55] In conjunction with this question, she writes of "переживание" (feeling through) and "представление" (representation), and she shows how both methods complement each other and how both are needed to do justice to Chekhov's plays. The two terms signal the fact that the playwright simultaneously forces the virtual recipient to observe the characters from the outside and at a distance, as in comedy, and from the inside with sympathy, as in a tragedy. The two point of views constantly replace each other and thus are one of the factors that account for the shifting distance in *The Cherry Orchard*.

A very sharp example of this ambiguous approach to characterization is the case of Firs and the way in which this figure is used at the end of the play. The old man is one of the most stereotypical and comic characters in the work. He is the proverbial old servant: deaf and with limited horizons, who continues to fuss around his master even when the latter is no longer a child. Firs acts as the near absurd chorus that comments on events. At the same time, the author chooses to use him in a serious way at the end of the play. On the one hand, even in the last scene, he repeats his not very profound remarks. On the other hand, the fact that he is old and sick and left behind definitely makes an unpleasant impression on the recipient. It is true, as some critics suggest, that his situation is not tragic because Lopakhin is retaining Epikhodov to look after the house and therefore Firs will surely be found. Nevertheless, the very fact of his abandonment serves to diminish the recipient's sympathy for the protagonists by showing one final moment of their self-centeredness.[56] Furthermore, this last scene—where a character, namely Firs, lies down completely immobile but not dead—flaunts the conventions of theater. An immobile body on the stage representing a corpse adheres to the conventions of traditional drama. However, the appearance of a body, but not a dead one, undercuts these conventions and makes a metatheatrical statement, emphasizing the separateness of textual and real worlds. The use of this device causes the textual world to collapse at the very end of the work.[57]

In addition, the ending of the work plays with genre expectations in still other ways. On the one hand, as Daniel Gerould notes, it should not be forgotten that it is normal for the ridiculous characters of comedy to be frustrated at the end, to have their plots and intrigues foiled. Traditional comedy always contrasts the ridiculous figures with positive ones, most often young lovers, and it is the latter's desires and plans that are fulfilled in the end. Also, the madcap freedom permitted during traditional comedy ends with the re-establishment of stability and societal norms.[58] That is not quite the case in Chekhov. It is true that the ridiculous characters are frustrated. However, this means that all of the characters are foiled because there are no completely positive figures in this work. Even the standing of the young lovers, Trofimov and Ania, is undercut throughout the play. Furthermore, order and stability are not restored at the end. The disintegration of the society created in this textual world—that, for a moment, it may have seemed possible to stop—is presented in the final scene as progressing unchecked. The last hold on the old order that the protagonists had, namely, the estate, has been lost. Ranevskaia will return to Paris where she will continue her downward slide. Gaev will go on making attempts at finding a job. Trofimov departs still the eternal student, and Lopakhin remains the unwilling owner of an estate, with a sense of having destroyed something beautiful. Thus, every recipient is left with a special kind of ambivalence and open-endedness that is not traditional in comedy. He does not leave the theater convinced that life has been restored to a stable and pleasant state, but rather bewildered by what has been presented to him.

It must be noted that the best traditional comedy contains an ambivalence that one does not find in tragedy. In other words, it is the nature of great traditional comedy that it, too, to some degree, manipulates the distance between the recipient and the textual world. It both engages his sympathy and keeps him at a distance.[59] J. L. Styan has demonstrated this point using two Shakespearean comedies, namely, *Troilus and Cressida* and *Twelfth Night*. He calls these works "dark comedies" and speaks of a "weighty and sinister effect." Furthermore, he states that, in tragedy, incongruity takes on a more grotesque character, whereas in comedy, it is more delicately balanced. Similarly, other critics speak of the violence of comedy for all of its supposed lightheartedness.[60] Yet for all the comparisons made, Chekhov's ambivalence, though certainly indebted to the works of William Shakespeare and earlier masters of comedy, is of a different, innovative sort. First, Chekhov does not balance and present personal with political or social events, as does Shakespeare. In fact, he takes great pains to hide and soften the political and social tensions that must have been very apparent during this time of change. Yet this is not due to the fact that Chekhov wishes to shun violence altogether. The playwright's comedic elements at times do have something violent in them. On occasion that violence seems to be due to viciousness, as with Jasha. At other times the possibility of violence, perhaps to oneself, is due more to despair, as with Sharlotta. Furthermore, Chekhov's incongruity has something more of the grotesque about it due to the serious masks placed on the protagonists. However, *The Cherry Orchard* is not a tragedy in the traditional sense. Instead, the grotesqueness of his misfits creates a sense of absurdity, of a stage cut off from the real world, and this moves the author in the direction of twentieth-century types of ambivalence.

Ambivalence, then, is the defining approach to genre in *The Cherry Orchard*. Chekhov consistently carries out his balancing act, fulfilling some comedic/farcical expectations, while frustrating others. Whereas in his earlier plays, the overall impression is that the works clearly lean toward serious drama, in *The Cherry Orchard,* it would be extremely difficult, if not impossible, to say which side is represented more strongly. One must look at this play as an example of a new genre, one that points to the absurdity of twentieth-century theater.

In conclusion, it is possible to state that in *The Cherry Orchard,* Chekhov creates a unique balance between distancing and engaging the recipient on the levels of structure, characterization, genre expectations, and language. This work is neither a traditional comedy nor tragicomedy, nor a typical realistic work. To begin with, the subject matter of the play, namely various forms of alienation, is very contemporary. A larger-than-life hero's sense of alienation was already a common topic of romantic drama. However, Chekhov's variety is much more modern and understandable to today's recipient. It is the alienation of everyday life, of mundane people who are unable to deal with the overwhelming social and cultural changes occurring around them. It has been said that Chekhov is the ultimate realist who brings the movement to its apex, and beyond whom there are no possibilities for realism. In some sense that is true. The playwright's presentation of alienation is stripped of romantic heroism. It is placed within a recognizable sociohistorical framework. Never to such a degree have characters been surrounded by a seemingly random collection of trifling details of everyday life. A sense of continuity with the real world is created by the myriad of offstage, invisible characters. As in real life no clear-cut answers or easy solutions are offered.

At the same time, Chekhov breaks out of realism, especially out of the parochialism that plagues the realist movement at the beginning of the twentieth century. He enters the realm of modernist experimentation. For example, in terms of composition, he does not offer the traditional causal plot, or the sweep of action toward a definite climax. For all of their realism, his characters are in some way misfits who do not conform to class expectations of proper behavior and who suggest the lost souls of absurd drama. Like many modernists, especially those associated with "theatricalism," the playwright experiments with the comedic genre. *The Cherry Orchard* fulfills traditional comedic expectations in certain areas, such as foregrounding language, reliance on incongruity of action to situation, farcical figures, and stage business. Simultaneously, Chekhov undercuts expectations by combining something of the depth and complexity of Golden Age comedy with twentieth-century instability and absurdity. On the one hand, his comedic characters have the kind of serious, even tragic, side as is found in a Don Quixote. On the other hand, the lack of farcical energy—the fact that at the end of the play stability is not restored, that not just a few villains, but all of the characters are foiled—points the play in the direction of modern developments. Furthermore, though rejecting the symbolists' transcendentalism and mysticism, the playwright shares their innovative approach to language. Like the symbolists, he tends toward utterances devoid of appellatives, a discourse that is not perlocutionary in its effect. Like them, Chekhov contrasts language with silence, that is noncommunication, showing the inadequacy of the word in expressing many of the important moments in life. Above all, this "Realist" realizes the symbolists' theoretical dreams of using rhythm as a principle of composition. The writer creates an extremely complicated orchestration of many elements that come together as an underlying rhythmic current that carries the meaning of the work, often in moments when actual utterances communicate little or nothing. However, the playwright avoids the extremes of the avant-garde, extremes that greatly confuse and distance even today's recipient.

Chekhov's crowning achievement, *The Cherry Orchard* is a bold work that does not hesitate to distance, yet combines radical innovation with both traditional and nontraditional emotive elements. At the end of his life, the playwright merges the two strands of dramatic writing that he had been developing throughout his life. *The Cherry Orchard* is an amalgam of one-act farces—with their humor, stage business, and incongruity—and of serious, philosophizing works that discuss the meaning of life, such as *Platonov* or even *The Three Sisters*. The reason for the great dramatic success of this final play lies in Chekhov's profound understanding of seemingly all twentieth-century recipients. For the modern recipient straddles, as it were, a fence: he lives in a technological, changed, and changing world, while emotionally, and, therefore, aesthetically, retaining ties with his past.

Chapter Two

Zinaida Gippius's *Holy Blood*

ONE OF THE earliest examples of distance manipulation is Zinaida Gippius's play *Holy Blood* (*Святая кровь*).[1] Albeit only a slight thirty-six pages in length, it is, nevertheless, a complex and subtle reaction to a number of issues. First, it participates in the symbolist search for spiritual answers to existential problems. More specifically, it is a concrete actualization of the philosophical discussions conducted in the Merezhkovskii circle. Second, though certainly not intentionally feminist, it does offer, within the very masculinized world of Russian symbolism, a unique treatment of the female protagonist. Third, it is another voice in the symbolist debate on the function of literature.[2]

Formally of great interest is the playwright's quite successful attempt to create a tragic mode in drama within a folkloric context. Furthermore, the work is innovative in its manipulation of distance. It contains such distancing elements as, for example, jarring subject matter, a surprising heroine, and atypical deixis. Simultaneously, Gippius's skill as a playwright leads her to temper the distancing effect with emotive techniques, both traditional and nontraditional in nature. By engaging the recipient emotionally, the techniques help create a work that is more than a writer's intellectual experiment. The emotive elements of this play include, among others, the usage of language, temporal references, and the arrangement of deictic segments. Above all, the author successfully captures the essence of the tragic mode and thus is able to elevate what would otherwise be a fantastic and not very probable tale to a higher, more spiritual plane.

It should be noted that Gippius actually wrote three plays. However, *Holy Blood* is the only one that breaks radically with traditional dramatic forms. For the most part, Gippius's experimentation occurred in the fields of poetry and short prose. Drama remained an occasional genre for her. Certainly she made no attempt to even publish *Holy Blood*. Yet her achievement in this one dramatic work is indisputable.

To begin with, the plot and story of *Holy Blood* are unusual. The central character is a young "русалка" ("water nymph"—a name sometimes bestowed on Gippius herself), who from the opening moments appears as a stranger among strangers. Water nymphs in general occupy a marginal position in the world, but here the protagonist is further marginalized by being brooding and passionate, rather than playful and lighthearted as expected of nymphs.[3] A song reveals to her that *rusalki* live long but eventually melt away without leaving a trace. Upset by this revelation, she questions an older nymph and is told that this is true, and also that there exist creatures, human beings, who have immortal souls. She then listens to the story of Christ's sacrifice and finds it inordinately moving and beautiful. As a result, she is seized with an overwhelming desire to acquire a human soul. An old witch supplies her with the information on what she must do in order to acquire a soul. Thus, the nymph leaves her watery world and moves in with two hermits—Nikodim, young and orthodox, Pafnutii, old, kind, and pantheistically unorthodox. Her body becomes human and she begins to learn about Christianity. Moreover, she develops a great love for the old monk. Her agony begins when she is informed by the old witch that in order to pass the final stage and receive an actual soul she has to choose between two paths, both of which are at first abhorrent to her. Either the old monk must baptize her and in the process lose his own soul or she must kill him despite the fact that she loves him. In the end, consumed with an even higher love for Christ, she commits the murder. Condemned by human beings for the deed, she accepts earthly punishment, as well as eternal sorrow, for the beloved life that she took. She does so with the conviction that her overwhelming and passionate love of Christ will eventually lead to redemption.

With the dominance of the everyday, the real, and the banal on the stage—both at the turn of the century and now—the story of this play distances today's recipient, and presumably was meant to distance the virtual recipient. First, the playwright presents a fantastic, fairy-tale-like setting within which she wishes to create a serious tragedy. To this day fairy tales have continued to be perceived as light, childish fare. Second, the seeming sanction of murder for the achievement of salvation creates the impression of a single-minded fanatical devotion to an unorthodox type of religiosity. Today's movies and other forms of popular entertainment are filled with murders of all sorts and gradually overcome the resistance of many recipients to violence. However, bloodshed, for the most part, continues to be presented within the framework of action movies, rather than serious, tragic drama. Furthermore, violence in art is usually not bolstered by religion. Third, the modernist recipient would have found disturbing the fact that epiphany is here achieved by a pagan, sinful heroine, a creature traditionally condemned to the status of a *nechist'* (unclean). For today's recipient this element is most probably lost. These estranging elements of the story can become clearer if placed within the context of Gippius's religious views and poetry. She had her own idiosyncratic definition of love, a definition borrowed from Plato and Vladimir Solov'ev, as well as from a host of fin-de-siècle notions.[4] While not decadent in origin, the author's ideas borrow from those of Fedor Dostoevski and Friedrich Nietzsche. Pantheism, with its emphasis on an intuitive, mystical, childlike approach to life, is used as an image of and bridge to the idea of a spiritual transformation through love. Furthermore, pantheistic nonintellectualism helps strengthen the emotional impact of the play. Nevertheless, the fairy-tale-like qualities of the story cause the murder of the monk to remain much more symbolic and hyperbolic than does, for example, the psychologically motivated rape perpetrated by a Stavrogin. The story appears as both a disturbing and a confusing factor that needs to be balanced by strong emotive elements. This was true for the modernist recipient used to the minimal demands of the *pièces bien faites* and is true for the contemporary recipient raised on popular movies and television.

This distancing subject matter is then presented within a form that clearly experiments with certain dramatic elements. Basically, Gippius manipulates the form of a *pièce à thèse* to make it more appealing to a modern audience. Beginning with the obvious aspects, one can consider the kind of setting that the playwright creates. In her stage directions, Gippius sketches a vague, fairy-tale-like scene: a moonlit meadow by the lake, a circle of pale and turbid water nymphs moving slowly as if in a dream. The scenery does not change much throughout the three acts, presenting the same bit of landscape from various angles.[5] At the time the play was written, a fairy tale-like set would appear most often in a ballet or opera. These are art forms in which the nature of aesthetic reception is quite different from that of serious, not to say, tragic drama, and ones in which the *rusalka* is presented lightheartedly as an idealized and benign creature. On the theatrical stage in 1901, veristic plays were still the staple fare, even though the symbolic works of somebody like Maurice Maeterlinck had already been produced.[6] Gippius's attempt to create a tragic mode within a folkloric context foreshadows the later experiments with folklore of such writers as Aleksei Remizov. Much the same is also true of today. Little has changed and in general fairy tales continue to be associated with children's literature, as well as opera and ballet.

Similarly nontraditional was her choice of a water nymph as protagonist, as well as the characterization of that nymph, both of which would have certainly undermined a modernist recipient's expectations. In Russian folk mythology, the *rusalka* is one of the "undead": a pregnant unmarried girl who after her suicide becomes a sexually threatening creature luring men to their death. The water nymph had already appeared in opera (*Rusalka*) and ballet (*La Sylphide, Giselle, Swan Lake*), and also in literature—though not in drama. However, Gippius's treatment of the character is unique. First, she de-emphasizes, though doesn't obliterate, the sexual and "unclean" elements from folklore. Undoubtedly, Nikodim's reaction to the heroine, as well as Pafnutii's references to "мерещется тебе искушение" (your dreaming of a temptation) and "неладные мысли" (bad thoughts) indicate that the former is physically attracted to her. Second, she avoids the operatic/ballet tradition that usually makes the *rusalka* a benign creature and focuses attention on the young male lover. Third, she rejects the symbolist practice of demonizing women within the concept of the "Eternal Feminine." For all of the theoretical statements of inclusiveness, the prevailing symbolist image of "woman" was a male-created "demonic eternal feminine." Examples of such an image include Aleksandr Blok's Kolumbina, Fedor Sologub's Al'gista, Innokentii Annenskii's Argiope, and Aleksei Remizov's Unkrada.[7]

Instead, the playwright makes the water nymph a passionate, loving, and kind heroine. From the beginning, her passion and unstoppable striving toward Christ are expressed both through her words, which continuously focus on the question of a soul, as well as through such stage directions as "молчит и смотрит на поляну, не двигаясь" (stands silent and looks at the meadow, not moving [p. 1]).[8] Furthermore, her innate goodness is emphasized by the fact that as soon as she hears that Pafnutii might lose his soul by baptizing her, she refuses to let him contemplate the deed. Such a reinterpretation of the traditional character of the nymph would definitely be distancing for both the modernist and the virtual recipients. Yet even for today's recipient, much less familiar with Russian folklore and/or symbolism, the characterization is still distancing. Though some of the historical nuances have been lost, it is the serious and tragic treatment of a fairy tale heroine that continues to be estranging in the second half of the twentieth century.

Gippius's choice of protagonist is in part dictated by her religious views, in which love (влюбленность) appears as a complex phenomenon that includes, among other ideas, Platonic androgyny, and which, moreover, must remain unconsummated. By joining a nonhuman and childlike creature with an elderly monk, the author creates a union that, at least partially, corresponds to her ideas. Simultaneously, the work subverts certain accepted images, notions, and forms of expression. Having de-emphasized sexuality, the author has the *rusalka* seek God—something that does not coincide with her "нечисть" (unclean) nature. Instead of demonizing, she juxtaposes her passion and love with the negative image of Nikodim's male Christian orthodoxy. In Gippius's textual world, the marginalized community of womanlike creatures is definitely more positive than the dominant male orthodoxy. Still, the author does not oversimplify, and Nikodim is contrasted with Pafnutii's kindly, pantheistic form of Christianity, and, furthermore, he is both chided and defended by the latter. Overall, however, the effect is that the "seemingly demonic Other is revealed as the truly human." And yet for all of Gippius's inadvertently feminist approach, in the end the playwright "advocate[s] escape from the watery world of [female] otherness" because "empowerment may be possible only in the world of men."[9] Many of the historically specific nuances of this interpretation would only be understandable to the virtual and modernist recipient. However, the image of the sexualized femme fatale contrasted with feminist views is a controversial issue still current for today's recipient.

Yet another distancing element is the whole composition of the play. The plot, though logical, is simple with very little action. It does not abound in the complicated and fast-paced intrigue so typical of much of nineteenth-century drama, especially of the more popular variety. Neither does it contain any of those magnificent, introspective soliloquies that in tragedy allow glimpses into the agitated mind of a protagonist in conflict with himself and the world around him. Furthermore, the play develops at a slow pace. In place of traditional plot and action, Gippius gives structure to the work by utilizing in an innovative fashion a series of parallelisms; these will be discussed later in greater detail.

Undoubtedly, the most radical and innovative experimentation with the form of this play occurs on the level of deixis and communicative functions. A combined deictic and communicative segmentation carried out on *Holy Blood* reveals very interesting manipulation on the part of the playwright, manipulation that functions both in a distancing and an emotive fashion. In terms of distancing (the emotiveness will be discussed later), in the first act, almost a third of the segments have nothing to do with the characters or the here and now as in normal traditional drama. Instead, they either pose questions or offer information about the general state of matters, the general characteristics of nymphs and human beings, or about religious beliefs. In other words, they are oriented toward a general there, as, for example, in the following:

Тетушка! Милая! Расскажи ты мне все, что знаешь о нас, о людях, об их душе!

Auntie! Dear! Tell me everything that you know about us, about people, about their soul! (p. 4)

Тогда меж нами родился Человек, которого они назвали Богом. . . .

Then among them was born a Man whom they called God. . . . (p. 4)

. . . можно ли так сделать, чтоб русалке, какой-нибудь, тоже иметь бессмертную душу?

. . . can one make it so that a nymph also has an immortal soul? (p. 7)

Another third of the segments are actual comments by the characters either about themselves or others who are present. However, few of these segments function as appellatives; in other words, they serve as attempts to exert influence upon the speaker's interlocutor. For example, the old nymph comments on the young one: "Опять закостенела! И что за ребенок! Ее и месяц точно не греет" (Again she's frozen up! And what a child! Really even the moon doesn't warm her [p. 2]). She then continues to brush out her hair without pursuing the matter further and seemingly not even expecting a response. Likewise, the young nymph's numerous invocations such as "Тетушка, милая," followed by questions, reveal her strong focus on the problem of the soul, but do not stir up any conflict or response, except an indulgent smile. An even lesser number of segments are statements of intended action.

Furthermore, the speech events in *Holy Blood* do not create conflict; very few of them are even designed to achieve a perlocutionary effect. Rather, they are comments about oneself or another who is present that elicit little or no opposing reaction.[10] Added to this is the fact that there are few spatial and temporal adverbs in this first act that would, as required by tradition, orient the scene toward the here and now. Also, one finds only a small number of segments that offer superfluous and realistic bits of information about the characters. These are bits that may be and usually are irrelevant to the action, but which, in a realistic drama, are an important technique for creating the illusion of reality and a sense of three-dimensional characters. Examples include "Старые косточки болят" (The old bones ache [p. 6]) or "приглаживая гребнем, тщательно расчесанные, редкие волосы" (with a comb smoothing down carefully combed, thinning hair [p. 3]). The overall effect therefore of the deixis in this act is to point every recipient toward a there and an offstage eternity (as opposed to the onstage eternal present). It directs him toward abstract ideas and general states, rather than focusing his attention on a dynamic here and now within the fictional world being presented.

A disturbing story, a setting and characters evocative of a fairy tale, a slow pace without the introspectiveness of traditional tragedy, a distal deixis—all of these elements undercut every recipient's expectations, thus distancing him. However, this distancing is balanced by other strategies, emotive in nature, that help make emotional identification possible, and allow for the creation of a tragedy, albeit of a nontraditional sort.

The first of these emotive strategies, traditional in nature, is the way the playwright deals with time. As mentioned earlier, verbal temporal markers are few in this text. However, a definite temporal frame is suggested by the seeming, though not actual, unity of time. The first act takes place at night, the second in the morning, and the third in the late afternoon and early evening. Though several days or even weeks must pass between the beginning and the end of the presented events, the three successive time periods hint at a conformity to the unity of time. Such unity, even if only apparent, functions emotively because it is a basic and familiar part of the framework of traditional plays.[11]

A further sense of familiarity is created through the relationship between the textual and the real worlds. As explained in the preceding chapter, realistic plays—familiar to every recipient—propose a continuity between onstage and offstage real-life events. In absurdist drama, on the other hand, no continuity exists and the recipient is presented with a metaphor of the existential isolation of the characters. *Holy Blood* follows the first, more traditional paradigm. Though the textual world is a fantastic one, it is clearly depicted as continuous with the real world. The protagonists' estrangement is not existential, but a result of circumstance and choice, a result that can and is changed. The deictic segments referring to an offstage there tie the drama's characters both to a transcendental world and to the world of mankind in general. The two monks each have a past, as well as connections to other offstage areas of the fictional world. This effect is created through such references as Nikodim's saying "Жили мы в селении . . ." (We lived in a village . . . [p. 17]) or "Завтра узнают люди о смерти святого и придут сюда" (Tomorrow people will find out about the death of the holy man and will come here [p. 36]). Eventually the nymph's actions unite her not just with Christ, but also with the rest of humanity. Such continuity fulfills the realistic expectations of all recipients, strengthening the emotiveness of the work.

Realism is further strengthened by the playwright's emotive use of language. With few exceptions, as in benedictions or quotations from the Bible, the language of *Holy Blood* is colloquial. Though not recreating naturalistically the spoken language of peasants, Gippius creates the illusion of homely and humble real people. She achieves this effect by inserting numerous colloquialisms (бултыхаться, пригорюнить), as well as diminutives (краюшек, божьи цветочки), substandard forms (никак for кажется, куражиться for вести себя нагло), and even dialectalisms (купава). In addition, she employs a simple syntax containing numerous repetitions, unfinished sentences, exclamations, and one word phrases—all characteristic of spoken language. Such fantastic creatures as the old *rusalka* and the witch begin to resemble kindly old peasant women of the sort that might have been someone's nanny. The use of such colloquial language in a written fairy tale or folkloric play is actually unusual. Rather, Gippius's choice of style suggests the bedtime story told informally by a parent using simple and familiar language. This familiarizing effect of language is further supplemented by small realistic details. Examples of these instances include the old water nymph brushing out her thinning hair and saying that her legs are not getting any younger or the witch complaining of aching bones.

A more ambiguous aspect of language is Gippius's use of humor. At times it is a gentle, deprecating kind of humor that humanizes rather than bites sarcastically, that allows the recipient to see matters in a new light (*ostranenie*), and yet supports the emotive effect of the language. Gentle deprecation of an alleged faux-pas can be sensed in such phrases as "Забавненькая девочка" (A comic little girl [p. 11]) or "Не дединька, а ведьминка! Немножко не угадала" (Not little grandfather, but little witch! Didn't quite guess [p. 29]). However, there are moments when the humor becomes biting, lending a touch of absurdity to the presentation, as in the stage direction "Рой русалок, бледных, мутных" (A swarm of pale, turbid nymphs [p. 1]). The stereotypical beauty and delicacy of the nymph is here transformed into something sickly and not especially appealing.

Familiarity is also achieved through Gippius's use of parallelisms. Due to certain spatiotemporal and narrational limitations, traditional drama tends to have a more symmetrical structure than prose fiction. To orient each recipient, traditional drama is often composed around a series of clearly contrasting parallelisms: the hero and the villain, the passive and the active character, and so on. Gippius also employs a number of parallel constructions, both thematic and visual. These parallelisms substitute for an action-packed plot and structurally fulfill a more important role than in traditional plays. First, the author juxtaposes females and males, with the former presented as kinder and as a marginal group. Even the old witch with her detached sense of humor is never actually harmful, as men can be. Old women (the old nymph and the witch) are contrasted with a young one who appears more active and passionate. The young Nikodim, on the other hand, is depicted far more negatively than the old Pafnutii. The former is a rigid orthodox, a man of reason and book learning, strict to the point of being uncaring. Pafnutii is more spiritual, certainly kinder. Yet the juxtaposition of the two is not oversimplified. Pafnutii consistently defends the younger man before the nymph, saying that though at times Nikodim makes mistakes and gets carried away, he has chosen a very difficult path to salvation. The path's very difficulty can lead Nikodim astray on occasion. Comparisons are also made between the pagan and the Christian worlds, most notably in the beautiful songs. The pagan realm is seen as being in harmony with nature, as associated with night and the moon. Overall, Christianity is depicted as being rigid, masculine, and abstract, with its songs solemn, even threatening, and written in an elevated style. The point is visually emphasized in the third act by the two songs delivered like an antiphony from opposite sides of the stage.[12] The playwright further complicates matters by portraying Pafnutii's pantheism as a bridge to the world of nature. Furthermore, the world of females, though kind, is impeded by its passivity, and is seen as imperfect and in some ways limiting. Only the spiritual union of the two groups is assumed to be regenerative. Continuously repeated and varied, the parallelisms gradually begin to function emotively in a nontraditional fashion, eliciting from every recipient an abstract, impersonal kind of understanding and identification. In some sense, though not as complex, they function in a fashion similar to Anton Chekhov's rhythm.

Finally, one can return to language and consider the interesting and important manipulation of deixis and communicative functions—this time in their emotive role. The deixis in the first act has already been described. The majority of statements refer the recipient either toward an otherworldly there or to a general state, are of a nonconflicting nature, and do not function as speech acts. However, these atypical deictic segments are then distributed in such a way as to increase emotiveness in the first act. Analysis shows that the two types—general and nonappellative but directed toward another—constantly interweave. Utterances referring to abstract ideas or general states are interrupted by statements, often expressives, about the speaker or his interlocutor. Though this distribution does not create drama in the traditional sense, it should be seen as an emotive replacement technique. This technique brings the there much closer and creates the illusion that a very personal presentation of the ideas is being given. It functions as a nontraditional emotive substitute for traditional action or moral conflict between characters. Consider, for example, the following series of statements made by the old witch:

Я для своей забавы помогаю. Всем помогаю. И вот таким рыбкам, как ты, и людям, когда случится. Чего хочется кому—то я сейчас и даю—на! И ничего за это не прошу: забавушка моя есть, мне и довольно. И тебя научу, как русалке можно душу бессмертную получить, коли уж захотелось. Сядем-ка, девушка, у меня ноги немолоденькие. Солнце подождет.

I help for my own amusement. I help everyone. Such little fishies as you, and on occasion people. Whatever whoever wants—that I give immediately—here! and I don't ask anything for it: I have my little fun, that's enough for me. And I will teach you how a nymph can receive an immortal soul, since that is want you want. Let's sit, girl, my legs aren't young. The sun will wait a while. (p. 8)

In the above passage, the witch begins by offering psychological motivation for her behavior—she enjoys it. Then she expands on what it is that she does—gives to each what he desires. Next, she returns to herself and pleasure. This is immediately followed by her promise to teach the nymph what she wants to know, acknowledging her need. The passage concludes with a realistic reference to her old legs and the sun. It is in a manner similar to this that all of the abstract distal information is interwoven with more personal statements.

Such a distribution, important for the characterization of the protagonist, is a vital element in the development of the tragic genre. The expressives, combined with the stage directions, constantly emphasize the focused and overwhelming passion of the *rusalka*, thus elevating the events of the drama to a higher plane. This engulfing passion in turn produces the emotional and irrational core that lies at the heart of all tragedy. Without it *Holy Blood* would simply remain a not very convincing fairy tale.[13]

Act 2 continues to focus every recipient's attention on the nymph, though the deixis is different than in act 1. Segments oriented toward a there and toward general information almost disappear. Instead, the majority of

Distance Manipulation

segments are directed toward a present you, and that you is the protagonist. Interest is created around the figure of the *rusalka* in two ways. First, the old monk makes statements that characterize her. Second, he uses the appellative function in order to elicit information from her—in other words, some form of perlocutionism is more visible. This process is by no means simple, as the nymph often avoids answering or gives false answers, thus heightening the suspense, especially as every recipient soon realizes that she is not a good liar and that she comes close to revealing the truth about herself. The following passage, a small fragment of the whole, illustrates this focus. In it, Pafnutii first comments on the nymph and then proceeds to question her, though the answers that he receives are not true:

О. Пафнутий. Ластится, как ребенок. Говорить не говорит. Может, несмысленная....

Русалочка (едва слышно). Умею.

О. Пафнутий (весело). Вот и благо. Скажи нам, не бойся, ты откуда пришла?

Русалочка. Я ... не знаю.

О. Пафнутий. Как не знаешь?

Русалочка. Не помню.

О. Пафнутий. И не помнишь, чья ты?

Русалочка. Не помню ...

F. Pafnutii. She's snuggling up like a child. Not really speaking. Perhaps she's dumb....

Nymph (hardly audibly). I can.

F. Pafnutii (happily). Well that's good. Tell us, don't be afraid, where have you come from?

Nymph. I ... don't know.

F. Pafnutii. How is that?

Nymph. Don't remember.

F. Pafnutii. And you don't remember whose you are?

Nymph. Don't remember ... (p. 13)

In this act, the infrequent references to time and the small realistic details, present in the first act, disappear. There is still no conflict in the traditional sense and the appellatives—with the exception of the nymph asking the monk to teach her how to pray—are still oriented toward eliciting information rather than producing true action. However, the singlemindedness of the deictic orientation toward a you secures its effect by channeling the attention of the recipient, creating an emotive effect, and continuing to develop a tragic mood.

Still another pattern of deixis can be noted in the third act. This act is twice as long as the others—one reason for its length is that without traditional action and intrigue the playwright needs more time to develop heightened tension. Gippius accomplishes this end by skillfully interweaving segments with different deictic orientations. Appellatives and statements of intended action are still infrequent, but at least the one in which the old monk states his intention of baptizing the nymph at the cost of losing his own soul leads to the dramatic act of murder. The majority of deictic segments are oriented either toward the I or the you. Their effect is augmented, first of all, by an increased use of expressives. Second, interest is heightened by a large number of segments that actually have a double orientation. Ostensibly directed toward something else, they in actual fact function as implied commentary, either regarding the speaker or his interlocutor. For example, when Nikodim says "В тишине мы жили, да в труде. А ныне люди нас нашли, и нет в нашем подвиге той сладости да строгости. Как мышлишь об этом, отче?" (We lived in quiet and in labor. And now people have found us, and the sweetness and the strictness have gone out of our labors. What do you think, father? [p. 18]), he really is implying that the nymph's appearance is a negative, disturbing factor and that he would like to see her leave. Similarly, when the nymph asks the question "Только скажи, если Бог хотел убить нас, зачем Он желание бессмертной души оставил?" (Only tell me, if God wanted to kill us, then why did He leave us the desire for an immortal soul? [p. 23]), she is really expressing her own personal needs, though without mentioning herself. Such indirectness captures every recipient's attention and forces him to become involved in deciphering the implied intention. In addition, the proximally directed segments are again intertwined with distally oriented ones. The percentage of the latter is much lower than in act 1, but much higher and thus more noticeable than in act 2. The playwright employs three devices simultaneously. She repeats her religious views to the recipient—after all this is a new type of *pièce à thèse,* in a most positive sense of the term. She makes her characters use these important religious truths as a kind of weapon in their opposition to each other. She raises the whole situation to a more spiritual plane. Finally, toward the end of the third act, the author increases the sense of urgency and tension by inserting segments that point to the passage of time in the here and now.

The fact that the actual murder is not depicted onstage does not detract from the dramatic effect. Usually, as in Chekhov's works, the sense of drama is diminished by this maneuver. In this case, however, the scene retains its dramatic effect because the events are filtered through the consciousness of another being who is very much emotionally absorbed by what is occurring. Such a presentation may actually increase emotive forcefulness.[14] Here, the suspense is built through the old witch's expressives directed simultaneously toward the nymph and her own growing nervousness:

Тут покоя кругом нет. И эта не идет. Чего она, бешенная? Просто опаска меня взяла. Забава, нечего сказать! Ихшум кругом. Совы, что ли, кричат. (Молчание.) Плетется. Чтоб ей разлететься, каверзной!

There's no peace around here. And that one's not coming. What's the matter with her, mad? Fear has really grabbed me. What fun, one can't complain! And noise around me. Owls, or something, are screeching. (Silence.) She's dragging herself. May she burst, the sly one! (p. 35)

Then, once the deed is done, Gippius vividly shows the nymph's condition, supplementing the latter's utterances with stage directions that describe her stony calmness: a mixture of great suffering and great joy. The *rusalka*'s statements once again point in two directions: some toward herself and her emotional state—that of great suffering—and others toward a there, toward the figure of Christ:

За муку ли даст Он, Чью волю я творила, вечные муки? За то, что ради Него я пролила кровь, которая мне дороже своей? Он знает—дороже своей! Где человек, что боялся бы мук после моей муки? Я ничего не боюсь. Я шла к Тому, Кто звал меня, Кто дал мне самый трудный из всех путей,—и Он встретил меня.

He whose will I was fulfilling, will he give me eternal suffering for suffering? Because for His sake I spilled blood which was dearer to me than my own? He knows—dearer than my own! Where's the man who would be afraid of suffering after what I've suffered? I'm not afraid of anything. I was going to the One, Who was calling me, Who gave me the most difficult of all paths,—and He met me. (p. 36)

As she does throughout the play, the author continues to combine two deictic orientations. She connects a tone of solemnity and seriousness referring to a religious world beyond the immediate environment of the protagonist with a strong personal passion. In this way Gippius elevates what could otherwise be just a sordid deed to the level of tragedy. Having first shrunk away from murder, by the end of the play the heroine grasps the terror and the suffering that accompany it. In this manner fear is changed to awe and the tragic mode is developed to its end.

Written in 1900, *Holy Blood* is one of the first Russian dramas to begin making demands of the virtual recipient by introducing elements that distance him. These elements create distance both by proposing strange notions, as well as by upsetting any recipient's expectations in terms of aesthetic reception and genre requirements. Later, much more radically experimental plays would be written. Such plays, however, do not undermine the achievement of Zinaida Gippius. She sets out to present an idea to her virtual recipient, an idea that is strange and not easily acceptable. The idea is that love of God is a frighteningly powerful force with truly miraculous transformative and regenerative powers, one that can override all other considerations. This is definitely a strong distancing element, but one that can be balanced with emotive elements. Historically, moreover, a fantastic, outlandish story has occasionally worked well in plays. One can consider, for example, Spanish drama of the Golden Age. As Eric Bentley rightly points out, a play such as Calderón de la Barca's *Devotion to the Cross* seems at first glance to "be an invitation to murder and incest." And yet it succeeds because of the passion that is expressed through the outlandish story, for, as Bentley writes, "If Christianity is . . . a bold, rash, even wild way of attempting to deal with a freakish, opaque, and recalcitrant world, then it is with some justification that the Christian dramatist examines extravagant doctrines and extreme cases."[15]

Additionally, Gippius chooses to present her wild ideas in the guise of a fairy tale peopled by nymphs and witches, asking her virtual recipient to accept it as a serious drama. Keeping anxiety and terror at a distance by means of the exoticism of the setting is a typical device of such "low forms" as melodrama. It also works against the transcendence of fear and pity into the emotions of awe and compassion—a prerequisite of the emotional catharsis offered in the "higher forms."

The author creates further distance by supplying every recipient with little action and conflict, even on the level of discourse, instead filling the first act with general utterances about states and beliefs. Yet she wants the recipient to be moved, to become involved, as in a tragedy. Moreover, the playwright creates a slow pace that impedes the achievement of a dramatic climax. These distancing devices are typical of the more lyrical and metaphysical products of symbolist drama, a subgenre evinced by the plays of Maurice Maeterlinck.

Nevertheless, emotional identification between recipient and protagonist is achieved. Distancing through choice of story, characters, and setting, as well as through atypical deixis, is counterbalanced by lively colloquial language, parallelisms, and the way in which the author interweaves and distributes her different types of segments. Above all, Gippius reveals herself as a playwright who understands that the essence of tragedy is not only logic and reason, but emotion and sacrifice. The author elevates the stature of the nymph—in many ways a simple soul, a "божьи детя" as she is called. She does so by relentlessly focusing on the nymph's overwhelming passion and by connecting that passion throughout the duration of the play with lofty religious ideas. And the playwright offers the spectator a sacrifice—the elderly monk so much beloved by the nymph. For "[death] is not only a terminal point in the aesthetic experience; it is the only ritual that can mirror the complexity of emotions that seek psychological expression at this precise point."[16] That sacrifice, along with the nymph's acceptance of suffering, transforms the fear into the higher sensation of awe, and the pity into compassion. In the end, dramatic success cannot be measured simply by Gippius's use of emotive techniques, both traditional and nontraditional, since each element is counterbalanced in *Holy Blood* by a distancing one. Neither does the author offer us psychological complexity to the degree that can be found in nineteenth-century realism. Missing also is some of the moral ambivalence and ambiguity that is usually associated with a Lear or a Hamlet. Though in many ways the play is subtle, with neither the heroine being unblemished nor Nikodim being a full-fledged villain, the very brevity of the work prohibits a fuller development of ambiguities. Rather, Gippius manages simultaneously to estrange each recipient, to shock him into a fresh perception of matters, and at the same time, to offer him that moment of emotional identification that lies at the core of aesthetic reception. She does so by fleetingly capturing something of the emotional essence of tragedy, what Federico García Lorca called *"la oscura raiz del grito"* (the dark root of the scream).[17]

Chapter Three

Fedor Sologub's *The Triumph of Death*

FEDOR SOLOGUB'S DRAMA, *The Triumph of Death* (Победа смерти), was written in 1906 and 1907. Sologub's closeness at the time to Vsevolod Meierhold's concept of *uslovnyi teatr* greatly shaped the work's form. Moreover, its composition was also inspired by the appearance of Aleksandr Blok's play, *The Puppet Show*, which premiered in December of 1906. *The Triumph of Death* serves as a useful example of two popular currents within modernist drama. On the one hand, as an attempt at a mystery play, it is part of the neomedieval current. For a number of reasons connected both with spiritual content and form, the medieval period had a great attraction for modernists. Examples of neomedieval works range from Maurice Maeterlinck's *Pelleas and Mélisande* (*Pelléas et Mélisande*) to William Butler Yeats's *The King's Threshold,* from Gabriele D'Annunzio's *Francesca da Rimini* to Paul Claudel's *Annunciation* (*L'Annonce faite à Marie*), and from Henrik Ibsen's *The Pretenders* to Stanisław Wyspiański's *Bolesław the Brave* (*Bolesław Śmiały*). In Russian literature after *The Triumph of Death*, Aleksandr Blok would add *The Rose and the Cross* (*Роза и крест*) to this list, and Sologub himself wrote *Vanka the Steward and the Page Jehan* (*Ванька ключник и Паж Жехан*). Like most Russian playwrights, Sologub turns to and employs the Western European medieval tradition with its much more developed and richer literature, rather than to the native Russian one.[1] On the other hand, *The Triumph of Death* lies within the neoromantic current because of its use of the popular genre of melodrama. In this respect, Sologub and other playwrights follow in the footsteps of such romantics as Victor Hugo in *Hernani* or Percy Bysshe Shelley in *Cenci*.

Sologub offers his recipients a story that is basically neutral in terms of expectations, at least when compared to *Holy Blood*. Yet the work is problematic in terms of eliciting an emotional response. Its problems can be attributed primarily to three elements. First, the playwright uses a style of language that is hermetic and elevated without being sufficiently "incomplete," emotive, passionate, or poetic. Second, the work's highly personal symbolism obfuscates the presentation. Third, melodrama, despite its popularity, sometimes may be too facile a genre to overcome a work's distancing effects.

As stated, at the time when the play was written, Sologub's ideas regarding drama and theater agreed in some respects with those of Meierhold.

Both, in very different ways, were part of the "theatricalizing" movement in drama, a movement that stressed the idea of "play." The ludic tone in a performance would supposedly return drama to its more elemental, vital, and ritualistic roots, and would therefore strengthen drama's transformative powers. The difference between the two men lay in the sources of inspiration and in the motivations that they proffered. Meierhold's approach was primarily aesthetic, and he sought the sources of "play" in earlier theatrical traditions such as the commedia dell'arte, the *balagan,* and Noh theater. He was interested in play as a means for renewing dramatic form so that once again it could begin to convey that which words alone could no longer capture. Sologub's approach was more personal, more psychological, more spiritual. He explained the desire for play by returning to childhood and the age of innocent participation. For him, play was an essential need of every human being and one that permitted him as an adult to recapture at least momentarily a certain spirituality usually lost after childhood.[2]

At least in theory, Sologub agrees with Meierhold on the means that were to be used in order to achieve the ludic tone. Both saw the need to foreground convention—in other words, to undercut recipient expectations. Foregrounding conventions is not a new technique and has been used for centuries for different purposes. Shortly before the advent of modernism, writers like Lev Tolstoy were employing the technique (later to be called *ostranenie*), both in order to achieve the sensation of greater realism and to present certain social criticisms. Sologub, like Meierhold and the other symbolists, foregrounds convention precisely in order to destroy the illusion of reality, to emphasize theatricality and the "unnaturalness" of the spectacle.

On a higher level of structure, foregrounding can be achieved through the stylization of genres. Sologub, like those who posit the idea of *uslovnyi teatr,* turns to other types of theaters, both historical (ancient Greek, medieval) and popular "low forms" as models, and "sources" for his own dramas. The earlier dramatic structures are sought out not simply to be copied, but more importantly to be reinterpreted and/or stylized in order to introduce ". . . nowe wartości artystyczne i podkreśl[ić] uniwersalizm tematyki podjętej przez dramaturga" (. . . new artistic values and to underscore the universalism of the topic taken up by the playwright).[3] "Low forms" refers to those popular, sometimes folk, forms that lie outside the field of high art. Through these works' crudeness, simplicity, emphasis on nonverbal elements, vitality, and naive emotionalism, modernist artists seek a revitalization of the higher forms. They see in them a source of "new blood" not eviscerated by overuse. Throughout Europe, artists turn to farce, melodrama, puppet theater, various European folk traditions (such as the *balagan* in Russia), and even non-European sources, such as Japanese Kabuki and Noh theaters.

Though agreeing in some respects with Vsevolod Meierhold and the tenets of *uslovnyi teatr,* Sologub's ideas about drama and theater also depart

Fedor Sologub's *The Triumph of Death*

at times from those of the director. For example, one tenet that the playwright fervently believes in is that a theatrical performance is the expression of the playwright's voice. He absolutely opposes the idea of a performance as a creation of the director. His is a totally solipsistic vision. Later, in the treatise *Theater of a Single Will*, he would state over and over with very little variation that "drama . . . exists in order to lead man unto Me."[4] As will be shown, such an approach to writing plays is reflected in certain aspects of dramatic form in *The Triumph of Death*.

Furthermore, Sologub's solipsism leads him to state that the theatrical performance is best experienced by a single, isolated recipient, separated from others by the darkness that reigns in the theater.[5] This idea diverges strongly from the point of view of all modernist writers and directors. They emphasize the communal aspect of theater and the added potential for reception whenever a group of recipients experiences the performance together and in the process acts upon each other.

Moreover, in some respects Sologub is closer to the ideas of the second generation of Russian symbolists than to those of Meierhold. For Meierhold, as for the writers of the first generation of symbolists such as Valerii Briusov, the new theater is defined primarily as a new form, a new structure. For all their lip service to "mysteries" and "the ineffable," Meierhold and Briusov do not treat theater as part of a broader quasi-philosophical, quasi-religious worldview. The serious desire for a pseudoreligious mystery play such as is attempted in *The Triumph of Death*—a play that could substitute for orthodox religion—echoes much more the ideas of Viacheslav Ivanov or Andrei Belyi. The second generation of symbolists' perception of drama, like that of Sologub, is primarily the result of accepting some of Nietzsche's ideas on art and religion, especially the notion that drama originally derived from Dionysian ritual. Both Sologub and the younger symbolists absolutely reject a strictly aesthetic and formal approach to art.[6]

Connections with the symbolists and with Meierhold notwithstanding, there is a uniquely Sologubian element that sets his oeuvre apart from that of his contemporaries. This element is the extreme existential pessimism observable in all of his work. The playwright carries within him a vision of a better world, but he is fully convinced that it is unreachable. Even in terms of art, he truly desires a new dramatic form, namely, the mystery play. Simultaneously, he presents this form as a mirage, unobtainable at the present stage of human spiritual and cultural development. Dul'cineia verbalizes this idea in the prologue when she says: "Опять зрелище остается зрелищем, и не становится мистерией" (Again the spectacle remains a spectacle, and does not become a mystery).[7] This pessimism, as will be shown, affects some of the formal aspects of *The Triumph of Death*.

Overall, this is a work that contains inconsistencies. Theoretically, Sologub would formulate his ideas a year later in the treatise *Theater of a*

Distance Manipulation

Single Will. However, even in the treatise he does not overcome all of his ideological and aesthetic contradictions. There would always remain in his approach to drama an inherent clash between the "theatricalizing" demand for ludic elements in a performance and the existential seriousness of the mystery play propounded by the second generation of symbolists.

It should be noted that Sologub wrote other types of dramas. Some, like *The Gift of the Wise Bees* (Дар мудрых пчел), fit into the neoclassical current. Others, like *Vanka the Steward and the Page Jehan,* are not just medieval, but above all folkloric. *The Triumph of Death* has been chosen because it represents two major modernistic currents—neomedieval and neoromantic. *Vanka,* with its use of Russian folklore, is more of an anomaly, finding an analogy only in Aleksei Remizov's works, *The Devil Play* and *The Tragedy of Judas, Prince of Iscariot.* The neoclassical current can be more usefully analyzed on the basis of Viacheslav Ivanov's radical work, *Tantalus.*

The plot of *The Triumph of Death* is based on a legend concerning the marriage of Charlemagne's parents. Sologub changes the names and the emphasis, but keeps the events of the original story. He begins with a prologue, actually added later, in which the figure of Dul'cineia confronts some of the other characters. Dul'cineia represents the force of ideal beauty and goodness. She tries to convince other characters (the King, the Poet, and the page) of who she is, but she is not believed. Instead, she is always taken for a lowly servant girl and laughed at for insisting on being somebody else. The prologue exhibits time shifts of the kind typical of symbolist plays. Toward the end of the prologue, Dul'cineia laments that because human beings continue to reject her, the play about to be shown will not become a true mystery, but will remain merely a spectacle. She also vows to continue her struggle for the acceptance of goodness and beauty, and for this purposes concocts a plan. She and her daughter will assume the guise of servants and she will also employ her magical powers. The curtain comes down on the prologue and the actual story begins.

The King has sent off to a faraway land for a royal bride. The bride, called Berta, arrives with two servants, Mal'gista and Al'gista, who are actually the forces of beauty. Berta herself is ugly, pockmarked, and lame due to an illness. On the wedding night, she allows her servant, Al'gista, to substitute for her in the King's bed. Al'gista does so, and then lightly stabs herself, pretending that it is Berta who has done so. Furthermore, she insists that Berta is really the servant girl. Because of her beauty she is believed, and the real queen is banished into the forest. Al'gista takes up her role as queen, bears a son, and in general for the next ten years is said to have a beneficial influence on the King. She is compassionate and caring and softens her husband's character.

After ten years, Berta's brother, in the guise of a minstrel, visits the court and exposes the fraud. It is revealed that Berta has been living in the forest and has given birth to a son there. At this stage, Al'gista, though warned by her mother not to do so, admits to the whole scheme, counting on the

King's love for her. She is tired of the deception and thinks that the strength of conjugal feelings will triumph. She is sadly mistaken. The King immediately rejects her and sentences her and her child to death. After she is dead, Al'gista appears, bloodied, before the King and once again pleads her case. She tells the King to choose love, to choose her, and thus to choose eternal life. However, the King, egged on by Berta, cannot break out of the strictures of his role. Society has certain laws and he will not ignore them, even though he admits his love for Al'gista. In retribution, the whole court is turned to stone. It is thus that Sologub uses an old legend to present his ideas that in today's world people will go on rejecting ideal beauty even if they come face to face with it. No solution is possible. After all, Al'gista dies while the humans who rejected her are deprived of death, the latter being a positive element in Sologub's worldview. It is a Pyrrhic victory at best.

Thus, the subject matter itself, that of a Neoplatonic world where the beauty of the ideal is hidden and accessible only to a few sensitive souls such as poets and artists, is not very surprising in any way. This is not the shocking story presented in Gippius's *Holy Blood* that distances recipients to an unprecedented degree. The ideas of Neoplatonism are deeply embedded in Western thought and keep reappearing periodically. However, two aspects of the presentation of the topic are uniquely Sologubian. The first is the author's extreme pessimism, which leads him to present a conclusion in which the only acceptable ending both for the ideal and the evil characters is destruction. The good perish, the evil are denied death (a positive phenomenon in Sologub's weltanschauung) and, turned into stone, are relegated into nothingness. Many modernists see the world around them in black hues, but the severity of Sologub's pessimism distances every recipient.

The second trait unique to the author's presentation is the fact that he mixes the Neoplatonic topic with a bit of social commentary. This is typical of all of Sologub's writing, and distinguishes him from the other symbolist writers of the time.[8] Among the symbolists, such a mixture would appear only later, as for example, in Aleksandr Blok's cycle of poetry *The City*. In *The Triumph of Death*, social commentary begins as statements about the ruling class, a class that through pride has cut itself off from the common people and has opened the door to active evil and deceit:

Много пышных обрядов придумали владыки, чтобы возвеличить себя выше нас.

The rulers have thought up many sumptuous rituals in order to exalt themselves over us. (p. 29)

Не ты ли король, обитающий в этом надменном чертоге и владеющий этою темною страною?

Are not you the king who inhabits this haughty palace and who rules this dark land? (p. 17)

Distance Manipulation

Strangely enough, because the language of the play is not differentiated to fit the personality and status of the characters, incongruities occasionally arise in the presentation of this social commentary. Even characters like the poet, who do not recognize real beauty and are on the side of the evildoers, begin to use negative epithets about the ruling class. For example, the poet states that "Настоящая Дульцинея живет в надменном чертоге" (The true Dul'cineia lives in a haughty palace [p. 21]). As the work progresses, the social criticism becomes broader and begins to encompass all classes. At one point, for example, Al'gista condemns everyone for having a slave mentality: "Но народ,—все эти простые люди, земледельцы и ремесленники, о, как они хотят быть рабами!" (But the people,—all those simple people, farmers, and craftsmen, oh, how they want to be slaves! [p. 40]). On the one hand, the social commentary appears somewhat anachronistic and jarring in the mouths of supposedly medieval characters. On the other, this commentary could theoretically concretize the Neoplatonic content and give it a unique flavor. Introducing sentiments close to the heart of all but the most elitist of recipients, it actually functions emotively to some degree—even if the emotiveness is not very strong. However, the commentary is not supported by the story of the drama and is often overwhelmed by the elevated language of the work.

A separate problem is the presentation of the subject matter in the form of a chansons de geste. Recipients are offered a story, a legend (despite the author's denials), and a tale that is not familiar to the majority of them, even if it was popular among symbolist artists. Yet even this tale, like the subject matter, should be less distancing than the witches and nymphs that populate *Holy Blood,* since the characters are at least human beings. Nevertheless, there is still the question of the "complexity" of the subject matter. Drama—for all of its core emotionalism—is not anti-intellectual and in fact great plays tend to carry profound ideas. Most effective is the presentation of ideas—with subtlety, complexity, and an ambiguity that inspires thought—in conjunction with strong emotions.[9] In *The Triumph of Death,* the presentation tends not to be very nuanced. There is a good and a bad side: Al'gista as a symbol of beauty is good, the King, who represents society and the blindness of mankind, is bad. Furthermore, in *The Triumph of Death* ideas seem to be all important, at times to the exclusion of any emotion.

The first, most obvious, and traditional distancing element in this play is the elevated style of the language. An elevated style can be minimalist in its elegance, as in neoclassical tragedy. However, this work contains the language of a hieratic ritual: solemn, opulent, and complex. The text is filled with archaisms: "опочивальня" (sleeping chamber), "личина" (mask), "праведный" (just), and "помрачить" (cloud); abstractions: "красота" (beauty), "безобразие" (outrage), "смерть" (death), "усталость" (exhaustion), "любовь" (love), and "жизнь" (life); participles: "воспета" (praised), "увенчана" (crowned), "пирующий" (feasting), and "разделиший" (having divided); elevated words: "воспеть" (praise), "вознести" (elevate), "низвергнуть" (throw down), and "возсиять" (shine); as well as traditional poetic terms: "дева" (maiden), "отринуть" (reject), "очи" (eyes), and "зорька" (dawn). Numerous sentences are long, with a complex syntax and a slow ponderous rhythm created by repetition,[10] as in the following:

> Опять не увенчана, не воспета, не полюбленная истинная красота этого мира, очаровательница Дульцинея, в образе змеиноокой Альдонсы.
>
> Again the true beauty of this world, the charmer Dul'cineia, in the image of Al'donsa is not crowned, not glorified, not loved. (p. 23)
>
> Пусть Берта закрыта своею златотканною вуалью,—я знаю, я помню ее изрытое оспою лицо, я знаю, что одна нога госпожи моей короче, чем другая, и хитро сделанными золотыми каблуками она скрывает это.
>
> Let Berta be covered by her gold-brocaded veil—I know, I remember her face pitted by smallpox, I know that one of my lady's legs is shorter than the other, and that she hides it with cleverly made heels. (p. 29)
>
> Обманщицу позорную и лютую казнить смертью перед народом,—бичу и розгам предать, обнажив ее тело, и сечь до смерти, и тело бросить в ров на съедение собакам.
>
> Put to death in front of the people this shameful and savage deceiver,—give her up to the whip and rod, having bared her body, and flog her to death, and throw the body into the ditch for dogs to eat. (p. 46)

The complexity of the sentences is made more distancing by the fact that the text is so heavily filled with referentials in the Jakobsonian sense. The exchanges in the play, though for the most part having a proximal deixis referring to characters and objects present on stage, are not really designed for any perlocutionary effect, but rather for the referential function of describing and offering information.

These referential utterances fall into several categories. Some have a "labeling" quality; that is, a protagonist present on the stage characterizes another one who is also present, as in the following statement in which the King defines Dul'cineia's supposed station in the hierarchy of the textual world:

> Ты—крестьянская девка Альдонса, та самая, над которой смеются мальчишки за то, что безумец назвал тебя сладким именем Дульцинеи, милой очаровательницы, прекраснейшей из дев на земле.
>
> You are the peasant girl Al'donsa, the same one at whom the little boys laugh, because some madman called you by the sweet name of Dul'cineia, that dear charmer, the most beautiful of maidens on earth. (p. 17)

Very frequently, a character describes those of his actions that occurred offstage, as in the following:

Властью моей безмерной любви, силою моих нестерпимых мучений, над жизнью и над смертью торжествующею моею волью купила я у земли и у неба и у темного подземного мира твое тело и твою душу и твою полночную тень.

With my immeasurable power, with the force of my unbearable sufferings, with my will triumphant over life and death, I bought from the earth and the heavens and from the dark underground world your body and your soul and your midnight shadow. (p. 51)

Occasionally, the referentials may be distally oriented statements about general states or ideas:

Владыки увенчанные и сильные открыли путь коварства и зла.

The mighty and crowned rulers have opened the way of perfidy and evil. (p. 29)

The ritualistic effect of referentials clothed in an elevated language is further solidified by the fact that there is no differentiation of style between the various characters. They all speak in exactly the same fashion. This treatment of dialogue agrees with Sologub's solipsistic definition of a play and a performance as the expression of the author's voice, split up among the voices of the characters. However, this practice goes against the illusionistic expectations of the recipient. It works to support the ritualistic qualities of the play, but also leads to psychological incongruities in terms of characterization.

Of course, poetic language does not need to distance, but can even add to the lyrical effect of the work. This result, however, is not the overall impression produced in this case. Sologub's combination of elevated lexicon, syntactic complexity, abundance of referentials, and nondifferentiation between characters serves to make the events of the work more remote. Keeping the fear and terror at bay is a common device of all melodrama.

Moreover, the already complex language of the text is further obfuscated by Sologub's own personal symbolism, without an understanding of which any recipient has difficulty in fully comprehending the work. For example, in the writer's textual world the character of Dul'cineia/Al'donsa symbolizes the ideal beauty that is present in the real world, but that is hidden from most people. The choice of the name Dul'cineia of course emphasizes the solipsism of Sologub's vision through a literary reference. As for Miguel de Cervantes's *Don Quixote*, what matters is the very personal perception of the individual *I* and not outward appearances. The author even inserts an oblique reference to the Spanish novel (p. 17). Next, in this symbolic dictionary, the living and dead water represent the offerings of Beauty: either spiritual life or death. However, the living water that is spiritual life is disdained by the other characters and seen fit only for washing floors. Additionally, in this textual world, the character of Mal'gista symbolizes the fateful force that controls the universe and moves people around like pawns on a chessboard. A frequent character in all of Sologub's ouevre is the young page, or youth (*отрок*) as he is labeled, who signifies the important moment of passage from childhood to adulthood. On the one hand, in Sologub's weltanschauung, the *otrok* still to some degree sees clearly like a child and is not blinded like adults. On the other, he is beginning to lose his childish innocence and is taking on an adult cynicism that will eventually completely cloud his vision.

Yet another aspect of Sologub's symbolism finds its roots in the frequent references to clothing and shoes. In the author's personal philosophy, clothes represent masks that hide the true nature of the protagonist. The more clothed the character the less the positive side of his or her nature can be revealed. Such is the case with Berta, for example. When clothed and shod, she is a cruel representative of the ruling class, urging the King to kill Al'gista. Her only moment of goodness comes when she runs barefoot and in rags through the woods.

The melodramatic and distancing aspects of language are reinforced by the stage directions. These have a literary quality, due once again to the lexicon and syntax. More importantly, they present an abstract medieval setting whose very geographical and historical exoticism distances:

Сени королевского замка. Стены сложены из громадных, грубо отесанных камней. В передней стене—огромная арка входа, через которую и видно зрителям сени.

The hall of the royal castle. The walls are constructed of huge, roughly hewn stones. In the front wall there is the huge arch of the entryway, through which the audience actually sees the hall. (p. 15)

The ill-lit, rough-hewn stones are like the stereotypical suggestion of a medieval castle without any historical precision. They remind one of images from so many movies about the middle ages, especially the more popular varieties—images that are familiar to and easily recognized by today's recipient, yet comfortably distant, creating the suggestion of a never-never land. It should be kept in mind that such a comfortable yet remote stereotype is one more element often utilized in melodrama. Sologub himself states in his postscript to the play that he wishes to ". . . оторвать эту трагедию от истории и даже от легенды" (. . . tear this tragedy away from history and even from legend [p. 55]). According to the author, this technique is needed in order to create a play that deals with certain abstract ideas in a symbolic fashion and not with any concrete historical event. Whether Sologub desired a more cerebral approach on the part of his virtual recipient is questionable in light of his stated desire for a mystery play. Be that as it may, the stage directions, though familiar to every recipient as a stereotype, as a cliché, further the distancing. However, they do so in a different fashion than the language. The work's usage of language creates a sense of remoteness through elevation. The stage directions remove the events to a familiarly comfortable, but safe distance. Taking into account language usage and the historical setting, perhaps only an individualized stage design, illusionistic in nature, would work emotively to counter the distancing effect of the first two elements.

Stage directions are usually the key source of information on the organization of scenic space. Here, it becomes clear that the symmetric arrangement of scenic space supports the ritualistic quality of the play. Thus, it contributes to the distancing effect upon any recipient. Symmetry in *The Triumph of Death* begins with the very first stage direction where three staircases—left, center, and right—lead to the great hall (p. 15). Later, two knights guard the entrance to the king's bedchamber, one on either side like statuary (p. 33). In act 3, Berta and her son, and later the twelve knights, move up the central staircase. In the latter case, the suggestion is of a line—single or double—moving up symmetrically. In fact, it is known that Vsevolod Meierhold emphasized spatial symmetry and proportion in his staging of the work. In the final scenes, the theatricalism and ritualism are emphasized, not by linear symmetry, but through a different arrangement. Here the crowd is described as standing pressed against the columns, with the central protagonists—like priests in some esoteric rite—left to play out the drama in the center (pp. 50, 53).[11]

The stylistic usage of language influences another level of the play's structure where distancing elements are strong, namely, characterization. Various definitions and descriptions have been offered in conjunction with the author's characterization techniques in *The Triumph of Death*. Some have suggested a foreshadowing of Pirandellian masking devices, though that seems doubtful. Of greater relevance is the relationship between Sologub's approach to characterization and the commedia dell'arte/*balagan* tradition. This tradition is visible both in plays written at the time (see Aleksandr Blok's *The Puppet Show*), as well as in Vsevolod Meierhold's productions of various works. Both Meierhold and Sologub wish to strip away the masks that often cover the true nature of people and events. In order to achieve this stripping, they try to create a two-dimensional, bas-relief type stage against which puppetlike characters perform. Each character represents a whole "cluster of associations," a cluster sometimes very familiar to the recipient, yet sometimes only a little or not at all.[12]

The end result of Sologub's practice is a tendency toward allegory reminiscent above all of Valerii Briusov's *The Earth* or Leonid Andreev's *The Life of Man*. Sologub takes a familiar character, like Dul'cineia, in order to change in many respects the content of that "cluster of associations" that the figure, as she is known from the Cervantes novel, usually represents. Here, Dul'cineia becomes an element in the author's personal symbolic web. Thus, she is much less familiar to any recipient than the characters of, for example, Blok's work.

In other words, it is a question of degree. Both the *uslovnyi teatr* as treated by Vsevolod Meierhold and Aleksandr Blok, as well as by Sologub, use two-dimensional figures taken from the common cultural treasury. Both sets of characters, therefore, distance because they do not have the expected three-dimensional depth. However, Sologub's characters distance more than those of Blok because the playwright severs them to a far greater degree from familiar cultural associations. Furthermore, these two-dimensional characters are in some way reminiscent of the figures of Western morality plays: serious, didactic, verbose, clearly representing an idea, and appearing as part of a symbolic web. Theoretically, such characters bring to mind medieval practice. However, medieval symbolism was not personal, but rather was the common property of all Christians living at the time in the Western world. Sologub's characters are part of the author's personal symbolic network and not part of anything known to any recipient.

Already in 1908, I. Jonson's review of the play refers to the characters as "субстанции" (substances), a notion that perhaps might suggest the later works of Dostoevski where characters represent different ideologies.[13] However, that would not be a correct conclusion, as Dostoevski's characters are more complex and ambiguous and the conflicts between them represent the clashes of whole systems of thought. Sologub's characters, unchanging images of a personal philosophy, differ from both *balagan* puppets and Dostoevski's "substances," as well as from medieval morality figures. They do, however, seem closest to the latter.

Two of the characters in this work show some change and therefore need to be briefly considered. Berta, while living in the forest, is momentarily revealed as possessing an internal beauty that disappears completely when she is clothed anew and reinstated as queen. However, the changes in her character are not motivated psychologically, but are purely a mechanical result of the author's philosophy and symbolism. For this reason, they will probably not elicit much of an emotive reaction from any recipient used to the psychological development of realistic characters. Al'gista's circumstances appear a little stronger. She starts by being a character willing to use deceit for a good cause, that of advancing beauty and true love, but eventually rejects such means, thus dooming herself.[14] However, all that is stated is that—because Al'gista has had a strong positive influence on the King during the ten years of marriage—she is convinced that he is ready to accept her for who she really is. The underlying motivation for the change is once again really only Sologub's philosophy. This is his illustration of the fact that people are not willing to accept beauty and goodness in the real world, no matter how much they are exposed to it. In the end, the only possible victory is a Pyrrhic one, with the King punished for his nonacceptance.

Some of the distancing effect of characterization can be attributed to the intentional, as well as unintentional, elements of composition. In terms of actual plot, the play offers no surprises. It is traditional and dense with no extraneous subplots to detract from the main story line. However, a number of other factors do distance all recipients. For example, there is the construction of the prologue. Inspired by Aleksandr Blok's *The Puppet Show*, which had appeared after Sologub had written the body of the play, the prologue of *The Triumph of Death* also tries to be a new kind of "fantasy satire," as George Kalbouss calls these types of works.[15] It mocks symbolist ideology and goals through a number of devices. The foremost of these devices is a sharp juxtaposition of two worlds: the ideal sphere of Dul'cineia/Al'donsa and the real one of the poet and the lady who visit an inn. The result is grotesque to some degree. The fantastic, poetic world of kings, pages, and maidens is constantly undercut by the trivial and base remarks of the poet. For example, Dul'cineia says: "Господин поэт, я ждала вас долго. Вы пришли сюда, в глубину времен . . ." (Sir poet, I have waited long for you. You have come here, into the depths of time. . . . [p. 20]). In response, the poet moves the statement into the realm of the prosaic by saying, "Этот кабачок называется «В глубине времен»" (This inn is called "In the Depths of Time" [p. 20]). For the poet, the living and dead waters are simply red and white wine. The sleeping king appears to be a doorkeeper to him. At every step, Sologub offers the kind of grotesque degradation of the ideal that is typical of theatricalism and the *balagan* tradition. For every recipient, this is an unexpected and distancing factor. It should be noted that in *The Triumph of Death*, the degradation is produced almost exclusively through verbal utterances, and that Sologub does not employ any of the visual and physical devices that Aleksandr Blok or Vsevolod Meierhold used with such success.

There are even more serious distancing elements that were probably not intended, but that stem from compositional weaknesses. Critics admit that the message of *The Triumph of Death* is unclear.[16] Questions remain as to why Al'gista, the symbol of beauty, agrees to deception. The text offers no satisfying answer. The passing internal beauty of Berta, already mentioned, is also a troubling moment. The Pyrrhic victory at the end leaves the recipient with no sense of closure. This is not a tragedy in which the hero transcends his guilt even if he must pay for it. Neither is it a comedy where by the end the situation is stabilized and returns to social norms. A substantial part of this ambiguity can be attributed to the flawed relationship between the prologue and the body of the play. The two are completely different in tone. The prologue is mocking, satiric, and grotesque. The body is overwhelmingly serious. The few satiric touches (i.e., pp. 31, 37) cannot destroy the overall seriousness and didacticism of the body, so strongly encoded in the language of the text. Theoretically, the juxtaposition of two antinomic parts could offer some new and interesting insights. In actual fact, in this play the opposition is never worked out properly and effectively and thus leads to a lack of clarity in the message. The two attitudes are completely different, yet they are neither reconciled in any way, nor contrasted in some subtle or informative fashion, leaving the recipient confused and distanced. Sologub was not alone in having difficulties with merging various disparate elements into one whole entity. The difference between jarring oppositions in a well-designed play and oppositions floating in a work with no integral structure is a fine one. One may admire the ambitiousness of the task that such writers set for themselves, yet realize that these experiments did not always fully succeed.

A number of other compositional elements are also employed in a distancing fashion. The first element is the ancient practice of not showing everything on stage, but instead having it related. It has been shown that in *Holy Blood* this method only increases emotiveness because of the old witch's personal involvement. Here, the effect is quite different. Like the ancient Greeks, Sologub uses a chorus to carry out the recounting. However, the communal voice of this chorus is broken down into individual parts. Moreover, this crowd does not fulfill the ethical role that it has in Greek drama, where it expresses the morality and standards of the community. In this play, it is a degraded, jeering assemblage of people that represents only the worst of society. An example of this technique occurs in the scene where the crowd describes the beating and death of Al'gista. Since the crowd is neither sympathetic toward Al'gista, nor itself personally involved in the action, the emotive forcefulness of the scene is not only not increased, but is actually decreased. The recipient is distanced because his sympathies are not engaged through a mediating character. A somewhat similar situation occurs in the scene in act 2 that takes place offstage. The voices of the characters are heard, but not seen, while the recipient is faced with an empty stage. Here, there is no obviously jeering and alienated crowd. However, neither does Sologub introduce any elements that would emotively affect a visually oriented recipient, as is the case in the nineteenth and twentieth centuries.

A further distancing element, also related to the chorus of Greek drama, is the use of song. The songs at the beginning of acts 1 and 2 hint at what is to occur. They do not comment or moralize on the subject. Instead, in a new twist on an old device, the voice of the people functions lyrically. The songs depart sharply from the tone of the subsequent utterances and create yet another jarring effect.

The final compositional element that needs to be mentioned is that of the voice that intrudes into the dialogue on several occasions. This voice suggests a rhyme to the poet in act 1. It states the principle theme at the very end of the play. The voice is clearly that of the playwright and is in keeping with Sologub's solipsistic approach to dramaturgy. However, its effect on every recipient is once again jarring. The voice's interruptions create an obvious break with realistic illusion, a break that is stronger than even the asides of traditional comedy.

Distance Manipulation

In short, the distancing elements of this play are very strong. First of all, the language functions in such a manner as to create the feeling of a hieratic ritual. As this is a very verbally oriented drama and not visually directed as an action-packed comedy or one of the new works in the *balagan* manner, language becomes an extremely important element in this work. Second, characterization—two-dimensional with overtones of medieval allegorical figures—elicits little identification from any recipient. Finally, the lack of an overall unity in the composition of the play may produce confusion. The question now is how and with what devices does Sologub try to balance these distancing elements.

While some compositional elements in *The Triumph of Death* distance, others function emotively. First, the work has a tight plot and moves causally from one event to the next. Second, one can consider symmetry. Symmetry of events and characters has always been much more marked in traditional drama than in other genres. The use of symmetry helps orient every recipient in a genre that has no narrator. Here, each act develops along the same pattern. At the end of each act "unrecognized beauty" is triumphant, if only temporarily. In acts 1 and 3, it is Al'gista. In act 2, it is Berta, momentarily shown to possess some deeply buried inner beauty. Furthermore, toward the end of each act, emotional intensification is achieved by increasing the number of characters on stage. A crowd that excitedly witnesses the events elevates the emotional intensity of the scene. This does not include the two times when a crowd is used to narrate an invisible scene and the whole effect is one of distancing. At the conclusion of each act, the crowd functions simply as a spectator.[17]

The compositional, as opposed to spatial, symmetry is also furthered by the relationship between Al'gista and Berta. They are opponents, yet each knows the other completely. Al'gista symbolizes beauty and creativeness, Berta oppression and blindness. The two opposites complement one another. Moreover, during the ten years that Al'gista is queen, the roles are reversed. It is Al'gista who is now concealed by the royal robes and, for all the good that she accomplishes, one may wonder what happens to her inner beauty. At the same time, Berta is released, allowed to "disrobe," and thus to reach her inner beauty.

The intensification of emotion that is noticeable on the compositional level also occurs to some degree on the level of language. First, the deixis is perfectly traditional, oriented for the most part toward the here and now. Second, what Keir Elam calls the "channel" is usually oriented toward the senses—the body or emotions—rather than the purely cerebral. The channel "registers the axes along which the communication unfolds (physical, mental, and emotional), the involvement of the speaker's body in the communication, and the individual characters' biases (toward the physical world, toward cerebration, toward their own bodies or their own emotional condition)."[18]

For example, when the King speaks of the anonymous voice of fate that calls to him, he describes this in a poetic fashion oriented toward the auditory and visual senses: "Невнятен твой голос, и темно лицо твое, словно туманною закрытое личиною" (Indistinct is your voice and dark is your face, as if covered by a dark mask [p. 16]). Similarly, when Dul'cineia demands from the poet that he recognize beauty, she states it in terms of concrete actions—singing her praise and crowning her: "Воспойте меня, господин поэт, и тогда король меня увенчает" (Glorify me, sir poet, and then the king will crown me [p. 21]). Thus, the so-called channel, by inclining toward action and the body in its choice of imagery and lexicon, increases the impression of dynamism and appeals to every recipient's senses. This, in turn, results in a sensation of basic emotiveness for the recipient.

Additionally, one notes the abundant use of expressives that underscore the emotional involvement of the characters and therefore increase the emotional tension of the whole work. The text is filled with such phrases as "Как я устал" (How tired I am), "Милая девушка" (Dear girl), "Я не боюсь" (I am not afraid), "Недотрога" (Touch-me-not), "спаси меня!" (save me!), ". . . и я завою на месте, где в землю впиталась ее обильно пролитая кровь" (. . . and I will begin to howl at the spot where her abundantly spilled blood has soaked into the earth), and "люблю" (I love). Expressives humanize the allegorical characters and help each recipient to respond to them at least minimally.

Still another emotive element is the appeal of the language to the most basic aesthetic responses through the use of rhythm. Sologub's rhythm is not as complicated, as masterly, or as important as is Chekhov's in *The Cherry Orchard*. In *The Cherry Orchard,* rhythm is a fundamental structural element. Here, it appears more in the nature of a decoration that does not extend deeply into the structure. Nevertheless, it is present and is, for the most part, a rhythm with a slow, ponderous tempo. Repetition lies at the basis of this rhythm. First, there is the repetition of words. For example, the words "зло" (evil), "сладкий" (sweet), and "золото" (gold) appear throughout. Second, sentences are often constructed around the repetition of syntactical patterns:

Когда ты меня любил, *когда* ты меня ласкал, *когда* ты нежные шептал мне слова, что были и блеск твоей короны, и твоя верховная власть!

When you loved me, when you caressed me, when you whispered tender words to me, what were to you either the brilliance of your crown or your supreme power! (p. 52)

Third, as in Chekhov's play, one also finds the repetition of various leitmotivs, linked directly to the ideas of the work. For example, the author dwells on the concept of deception (обман) and weaves it throughout the play. Deception perpetrated by Al'gista on the King makes continued life with her impossible, though the deception of Berta and her father does not seem to bother him—another inconsistency. The text is filled with such phrases as "сеть обмана" (the net of deceit), "петли обмана" (the nooses of deceit), "жертва обмана" (the victim of deceit), "обманщица" (deceiver-feminine), and "сын обманщика идет с обманом на обман" (the son of a deceiver is moving toward deceit with deceit).[19] Next, repetition also occurs on a more basic level through the use of alliteration: "Я чувствую странную усталость. Сядемте здесь, моя госпожа" (I feel a strange exhaustion. Let us sit down here, my lady [p. 21]), "Забили, замучили. Долго хлестали безпощадные бичи" (They have killed, tormented. For a long time the merciless whips whipped [p. 47]), and ". . . но псы не тронули ее, и выли над ее телом, выли в тоске над телом ласковой госпожи" (. . . but the dogs did not touch her, and they howled over her body, they howled in sadness over the body of a kind mistress [p. 47]). Finally, rhythm is created through sentence length. Into the preponderance of long solemn sentences, Sologub interjects series of short sentences expressing excitement, as in the following passage:

—Смотрите, здесь Альгиста!
—Замученная королева встала!
—И ее сын.
—Горе нам,

—Look, there is Al'gista!
—The tortured queen has risen!
—And her son.
—Woe unto us. (p. 50)

An overall rhythmic quality is created through the language, though not one as integral to the understanding of the story, as in Chekhov's play.

An appeal to the emotions is also made on the level of characterization. Here, the major emotive element is the nature of Al'gista. George Kalbouss calls her a "romantic" character, by which he means "a general state of being in which a dramatic personage's motivation and decision-making is ruled by the heart." She is a character with whom any recipient can identify, at least at certain points in the play, such as, for example, when she decides to uncover the deception that she has perpetrated and kept up for ten years. For all of Mal'gista's logical and rational arguments, it is Al'gista's heart and emotions that push her toward the revelation. The romantic aspects are not deeply explored in the work, and in some sense function as a cover for arbitrary actions that simply reflect the author's ideas. Nevertheless, on a superficial level at least, the character's words, the expressives assigned to her, and the motivations given for her actions are depicted as resulting from emotions.[20]

Language, characterization, composition, and setting are all part of a broader strategy to increase emotiveness in *The Triumph of Death*, namely, the author's recourse to melodrama. As has been mentioned, the use of low forms during modernism is widespread. In this case, Sologub turns toward a romantic device, namely, the use of melodrama. Further back, such plays as Christopher Marlowe's *Tamburlaine* or William Shakespeare's *Richard III* use the same technique. Melodrama is a popular art form that is designed to function in an intense though facile manner, primarily inducing the feelings of fear and pity. It distances not by alienating, but by removing events to the familiar, safe distance of a never-never land. Even the most violent emotions are made less threatening by the unreality of the setting. By the twentieth century, it comes to be greatly disparaged, mostly due to the results, or rather failures, of the Victorian repertoire. However, it is unfair to judge something by its weakest members, and Victorian melodrama "was the lag-end—the rags and tatters, if you will—of something that had once been splendid."[21] In some sense, melodrama is the core of drama, the immature, but highly emotional play that we all participate in as children. The problem, of course, is that it never matures. Be that as it may, elements of melodrama can be used splendidly as in the works of the authors cited above.

What, then, are the elements of melodrama that appear in *The Triumph of Death* in order to increase its emotiveness? First, as mentioned earlier, there is an exotic and abstracted setting that keeps terror at bay by situating the action in the familiar yet remote land of tales. The medieval decor is further supported by a number of devices that are common in melodrama. The lighting, for example, is exaggerated, with strong contrasts between dark and light, often just one spot picked out by moonlight on a dark stage (pp. 15, 47, 49–50). The stage directions call for mysterious moans and rustles to fill the castle (pp. 33, 48). Cries ring out (pp. 45–46, 48–49), dogs howl (p. 47), and Mal'gista laments (pp. 47–48). There is much violent, rapid motion that emphasizes the frenzy of emotion: Mal'gista running across the stage (p. 34), then throwing herself at the supposedly wounded Berta (p. 35). Act 2 opens with Al'gista "rushing about the hall" (мечется по сеням [p. 38]), and this is followed by a struggle between mother and daughter (p. 45). The plot of the story calls for deception, an alleged knifing, intrigue, and a bloody killing of mother and child. Bloodied clothing is twice mentioned in the stage directions (pp. 47, 49).

Besides these most superficial of melodramatic elements, there are others that are more important. The stylistic usage of language fulfills a dual function in this work. On the one hand, the use of repetition and rhythm elicits an emotional response. On the other, the elevated language with abstract words and complex sentences distances. Simply stated, the emotional hyperbole of melodrama does not accord with a muted, realistic style. High rhetoric is called for and then it becomes a question of the playwright's skill in determining how successful he will be. Christopher Marlowe, William Shakespeare, and Victor Hugo all create splendid examples of lofty and moving rhetoric. Sologub is less successful. Though his language is in some measure beautiful and rhythmic, it lacks the poetry and the convincing passion of his predecessors. Perhaps after a century of overuse, it becomes more difficult to produce a convincing yet lofty style.

Sologub does present, as required by melodrama, an unmitigated villain—the King. Shakespeare in his melodrama uses passionate rhetoric, great poetry, and subtle characterization in order to make the figure of Richard at least to some degree ambiguous. In this way, he leaves the door open to some form of recipient identification with the protagonist. The play's "incompleteness" even permits productions where Richard is portrayed as the victim of his infirmity. That is not the case with Sologub's King. He is easily deceived by Al'gista, just as easily deserts her, and never for a moment is he capable of breaking out of his protective shell of *ruler*.

Overall, as in melodrama, there is no transcendence of terror in *The Triumph of Death*. This is due to a number of factors. First, there is not enough complexity or moral ambiguity, a trait that tragedy requires. Tragedy can have villains and heroes, just like melodrama, but they are always more complex and nuanced. Great melodrama moves its characters in the direction of tragedy. That is not the case in Sologub's play. Here, the characters never hesitate. If one considers Al'gista for a moment, one sees that she is completely single-minded. Being focused is one thing, but having no doubts is another. She chooses deception as a means for advancing beauty without ever questioning those means. In that respect, she is like a simple black-and-white character in melodrama, and that is further emphasized by her "romantic" nature. Second, the author does not offer an ending where suffering is accepted as punishment for the hero's hubris, or as part of the great deed that has been carried out by the tragic protagonist.

Thus, as in melodrama, this work purveys the emotions of fear and pity, but not of awe and compassion. Pity for Al'gista is created through the dramatic setting, the bloody clothes, the laments of her mother, the hatred of Berta, and the villainy of a king who can discard a supposedly beloved wife after ten years. Similarly, fear is built up as Mal'gista emphasizes the dangers facing her daughter if she confesses to who she is. A possible suggestion of transcendence is offered when Al'gista decides to reject further deception. However, it is never developed far enough. This inability of twentieth-century melodrama to move in the direction of tragedy occurs frequently and not just in Sologub's work. For the moment, the genre seems to have exhausted its potential.

In conclusion, one can state that Fedor Sologub's drama, *The Triumph of Death*, is an interesting experiment which reflects some of the most important needs and tendencies of the modernist search for a new drama. A widespread phenomenon, exemplified also by Sologub, is the intense interest in the middle ages that many modernists exhibit. This comes from a feeling of communality with a period that is generally perceived to be equally unstable. The difference between the two periods lies in the fact that upon the political and social instability of its times, the medieval mind imposed a rigid structure of various forms that were to help people deal with every conceivable situation.[22] Sologub shows how modernists attempted to adapt some of the medieval artistic forms to their own needs—from the use of symbolism and old stories to revivals of original works. However, *The Triumph of Death* underscores the complexity and difficulty of adapting and stylizing the traditions of earlier ages. Medieval mystery plays were often verbose, heavily didactic, allegoric, and slow. Yet they succeeded because they spoke to a community of believers through a recognizable system of symbols that could truly transform the work into a quasi-religious event. Even today, if care is taken, a medieval work may be staged successfully since its symbolic system is so deeply ingrained in the Western mind, regardless of whether an individual is actually a believer. It is also more accepted simply because it is old. When a twentieth-century writer adapts a historically distant dramatic structure for his own age, he must be careful. As *The Triumph of Death* demonstrates, an old form employed to deal with a modern approach to a subject may be alienating for today's recipient. Furthermore, symbolism must be communal at least to some degree in order to be comprehensible.

Further difficulties arise when modernist writers try to employ popular genres in the service of high art. Popular low forms, such as melodrama, have their limitations. Melodrama, for example, is a somewhat facile genre. For it to succeed, every element that goes into its creation must be successful and smoothly merged into a united whole. The language must be lofty, but also great and passionate. The setting must be exotic and elicit the proper mood. The characters must be dramatic and have flair—featuring villains seething with evil and heroes akin to angels. The work must be filled with high-paced action and intrigue. In comparison, a high genre such as tragedy has a core of awe and transcendence so strongly emotive that every movement in the direction of that core will contribute to the emotiveness of the work. Among the popular forms, melodrama may have become especially vulnerable after its overuse during the Victorian period.

On a more general level, *The Triumph of Death* reveals to us that elements in a dramatic work have varying strengths and are of varying importance. Language, the whole verbal text, is a powerful element. Thus, if used in a distancing fashion, it must be carefully balanced. It can, as in Gippius's play *Holy Blood,* incorporate both distancing and emotive elements within itself: atypical deixis versus emotive distribution, abundant referentials versus the use of a colloquial style, and so on. As with *The Triumph of Death,* language may also be very poetic and lofty, employing an elevated lexicon, complex syntax, and abundant referentials—yet still remain emotive.

However, there are two necessary conditions for safeguarding emotiveness. First, as shown by Shakespeare, the poetry of the text must be great, passionate, and stirring. Second, the playwright needs to take into account the specific character of dramatic language. In order for dramatic language to succeed, it must be characterized by a certain, as Keir Elam calls it, "incompleteness." This means that it must contain a high degree of deictic pointers, which, during the course of the play, are contextualized by nonverbal means, be they gestures, objects, action, or movement. Only then will the connotative and denotative dynamism of the sign, that is, the word, be fully realized in all of its richness. Thus, a language such as can be found in *The Triumph of Death* is in some sense too complete. It is more the language of poetic prose than of drama, with its abundance of complex sentences, participles, elevated lexicon, and a small amount of indexical expressions that might be "disambiguated" by nonverbal elements. As the text of this play stands, the language of the work is not completed or complemented by nonverbal indices. Sologub does not introduce a sufficient number of actions, gestures, visual images, music, dance, or even silences to break down the closed linguistic structures.[23]

Overall, Sologub's play *The Triumph of Death* serves as a useful example of the ambitiousness of modernist experimentation, as well as of the difficulties faced by these artists. Both the perceived closeness of medieval art, as well as the desire to incorporate low, popular forms into high art, carry with them inherent dangers that writers overcome with varying amounts of success.

Chapter Four

Aleksandr Blok's *The Puppet Show*

AN INTERESTING and successful example of transforming a historical genre occurs with Aleksandr Blok's dramatic work, *The Puppet Show* (Балганчик). Written in 1906, it is a seemingly slight playlet that to the surprise of everybody, including the author, became one of the pivotal points in the development of Russian drama and theater. The work's significance stems from its innovative and complex use of commedia dell'arte. The writer combines elements of *commedia* with elements of symbolist neomysteries to create an amalgamated genre that is sometimes called a fantasy satire.[1] *The Puppet Show* was a major source of inspiration and success, not just for the director Vsevolod Meierhold but for the whole Russian movement of "theatricalism." With its emphasis on the visual, ludic, and carnivalistic, it presages the developmental patterns and spirit of much of twentieth-century theater, and even of more popular forms of performance entertainment.

For some time before the appearance of this play, Blok had been participating in the "Wednesdays" organized by the symbolist Viacheslav Ivanov. Besides Ivanov, the meetings brought together such diverse personalities as Valerii Briusov and Vsevolod Meierhold. The group tried to formulate the concept of "mystical anarchism." It discussed the creation of a new, national, yet deeply religious theater, as well as of a new journal, both of which were to be named *Fakely*. The theater and the journal were to develop the group's "visionary programme of Symbolists individualism yoked with collective, communal action."[2] The participants had great ambitions of attracting even such aesthetically and theoretically distant writers as Maksim Gorky and the *Znanie* group. The actual results were more modest. Only the journal ever appeared; the theater never materialized. Nevertheless, an important outcome of these meetings was that—at the urging primarily of Georgii Chulkov—Blok sat down and within the space of a month rewrote his 1905 poem "Balaganchik" into the drama *The Puppet Show*. The work is an ironic reaction to a group that advocated a national religious theater.[3]

What was probably not recognized at the time by his fellow writers but what has now been well established is that the play appears at a very difficult time for Blok. Though doubts about his neoromantic, Neoplatonic ideas had been creeping into his poetry since 1902, the spiritual disenchantment seems to come to a head in 1906. This occurs partly because of the failure of the 1905 revolution, partly as a result of the writer's marital problems, and certainly also for artistic reasons. Chief among these artistic reasons is Blok's need to escape from the single-voiced, static character of the lyric poem. That need for dramatic multivocalism, sometimes even for the rudiments of drama, can be observed in much of symbolist poetry, not just Russian.[4] Blok himself writes of his condition at the time, saying that he was close "до тления, на границы которого я прошел в прошлом году" (to decay, on the boundary of which I found myself last year). He also states in his diary that the play served as a kind of therapy "вышедшие из недр департамента полиции моей собственной души" (coming out of the bowels of the police department of my own soul).[5]

Certainly no one was prepared for the strength of reaction and depth of passions that the staging of the work by Vsevolod Meierhold in Vera Komissarzhevskaia's theater in December of 1906 would arouse. Even at the play's premiere, the outburst of emotion was unprecedented. Georgii Chulkov, who was present and who was one of the few symbolists to react favorably to the performance, wrote: "Я никогда ни до, ни после не наблюдал такой непримиримой опозиции и такого восторга поклонников в зрительном зале. Неистовый свист врагов и гром дружеских аплодисментов смешались с криками и воплями" (Never before or after did I observe such implacable opposition and such an ecstasy on the part of admirers in an auditorium. The violent whistles of enemies and the thunder of friendly applause mixed with shouts and howls).[6] It was to be expected that the adherents of realistic theater would react critically to Blok's latest work, but that many of his closest friends felt themselves mortally offended was more surprising. Andrei Belyi, for example, repeatedly returned over the course of several years to the work and to his anger, bitterness, and disappointment. The work permanently damaged Blok's friendship with Sergei Solov'ev. Blok himself was surprised at the reaction, and he insisted on emphasizing both the trifling nature of the work, as well as his continued adherence to symbolism and to the ideas of Vladimir Solov'ev.[7] In fact, as V. P. Zarovnaia states: "Блок скорее склонен был увидеть в 'Балаганчике' 'ничтожную декадентскую пьеску, не без изящества, с какими-то типиками, неудавшимися картонными фигурками живых людей,' чем согласится с обвинением в поругании собственных святынь" (Blok was more willing to see "Balaganchik" as "a trifling decadent playlet, not without refinement, with types of some sort, unsuccessful cardboard figures of living people," rather than agree with the accusation of having profaned his own holies).[8] Yet in this play the author certainly set aside the symbolists' uncritical worship of Vladimir Solov'ev's philosophy. Simultaneously, Blok retained the greatest respect for Solov'ev's literary work, and even admitted to the influence of Solov'ev's play *White Lily* on his own *Puppet Show*.[9]

Aleksandr Blok's *The Puppet Show*

For the director Vsevolod Meierhold, the staging of *The Puppet Show* was a momentous event. Not only did it raise him to the status of a cult figure among the younger generation of artists, but it was also a defining moment in the development of his own theatrical ideas. As Konstantin Rudnitskii puts it: "'Балаганчик' изменил судьбу режиссера, предопределил все метаморфозы, которые совершились впоследствии в его искусстве" ("Balaganchik" changed the director's fate, predetermined all the metamorphoses which subsequently occurred in his art).[10] Overall, the play and its performance are "яркими событиями в истории русской культуры. Их воздействия и отражения в самых разнообразных культурных текстах весьма многочисленны" (colorful events in the history of Russian culture. Numerous are the examples of their influence upon and reflections in various cultural texts).[11]

At first glance, the most obvious innovation in *The Puppet Show* is the use of elements of commedia dell'arte, a genre that experiences a great revival at the beginning of this century. As discussed in the previous chapter, the use of so-called low forms in drama and theater becomes popular at the end of the nineteenth century and continues into the early twentieth. Among these, the "low form" undoubtedly most often applied throughout Europe is that of the commedia dell'arte. It is important to remember that *commedia* actually appears "as one element in a matrix of contiguous phenomena that coexisted with it, expressed a similar sensibility, and, in some instances coalesced with it."[12] These phenomena include the cult of the circus and the clown, *Kleinkunst* as a German branch of art nouveau, primitivism as expressed through cubism, and the idea of the director as a puppet master. In the Russian case, one must add an interest in the folkloric *balagan*, as well as the masquerade with its ties to the works of Aleksandr Griboedov, Aleksandr Pushkin, and Mikhail Lermontov.

Though there were attempts at puristic revivals of the original sixteenth-century Italian art form, for the most part what artists used was a much enriched tradition of *commedia*, and one that has gone through many permutations. The individual artist decides which elements of the tradition he wishes to emphasize in his work. The first important variation on the genre occurs in the eighteenth century when it enters written "high" drama. Within this movement are located Carlo Goldoni's sentimental plays with their touch of the rococo. However, it is Goldoni's contemporary, Carlo Gozzi, who made a more lasting impact. Gozzi combines playfulness with a violence and a "skirting of tragedy," which, in some ways, is closer to the original sixteenth-century Italian form. Significantly, he also alternates verse with prose. During the romantic period, E. T. A. Hoffman moves the genre in the direction of sinister and grotesque effects with an undercurrent of social subversiveness. Hoffman also turns the *commedia* characters into doll-like creatures in order to underscore their helplessness. On the other hand, his fellow romantic, Ludwick Tieck, used the *commedia* form to pose metatheatrical questions and was certainly ahead of his time in his conscious foregrounding of convention. Somewhat later, *commedia,* and especially the figure of Pierrot, became an important part of French nineteenth-century theater. As the creation of Charles Deburau and the Théâtre de Funambules, Pierrot combined irony and social subversiveness with poignancy and pathos. In later versions, especially those of the French symbolists, Pierrot is often identified with Hamlet, dandyism, and the artist. To his poignancy is added stylized decadence and malignancy, as well as sexual perversity and ambivalence. Such elements can be seen in the work of Paul Verlaine, Jules Laforgue, and in England, in the drawings of Aubrey Beardsley. In Russia, the influence of the French symbolists is very important, though often denied.[13]

There are a number of reasons why the *commedia* is so attractive to the modernist writer, even if its use also carries with it possible dangers. First, is the fact that *commedia* characters are both stereotypical, as well as fluid and accumulative. They evoke certain definite expectations, yet since they are not tied to a role, they simultaneously change and evolve. Moreover, from earliest times they accumulate the personality traits of the actors playing them. Thus, they offer an attractive "interplay of the familiar and the unexpected." In other words, these characters are "noncoincidental" with their role—they can be moved from plot to plot, but in a way that is much richer than the stock types of melodrama. Furthermore, while a traditional tragic hero is "a function of the plot fate assigns him," and is in many ways "unambiguous and inflexible," *commedia* figures allow a playwright to keep redefining his position.[14] This type of drama functions as an incomplete object, a process that allows one to reflect on the subject matter of the work from many points of view. The masks simply, as it were, freeze for a moment one or another interpretation.[15]

An important part of characterization in *commedia* is the use of masks, and masks are the second aspect of the genre that modernists find attractive. Masks are an effective means for presenting the theme of alienation. Tension between an actual face, a poetic ego, and the mask or masks can be used to depict an internal psychological state of division and estrangement. Such tension can also be used to show the difference between a private and a public face. On occasion writers even go so far as to insist that the individual is completely shaped by society and has no private face. Furthermore, the use of masks automatically foregrounds the relationship between the stage and every recipient because it definitively breaks the illusion of a conventionalized reality. Therefore, it becomes a useful tool for posing metatheatrical questions, something that the modernists, in their search for new forms, are constantly doing.[16]

The search for new forms is often formulated by modernists as a return to the essence of theater and drama. Modern theater wishes to return to a new and "revitalized" kind of absolute—"concrete images of man's essential fears, hopes, and beliefs."[17] This search for essential sensations is a response to the modernist conviction that, first of all, language has become too conventionalized and ineffective from over- and misuse. Second, it stems from a belief that drama's roots lie in visceral, primitive rites. Therefore, if drama is to serve as a quasi-religious ritual—the Nietzschean-inspired and stated goal of many a modernist—it has to return to these sources. Here again masks are a simple and visually bold means for presenting such essential emotions.

Mistrust of the word, its supposed inadequacy, and a conventionalized and even deceitful character led to an interest in yet another aspect of *commedia,* namely, its improvisational nature, as well as its use of nonverbal elements, including stock tricks and stage business. The concept of "plasticity," for example, is stressed by Vsevolod Meierhold in his writings of the time. By "plasticity," Meierhold seems to mean a whole rhythmic orchestration of improvisation, movement, gestures, stage business, and masks that communicates its own message, and that, significantly, forces the recipient to become a participant. For improvisation is also seen as a powerful means of abolishing the fourth wall in the theater and of actively drawing in the recipient. Directors like Vsevolod Meierhold and Nikolai Evreinov are opposed to the fourth wall in the Stanislavskian sense. They see in it "an embarrassingly naive juxtaposition of the real and the conventionally realistic, the grotesque contradiction between the two being conveniently ignored."[18]

The struggle against the Stanislavskian fourth wall is one aspect of the playwrights' radicalism. It is precisely this spirit of revolt that the modernists find in *commedia,* both in its original Italian form and in the version of the Théâtre de Funambules. Artists, as well as the authorities, perceive *commedia* as a satiric, subversive, and dangerous art form. It is the figure of Pierrot that is most often associated with a spirited defense of the poor and socially downtrodden. Such a subtext to the genre fits the mood of the modernist playwrights. All of these artists are trying to subvert traditional drama and theater. Moreover, they are attempting to present the plight of what they see as the poor, abused artist reduced in contemporary market-oriented society to the status of a clown, or at best that of an artiste.[19]

Metatheatricalism is present in *commedia* not only on the level of characterization, but also of composition. *Commedia* often presents a play-within-a-play, a theater-within-a-theater, contrasting the "straight" unmasked inamoratas with the masked figures. Philosophically, such a form expresses the baroque notion of a *theatrum mundi* with its juxtaposition of different worlds and different realities. However, the symbolist *theatrum mundi,* unlike the baroque one, is "not a one-for-one correlation between the composing elements of the different worlds, . . . It is in the boundaries between the realities presented on the . . . stage that the disharmonies of the age are expressed."[20]

Furthermore, with the onstage blurring of the boundary between reality and appearance, existence as a whole is put into question. The individual ego, perceived differently by different characters, becomes tenuous and ambiguous. Similarly, both the ideal world and the sensual, material one become confused and interconnected.

The most complicated and ambiguous aspect of *commedia* that draws the attention of the modernists is its use of the grotesque and the carnivalistic (in the Bakhtinian sense). On the one hand, in traditional theater, and in fact, in all forms of traditional art, the grotesque is clearly seen as a distancing factor. On the other hand, the jarring, bizarre, sometimes even sinister juxtaposition of opposed realities and contradictory moods and elements that are found in the grotesque suddenly begins to make sense to the modernists and seems to be the most "realistic" way of perceiving events. Modernism is the first period in Western development when the depth and breadth of changes in every sphere of existence reach such acute and overwhelming proportions that absurdity becomes a comprehensible attitude toward life. As the twentieth century progresses, the grotesque becomes more than a technique, certainly more than a mere distancing technique. Technological advances create the impression that human beings themselves have become depersonalized and turned into machines. The grotesque, which traditionally dehumanizes people by emphasizing the bizarre or by turning the individual into a body part, an animal, or an inanimate object, seems to portray aptly the essence of modern life. In importance it reaches the stature of a worldview. Vsevolod Meierhold, citing *The Puppet Show* as an example, writes about the grotesque, seeing it as the way of the future that would unite the concept of "representation" in theater with that of "presentation." He lauds the subtlety and enormity of the phenomenon as equal to the achievements of the great Gothic cathedrals. Similarly, the carnivalistic and ludic elements of *commedia*, as well as of various other rituals, begin to resonate with modernists. The original carnivalistic elements of ritual are simultaneously deeply cathartic for the community and distancing. They remove the community's violent and subversive feelings into an aesthetic form. The acuteness of problems in the twentieth century attracts modernist artists to the mask of the clown. This mask allows artists to hide their dead serious feelings to present the problems through nonserious means. Though the fashion for commedia dell'arte eventually disappears, it can be said that its spirit persists and even grows throughout the twentieth century. Its flamboyant, violent, sexually ambivalent, highly stylized, and above all subversively nonserious way of dealing with serious questions can be detected in the most diverse cultural phenomena. Examples from "high art" include the works of Samuel Beckett, Friedrich Dürrenmatt, Federico Fellini, and Peter Brooks. Popular manifestations range from Boy George through Monty Python and Madonna to David Bowie.[21]

Of course, for all of its usefulness, the application of *commedia* also carries inherent dangers within itself, two of which stand out in particular. First, the masked stereotypical characters of *commedia* can fulfill a useful function only if they are familiar to the recipient. Only if the recipient shares in the communal memories of generations contained in a given figure can he reinterpret it in the new context, understand its significance, and thus understand the play. The other possible problem is that the twentieth-century recipient, raised on the expectations of nineteenth-century realistic drama, often does not respond to the primal, simplified message of the mask. "The mask robbed of psychological meaning is empty for modern audiences. The abstract, symbolic mask has academic connotations only, no inherent spiritual meaning."[22] Nevertheless, despite the dangers, the *commedia* was used extensively and to spectacular effect in the great dramatic, theatrical upheaval that occurs at the beginning of this century. Within this upheaval, *The Puppet Show* had its own, not insignificant, role.

Turning directly to the play, Blok's application of *commedia* elements and devices works in two directions, both distancing the recipient and functioning emotively. Furthermore, *commedia* penetrates all levels of structure so as to create an intricate web interwoven throughout the whole work. It needs to be noted in terms of any recipient's expectations, both at the beginning of this century and throughout it, that realistic plays continue to dominate the stage. Moreover, the closest most recipients ever get to *commedia* is farce and its abundant use of slapstick and stage business. Farce is a popular genre that frequently appeared on the stage and later on the movie screen. Thus, it is the characteristics of farce that are familiar and therefore perceived as "normal."

Among the distancing effects of *commedia* in *The Puppet Show*, the question of metatheatricalism is one of the strongest and most visible. The opening lines of the play create confusion about what is happening. The stage directions state that the curtain should rise on an "Обыкновенная театральная комната" (A normal theatrical room [p. 6]).[23] A twentieth-century recipient's expectation would be for the curtain to open on a stage set that suggests, through an arrangement of conventions, some definite location, either in the real world or in a fairy land, but in any case not the theatrical stage itself. After all, the empty stage of the Shakespearean theater has long been forgotten and filled with ever more elaborate sets. Thus, from the first, a metatheatrical discussion is begun, and the theatrical illusion of a conventionalized reality is shattered. Form and content merge when both the mystics and Pierrot appear in the opening scene. The two belong to completely different "theatrical codes." The mystics come from symbolist neomysteries—Pierrot, of course, from *commedia*. Moreover, the playwright complicates matters even more by "contaminating" the codes and having Pierrot on occasion use elements of the symbolist code.[24] By blurring his virtual recipient's expectations from the beginning of the work, Blok makes it more difficult for him to respond to any set of expectations. Immediately, every recipient is challenged to think and make sense of what is taking place in front of him. In a sense, this scene is somewhat reminiscent of the first scene in *The Cherry Orchard*. There, too, elements of comedy and a traditional exposition are mixed with lyric, reflective moments that undercut the farcical "energy."

The metatheatrical discussion is also carried out through a number of other devices. Inspired perhaps by the work of Ludwig Tieck, Blok introduces the play-within-a-play. The playwright does not explicitly state that there is a stage on the stage—as Vsevolod Meierhold actually designed the premiere performance. However, by writing that the play opens in a "normal theatrical room" and then at the end of the play inscribing into the stage directions "Но внезапно все декорации взвиваются и улетают вверх" (But suddenly all the decorations soar up and fly up [p. 17]), he seems quite clearly to suggest something of the sort. When the scenery flies up and disappears, each recipient is returned to the theatrical stage—in other words, to reality. The distancing effect is further strengthened by the obviously paper flats through which Harlequin hurtles himself into nothingness and that again accent the contrast between the artificiality of performance and the "naturalness" of reality. Also, in the same vein are the visibly cardboard sword and helmet in the ball scene, as well as the "паяц" (clown) who bleeds cranberry juice. All of these elements break the illusion of reality for the recipient and keep him aware that he is watching a created, artificial world.

Furthermore, like Anton Chekhov in *The Cherry Orchard*, Blok participates in a metatheatrical discussion in which in one moment he employs various forms of stage business and in the next he proceeds to undercut comedic expectations. Pierrot falls down (pp. 11, 18), Harlequin jumps and dances (pp. 12, 16–17), the mystics disappear into their suits (p. 11), the clown bleeds (p. 16), and the Author runs off in fright (p. 18). As in a farce, there is violence, as well as violence with sexual innuendos. Harlequin strikes Pierrot (p. 11). The male in the second pair of lovers chases the woman (p. 13). The knight slashes the mocking clown (p. 16). All these examples fit into the norms of both *commedia* and farce. Traditionally, this kind of stage business tends to be a distancing factor since all recipients begin to look down on the characters engaged in it. At the same time, in a traditional comedic context there would be a sense of familiarity with such gags and thus a certain emotive effect. In *The Puppet Show*, as in Chekhov again, the combination of stage business and disappointed expectations opens up, in yet another form, the metatheatrical discussion of genre.

On a more explicitly ideological level, metatheatrical questions are debated through the character of the Author. He is a proponent of realistic theater, but the effectiveness of his words is undercut by the fact that, puppetlike, he is repeatedly yanked off the stage by stronger forces. The Author hears the dialogue of the other characters, but he cannot recognize their theatrical code. Moreover, he blames the actors for his work going awry and seems oblivious of the "abstract author." Simultaneously, through the character of Columbine the whole question of realistic illusion as created through conventions and the self-deceiving idealism of symbolist mysticism are further spotlighted. Not only is it uncertain whether Columbine's *kosa* is a braid or a scythe or both, but she is also a figure completely defined by the subjective point of view of the other characters. Furthermore, Blok uses her to present the existential problem of identity and self, a matter that was greatly troubling him at the time that this play was written. In Columbine, the social and public mask has completely obliterated the individual and real face.[25]

In *The Puppet Show*, metatheatricalism is also intertwined with the very complex phenomenon of the carnival-grotesque—in the Bakhtinian sense. The most obvious aspect of the whole problem is the fact that Blok adds metatheatrical overtones to the carnival ritual of crowning-discrowning. First, the author makes the mock king a queen, namely, Columbine. Second, the mock king/queen returns yet again at the end of the play. She is discrowned by turning into a cardboard figure that falls in the snow and over which Pierrot and Harlequin perform their mocking dance. Then she puts in a subsequent ambiguous appearance, once more in the process transforming herself from the figure of Death into that of a young girl. As Timothy C. Westphalen writes: "Thus, *The Puppet Show* moves beyond a mere enactment of the carnival ritual to become a meditation upon the very mutability of the ritual itself. The play offers not so much ritual as meta-ritual."[26]

A more slippery question is how different recipients will respond to Blok's use of the grotesque. Traditionally, as has been noted by previous scholars, the grotesque was created by spinning a web of devices, devices that together distanced the majority of recipients. Undoubtedly, in *The Puppet Show*, the grotesque also distances many recipients on the emotional level. It is strong and discourages personal identification with any of the characters. Its strength comes from the fact that it involves many levels of structure. Certainly caricature and the fantastic can be found in this play, from the lifeless suits of the mystics to the three pairs of lovers who are parodied. As is typical of the grotesque, one way in which a sensation of the fantastic is achieved is by turning animate beings into objects. In the case of the mystics, for example, as their fear and dismay increase they become progressively reified, turned into body parts and pieces of clothing. The text contains statements such as "Руки всплеснулись. Фалды сюртуков раскачиваются" (Hands fly up. The folds of the frock coats swing [p. 9]), and "Рукава сюртуков вытянулись. . . . Головы ушли в воротники. Кажется на стульях висят пустые сюртуки" (The sleeves of the frock coats stretch out. . . . The heads disappear into the collars. It seems that empty frock coats hang on the chairs [p. 11]). Next, the textual world evades logical interpretation because it is governed by more than one theatrical and cultural system. The mystics come from the world of neomysteries—Pierrot, Harlequin, and Columbine from the world of *commedia*. Each of the three pairs of lovers is again from a different "theatrical code" and thus a different kind of textual world. The first pair belongs to the Neoplatonic idealism of the playwright's early poetry. The second emerges from the sensual, debased vision of love that corresponds to Blok's city poetry. The third represents a peculiar vision of the middle ages. The different codes and worlds are constantly being alternated, juxtaposed, and in turn given prominence, thus making the work seem confusing and open-ended. Furthermore, there is a constant juxtaposition of opposing moods. The pompously solemn expectations of the mystics are contrasted with the lyric reflectiveness of Pierrot and the whirlwind energy and merriment of Harlequin. Then the focus returns to Pierrot, but in a more narrative style of discourse, and so on. Additionally, one can find in *The Puppet Show* a parody of genre conventions, something typical of the grotesque. For example, Maeterlinckian neomysteries with their focus on death as the defining moment of existence are parodied in the mystics' pompous preparations for the arrival of death—who turns out to be a pretty and fickle young girl. Moreover, Blok mixes different styles of language. The mystics speak an elevated, bizarre language: "Наступит событие" (An event will occur); "О, вечный ужас, вечный мрак!" (Oh, eternal horror, oh, eternal darkness! [p. 6]). The style of Pierrot is colloquial with simple lexicon and syntax, as well as incomplete sentences. However, on occasion he uses verse: "И вот, стою я, бледен лицом, / Но вам надо мною смеяться грешно. / Что делать! Она упала ничком.... / Мне очень грустно? А вам смешно?" (And here I stand, with a pale face, / But it is sinful for you to laugh at me. / What should I do! She fell flat on her face ... / Am I very sad? Is it funny for you? [p. 18]). On the other hand, the Author speaks colloquially and always in prose. This constant juxtaposing and interweaving of disparate elements creates a grotesque feeling and an open-endedness, since no single point of view or system dominates. In other words, it distances.

At the same time, it must be kept in mind that reaction to the grotesque as a phenomenon is determined and influenced by the historical period. Blok's contemporaries were undoubtedly more shocked by his use of the grotesque than today's recipients are. As the twentieth century progresses, though the grotesque continues to impede traditional personal identification, it yet becomes one of the principal techniques of art and a dominant worldview. The events of our century have been so extreme that the grotesque now appears as the most convincing, most natural response to existence. In other words, though distanced in terms of personal identification with a character, today's recipient on some emotional level responds emotively to the grotesque. It is enough to consider the works of the most diverse group of writers to see how frequent the use of the grotesque has become. It even dominates works that are very highly personal. Examples range from Friedrich Dürrenmatt and Günter Grass through Frantisek Hašek, Vladimir Mayakovsky, Liudmila Petrushevskaia, Mikhail Bulgakov, Stanisław Ignacy Witkiewicz, Bruno Schulz, Stanisław Różewicz, Eugène Ionesco, and Jean Anouilh to Carlos Fuentes and Gabriel García Márquez. Thus, for recipients in the second half of the twentieth century—recipients much more exposed to the grotesque as a worldview—the degree of distancing caused by it diminishes.

One of the techniques that has been employed in creating the grotesque is the use of masks—be it actual three-dimensional creations or faces masked by makeup. Overall, Blok's masks in *The Puppet Show* function in a distancing fashion. First, all of the characters are "masks" in some way; there are no exceptions. Besides the three *commedia* figures and the masked guests at the ball, Blok suggests the same situation for the mystics and the Author. The mystics are described at critical moments as inanimate parts; their faces and hands disappear and only suits are left. It is known that when Vsevolod Meierhold staged the work he created cutouts of figures behind which stood the actors, showing only their hands and faces.[27] Similarly, the Author, yanked back by an invisible force (by a visible rope in the original production), is presented as a puppetlike creation. Such complete masking goes beyond what the original *commedia* does, since there one always finds the unmasked inamoratas who are closest to the recipient and who offer him at least a momentary illusion of entering reality. The practice in modern drama and theater has most often been to mask the secondary characters but to leave the protagonist unmasked. The protagonist then is the figure with whom the recipient associates himself, while gradually being educated in the use of masks through the secondary characters. Blok certainly adds elements to the protagonist Pierrot that make him much more emotive than the other characters (this will be discussed later). Yet even he in the end remains a mask.

Furthermore, since the characterization offered in this work is slight, the role of the mask increases. The playwright depends strongly on the collective cultural memory of his virtual recipient and his familiarity with the *commedia* tradition. Blok expects that the virtual recipient will interpret the characters by recognizing the masks that he has put on them. Unfortunately, that knowledge cannot be treated as a given. As the twentieth century has progressed, familiarity with the *commedia* figures has diminished culturally, even if its spirit may have lived on in various ways.

However, it should be noted that, except for the guests at the ball who are wearing true masks, the rest of the dramatis personae are "masked" only with the help of makeup and costume. Pierrot, for example, has, as tradition dictates, a floured face with two rouged spots on his cheeks. The author's decision for a more flexible and fluid type of masking results from his desire to emphasize the uncertainty of the private and the public, the individual and the stereotypical. A true mask, completely immobile and with "[i]ts strong indexical properties, leaving no room for uncertainty about role and actor, would seem to be unfit to express that very uncertainty" of roles.[28] That is precisely the reason why, for example, Luigi Pirandello's play *Six Characters in Search of an Author* is almost always staged without masks, despite the author's explicit stage direction to the effect.

In brief, one sees that many commedia dell'arte elements in this work function in a distancing fashion: the metatheatrical discussion on veristic versus antiveristic theater, the grotesque vision of the world, the masks that simplify into absolutes. In some instances, these features become even more distancing then they would be normally because Blok mixes theatrical codes and thus undercuts the genre expectations of the recipient. *The Puppet Show* is not simply a *commedia* play, but a play on *commedia* elements, combined with a parody of other, serious forms of drama. Every recipient is constantly being shunted from one form to another, never allowed to sit back comfortably and become passively certain in his knowledge of the kind of work that he is experiencing.

There are, however, three *commedia* elements that Blok uses in an emotive fashion. The first of these is his construction of the figure of Pierrot. The author begins by trying to awaken communal cultural memory through a statement in the stage directions that his Pierrot is "как все Пьеро" (like all Pierrots [p. 6]). In other words, he does not limit the character to a single interpretation but offers each recipient the possibility of dipping into a rich and varied tradition of creating this particular character. That effect, of course, demands that the recipient respond actively and engage himself in the interpretative process. It is even more of an invitation for any director to be creative and subjective in his staging. This runs contrary to the general modernist tendencies, where playwrights often create puppetlike characters but at the same time try to control the whims of directors by giving them elaborate stage directions.

After this introduction, Blok himself fleshes out Pierrot more than the other characters, dipping into several traditions in the process of characterization. First, there is the lyric side of Pierrot, the sad lover of Deburau's creation.[29] He is given lyric monologues in which he expresses his feelings for Columbine. Often these are self-pitying laments reminiscent of Jules Laforgue's version of the character: "Я пойду бренчать печальною гитарою" (I will go to strum my sad guitar [p. 6]) or "Слышишь ты, Колумбина, как сердце бедное / тянет, тянет грустную песню мою?" (Columbine, do you hear, how my poor heart is / intoning, intoning its sad song? [p. 7]).

Furthermore, Pierrot's lyric side is "contaminated" by images and expressions typical of Blok's early symbolist phase, such as, for example, "вьюга" (storm), "вечный мрак" (eternal darkness), and "зеленела звезда" (a star shown green). He endears the audience with his bewilderment over Columbine's identity and his fool's role, as when he is patronized by the mystics: "Наш бедный друг сошел с ума" (Our poor friend has gone out of his mind) or "Простим великодушно простеца" (We will graciously forgive the simpleton [p. 10]). Despite lapses, Pierrot reveals a deep devotion to his fickle love, even in the final monologue while reproaching himself for his moment of weakness and laughter, as well as emphasizing his sadness over losing her. This emotionalism is strengthened by the abundant use of expressives and by a proximal deixis that focuses on Pierrot's emotions and desires. Finally, the lyricism is underscored through the character's artistic talent: he is a poet who speaks in verse and a musician who plays the flute. Thus, his sensitivity is revealed.

Artistic talent does not preclude a weak side to Pierrot. As V. P. Zarovnaia writes: "Все в нем—не порывы, а воздыхания, не действия и чувства, а их отдаленное, слабое подобие" (Everything in him is not a gust, but a sigh, not an action and feeling, but a distant, weak likeness).[30] Pierrot becomes uncertain when the mystics question the identity of Columbine and he immediately doubts his own intelligence: "Или вы правы, и я—несчастный сумасшедший. Или вы сошли с ума—и я одинокий, непонятный вздыхатель" (Either you are right, and I am an unfortunate madman. Or you have lost your minds, and I am a solitary, misunderstood dreamer [p. 10]). He falls under the weight of Harlequin's hand on his shoulder [p. 11]). Twice during the course of the play the character collapses on the stage and lies helpless: a victim and a puppet whose strings have been cut. At the end of the work, Pierrot in his confusion directs rhetorical questions to the playwright. He blames the writer for placing him, Pierrot, in an inexplicable reality—perhaps the presented world, perhaps the reality of the actual theater: "Куда ты завел? Как угадать? / Ты предал меня коварной судьбе" (Where have you brought me? How can I guess? / You have sold me to an insidious fate [p. 18]).

Thus, there are elements of a Hamlet in this Pierrot: his indecisiveness, his lack of strength in dealing with situations. This accords with the modernist set of associations: artist = poet = clown = Hamlet. The equation often also includes Christ—in the image of the suffering innocent.[31] Perhaps there are touches of that here.

Pierrot's lyricism and expressiveness are sometimes contrasted with a less kindly face. He mockingly dances over the body of his beloved Columbine, who has fallen down in the snow and been turned into a cardboard cutout. Then he walks off "as a brother" with his own rival, Harlequin (p. 12). In this example, one can see another "contamination" of the *commedia* tradition with modernist elements where Pierrot is on occasion presented as sly, even with a streak of cruelty. As such he appears, for example, in some of Jules Laforgue's work.[32]

Distance Manipulation

Though children can also be cruel, for Blok, Pierrot's childlike side is pure, innocent, and direct.[33] In Pierrot, the childlike is weak, easily concealed by other traits. It is there, however, as in the stage directions that "Он говорит голосом звонким и радостным, как первый удар колокола" (He speaks with a ringing and joyous voice, like the first stroke of a bell [p. 9]) or "звонким, детским голосом" (with a ringing, childlike voice [p. 10]). The joyfulness is most often combined with a helplessness, as when at the end of the play he looks around and questions, not even states, with reproach, "Мне очень грустно? А вам смешно?" (Am I very sad? Are you happy? [p. 18]).

Pierrot also plays an important part in the development of the theme of alienation, self-alienation, and doubles. Pierrot the clown is a mask for the poet; the mask "protects him and refracts his feelings." Furthermore, there seems to be an interweaving of a more superior face with a more inferior face, a good face with a bad face.[34] It is as if the poet were both proud of himself and happy with his behavior one moment, then full of self-reproaches and self-irony the next. Moreover, Pierrot's constant, abrupt, and unmotivated changes of behavior underscore the illusion of appearances, the oscillating seductive fictions that seem to be constantly replacing one another. Pierrot is a product of his environment, and his changeability, placed in the context of a perpetually transforming textual world, reveals the reasons behind the poet's alienation. Alienation is a normal result of the incomprehensibility of both the world and the self. Pierrot's confusion persists until the very end of the play, when in an accusatory voice he hurls questions at the abstract author and tries to make sense of his sadness and of the recipient's gleefulness.

Thus, Pierrot is more fully drawn than the other characters. In this way, he functions as an emotive element in the play. It must be stressed, however, that the effect is equivocal, for though more developed, he still remains a mask, a puppet. The changes in his behavior, the different sides of him that suddenly become visible, are not psychologically motivated. They are not a response to any event or changes in a situation. The character is simply arbitrarily moved around by the playwright and placed in different realities and contexts. It is the playwright's decision that calls forth one or another of the Pierrot images found in Western tradition.

Another emotive element that involves Pierrot, and appears not only in *commedia* but in many other genres, is the love triangle. In a certain sense like Chekhov's holiday/social occasion in *The Cherry Orchard,* the love triangle functions emotively because of its great familiarity to all recipients. Though the triangle is neither as pivotal nor as cathartic as the social occasion in Chekhov, its emotive strength is increased by generating sympathy for the figure of Pierrot. On the other hand, Blok does add a twist to the traditional motif, by making Pierrot retain his friendship with Harlequin, despite the fact that his friend takes away Pierrot's beloved, Columbine.

Finally, when it comes to emotive aspects derived from *commedia,* one can consider the complicated matter of the "carnivalistic" (in Bakhtinian terms) spirit of this work. Martin Green briefly delineates this spirit as brittleness, flamboyance, violence (sometimes with sexual innuendoes), decadence, stylization, sexual ambivalence, and a nonserious presentation of serious questions.[35] Several of the characteristics mentioned by Green fit into Mikhail Bakhtin's more detailed model of carnivalization. Though some elements of Bakhtin's model are missing in *The Puppet Show,* and a few others appear in a somewhat tenuous or equivocal form, most can be easily found and help to create the carnivalistic mood of this work. Not really present is audience participation in a carnivalistic sense. Present but tenuous is the idea of renewal. Furthermore, somewhat equivocal is the nature of laughter in this play. It is present in its derisive, ridiculing form in Pierrot's narrative monologue (p. 12). However, its rejoicing, renewing aspect is much less emphasized. Ambiguous also is the question of new relationships. Blok certainly disregards status and hierarchies, placing on the stage characters from very different theatrical codes and cultural fields. However, it is difficult to speak of relationships between them. It is more a question of physical proximity and contiguity, with rather limited reciprocity.

On the other hand, the carnival's tradition of dependence on stylization is clearly visible in *The Puppet Show.* First of all, this includes the use of language. Blok employs a strange, grotesque language for the mystics and then parodies it. He also juxtaposes it both with the simple yet poetic style of Pierrot, as well as with the prosaic and colloquial language of the Author. Next, carnivalistic stylization often uses ridiculous and even obscene gestures. An example of that effect in this work is the *pajac* who sticks out his tongue at the knight (p. 16). Stylization also means the invocation of traditions or fashions, either with a serious or a parodic intent. Here, for example, the vogue for a vague symbolist Neoplatonic idealism is parodied in the mystics—beginning with the emphasis on their fashionable dress. The juxtaposition related to stylization leads in turn to Bakhtin's mésalliances, which are also present in *The Puppet Show.* Even if relationships are not formed, certainly opposites are juxtaposed. The "high" of medieval courtly love clashes with the silliness of the clown. The childlike simplicity of Pierrot meets the esoteric and jaded subtlety of the mystics. These mésalliances in turn serve to create a sense of "profanation." For example, symbolist sanctities, such as the worship of and yearning for the ideal sphere, are ridiculed through the characters of the mystics, as well as through the first pair of lovers. Moreover, parody, which Blok often employs, is certainly present, and it even takes on the form of doubles as mentioned by Bakhtin. Much has been written about the complicated system of doubles created in this work. Its use is in keeping with the carnivalistic tradition.[36]

Distance Manipulation

Obviously present is the crowning-discrowning ritual, with Columbine fulfilling the role of the mock king. As with traditional carnival, the ritual here is used to undermine the status quo, authority. In this case, however, it is the authority not of political systems, but of cultural systems and traditions. The whole crowning-discrowning ritual is a clear pointer to the fact that Blok embraces another element of the Bakhtinian model—namely the "two-in-one," the idea that every image carries within itself the suggestion of itself but also of its opposite. Pierrot, for example, is both the dreamy lover and the mocking buddy of Harlequin. Moreover, the ritual of crowning-discrowning involves violence, and violence is one of the elements cited by Michael Green as being characteristic of the spirit of *commedia*. There are other examples of violence besides the ritual in *The Puppet Show*. These include the falling of Pierrot under Harlequin's touch, the decapitation of the *pajac*, Harlequin's annihilating jump into nothingness, and even the Author being yanked off the stage.

Certainly carnivalistic eccentricity, or the exoticism of decadence as Martin Green would have it, are present in this work. The eccentricity and the strangeness come from the various forms of parody, from the juxtaposition of disparate elements. Additionally, the sensuality often associated with decadence can be seen in the predominance of channels geared toward the visual, auditory, and emotional. In Pierrot's and Harlequin's utterances, ideas and descriptions are often expressed by appealing to the auditory: "бренчать" (jingle), "слышишь" (do you hear), "поют" (they are singing), "звеня" (ringing); or the visual: "свет" (light), "нарумяню" (I will rouge), "бледное" (pale), and "сумерки" (twilight); or even the tactile: "зимний день" (wintry day), "морозный туман" (frosty fog), "щекотало" (tickled), and "морозные иглы" (frosty needles). Furthermore, decadence is also present in the pessimism of the work, in the fact that Blok de-emphasizes the renewal aspect of carnival.

Next, the relativistic perspective of carnival can also be found here. The constant juxtapositions, the ephemerality of every situation, scene, and point of view, lead to an open-endedness. The author's voice favors a certain stance, namely that embodied in the figure of Pierrot whose lyrical creativity is the closing note of the work. Nevertheless, not a single point of view is presented as wholly good or convincing; each is to a greater or lesser degree ambiguous. Though Blok does not dwell on the sexual ambivalence of Pierrot, as certain modernist presentations do, he does suggest a weakness in his protagonist that is contrasted with the vigor of Harlequin.

And finally, two characteristics that Green associates with the spirit of *commedia* in its modernistic and postmodernistic version are brittleness and flamboyance. Both of these traits are present in *The Puppet Show*. "Brittle" can be taken here as meaning both "brilliantly sharp" and "fleeting, transitory, easily disrupted."[37] The sudden, jarring jumps between scenes and moods are combined with characters who are strongly differentiated from each other and drawn as very distinct, even if only in the barest of outlines due to the brevity of the play. Also, the ideas, emotions, and impressions are fleeting, since each of the scenes is so short. The recipient can barely register them before being forced to receive new ones. This abbreviated method of dealing with what are essentially very serious themes gives the work an air of flippancy typical of the early twentieth-century mind-set, such as, for example, that found in the novels of Evelyn Waugh. Overall, such flippancy is more frequent in western Europe than it is in Russia. Similarly, one can describe this play as being flamboyant both in the sense of "richly colored, resplendent," as well as "marked by striking audacity and verve."[38] The constant changing of theatrical codes and semantic and cultural fields certainly gives the work a colorful, motley texture. The audacity of dealing with so many serious and complicated themes in a play whose performance lasts about eighteen minutes is nothing but flamboyant.

Thus, it can be seen that *The Puppet Show* is part of the carnivalistic tradition. The fact that it openly uses *commedia* figures, as well as its brittleness, identifies the work as belonging to the early twentieth century. However, Blok's usage of the carnival tradition is more complex than just those two elements. The spirit of the work, especially its absurd and grotesque side, should resonate with and function emotively for all twentieth-century recipients. As the century progresses, perhaps the flippant brittleness grows weaker. Yet an absurd, violent, relativistic, and nonserious way of dealing with deadly serious issues only grows in a world that seems to become more frightening and alienated as time passes.

Moving outside the sphere of *commedia,* there are a number of elements in *The Puppet Show* that need to be discussed in reference to the manipulation of distance. To begin with, on the compositional level every recipient is distanced because of the absence of a traditional, dynamic, and causal plot. The play in fact has been called antidramatic. Action and intrigue would have been expected from farce. Instead, if one applies C. Brémond's definition of action,"it appears that we will always find the intention of action"; however, "the intention of action is always related to an object that is . . . unattainable."[39] Therefore, the action is never completed. Additionally, each recipient is presented with a sequence of scenes linked by association, by symbolic and thematic threads. For example, the figure of Pierrot is one of the linking threads that appears in every scene. The structural axis seems to be Columbine, whose identity remains a mystery, subject to the perception of this figure by the other characters. Even though her carnivalistic discrowning is not shown on stage but only narrated, it is this event that "becomes the hinge on which the play swings."[40] Thus, what should be the climax of the work is only narrated and not shown. The epic qualities of the narration—as well as the grotesque, ironic stance of Pierrot as narrator—reduce the scene's emotive forcefulness as compared to, for example, the witch's retelling of the murder in Zinaida Gippius's play *Holy Blood*. Thus, in this case the antidramatic effect is only strengthened. Moreover, there is no direct cause and effect based on action and reaction between scenes and characters, as would be the case with the composition of a traditional play. Instead, as has been stated, characters are often contiguous; they appear simultaneously in the same place, but they do not interact. Rather, the relationships between them are based on associative juxtapositions of ideas and emotions.

On the thematic level, complexity becomes another distancing factor in *The Puppet Show*. Though traditional farce abounds in intrigue and conflict, it is not known for its intellectual depth. Ancient Greek and Golden Age comedy of the sixteenth and seventeenth centuries on occasion exhibits profundity and complexity, as in the works of Aristophanes, Shakespeare, Lope de Vega, or Molière. This, however, is not true of the overwhelming majority of nineteenth-century comedies. Aleksandr Griboedov's *Woe from Wit* and Nikolai Gogol's *Inspector General* are really exceptions.[41] Standard fare of the period tends to be shallow and nonintellectual. Moreover, it must be remembered that the mask itself is rather a simple device, which can increase the dramatic essence of a work by "embody[ing] ideas analogically," though the playwright must be careful not to overburden it.[42] Blok's short work, however, presents a bewildering array of ideas and themes in an exceedingly small number of pages and in a highly elliptic form. These include the illusion of appearances; the ambiguity of the alienated *I* as presented in the whole problem of masks; criticism of symbolist neomysteries preoccupied with death and simplistic realistic verism; the eternal love triangle; the concept of the Eternal Feminine; and the transcendence of art, sensual joie de vivre. Each of these themes is briefly sketched, introduced, and interwoven with others in a complex web of meaning and implications, permutations, and variations, all of which are not easily understood or disentangled.

At the same time, it must be acknowledged that, though complexity distances the twentieth-century recipient seemingly encountering signs of a comedy, over time it can challenge him intellectually. This will not elicit a traditional type of identification with a protagonist, but it will awaken interest. The recipient may begin to appreciate the subtlety in the presentation of the ideas both from an intellectual and an aesthetic point of view.[43]

Of the whole complex web of subjects, one stands out in *The Puppet Show* as being emotive in and of itself and being presented in an emotive fashion. This is the phenomenon of alienation, which is one of the most pervasive and important themes in this play and one that has been well documented.[44] At least since the Renaissance, the textual world of drama has been anthropocentric and the virtual recipient's focus and sympathies have been directed to the fate of a given protagonist or protagonists. Beginning with romanticism, more ambitious and avant-garde drama has tended to emphasize a state of alienation of the hero from the world around him. Examples include Alfred de Vigny's *Chatterton,* Friedrich Schiller's *Don Carlos,* Adam Mickiewicz's *Forefather's Eve, Part III,* and Juliusz Słowacki's *Kordian.* With modernism, a sense of alienation from the rapidly evolving surroundings, conditions, and shape of life, often leading to a sense of self-alienation, has been one of the dominant themes of all Western art. During the twentieth century those feelings have only grown and spread to ever broader circles of people. Thus, alienation as a theme is not only familiar to today's recipient, but also, as it were, close to his heart. Of course, the emotiveness of the theme will depend greatly on its presentation, on the form of the dramatic work. Many experimental plays try to present alienation by estranging the virtual recipient, by pushing him away emotionally, and thus having him experience the condition himself. Such, for example, are the tendencies of absurd drama, as in the works of Eugène Ionesco, Jean Anouilh, or Samuel Beckett. However, the theme of alienation can also be presented in a way that awakens the sympathy of the recipient for the protagonist.

Blok's presentation of the theme in *The Puppet Show* is multifaceted. He depicts the estrangement of the mystics from reality. He refracts his own personal and biographical dilemmas both as husband and as author into several characters: Pierrot, Harlequin, and Author, for example. His juxtapositions of various realities and the blurring of boundaries so that everything becomes illusory and deceptive "signalled his acceptance of the earthly reality around him, but a reality that was shifting, elusive and disturbing, and had to be expressed in his 'cruel harlequinade.'"[45] Some of the aspects of his presentation distance every recipient, such as, for example, the contrasting worlds. However, his presentation of the theme of alienation in the figure of Pierrot functions emotively. By focusing on the childlike bewilderment of Pierrot, his faithfulness to Columbine, his artistic sensitivity, and his lyricism (use of verse, expressives, channel, and deixis), the playwright enlists each recipient's sympathy toward this character. This is a figure lost in a world that he does not understand. Pierrot's final monologue clearly reveals his confusion and estrangement from the world around him, and it does so in emotive terms.

One entirely separate level in *The Puppet Show* functions emotively, namely, the usage of language in this work. It has been shown how strongly language can affect the reception of a play. In *Holy Blood,* it makes a distancing subject matter and story personal and understandable. On the other hand, in *The Triumph of Death,* it distances the recipient due to its abstract, elevated, undifferentiated, and "complete" character. Blok's usage of language in *The Puppet Show* is not without ambiguities, but overall it is emotive. In some ways the usage of language in this play resembles that of *Holy Blood.* This is a work with a large percentage of referentials. The referentials may relate events that have occurred or will occur offstage. For example:

Distance Manipulation

Сквозь улицы сонные
Протянулась длинная цепь фонарей

Through the sleepy streets
a long string of torches has passed. (p. 6)

Ах, тогда в извозчичьи сани
Он подругу мою усадил!

Ah, then into a cab-sleigh
he seated my girlfriend! (p. 12)

Moreover, referentials may be descriptions of conditions present on the stage:

Не видно ни зги.

It is pitch-dark. (p. 9)

Лица, скрытые облаком мглы,
Озаряются тусклым блеском!

The faces, hidden by a cloud of fog,
are lit up by a dim luster! (p. 16)

After referentials, expressives and phatic statements are most numerous. Expressives help increase the emotiveness of the work in a new substitutive way, as they did in *The Cherry Orchard* and *Holy Blood*. Most often expressives appear in the utterances of Pierrot, such as, for example, in the following:

... как сердце бедное
Тянет, тянет грустную песню свою?

... how my poor heart
intones, intones its sad song? (p. 7)

Мне очень грустно?

Am I very sad? (p. 18)

However, expressives can also be found in the statements of many other characters, as in those remarks of the first pair of lovers:

... Кто-то темный стоит у колонны
И мигает лукавым зрачком!
Я боюсь тебя, влюбленный!

Someone dark is standing by the column
and winking with a sly pupil!
I am afraid of you, beloved! (p. 13)

Aleksandr Blok's *The Puppet Show*

On the other hand, the numerous phatic expressions create the illusion of movement, a substitute for true perlocutionism, with the characters constantly checking to see if the communication channel is open:

Ты слушаешь?

Are you listening? (p. 6)

Милостивые государи и государыни!

Excellent gentlemen and ladies! (p. 11)

Посмотри, . . .

Look, . . . (p. 13)

In terms of sheer numbers, appellatives are in last place in this text, and therefore perlocutionism of a traditional kind is low.

When one considers deixis in *The Puppet Show*, one realizes that over a third of the statements are distally oriented and refer to an offstage *there*. Sometimes this *there* is a general statement about matters, states, and events that are to come, as in the utterances of the mystics:

Наступит событие.

An event will occur. (p. 6)

Приближается дева из дальней страны.

A maiden from a faraway land is drawing near. (p. 7)

At other times the distal orientation comes from the narrating of events that concern the speaker, events in which he was involved or intends to be involved, as in Pierrot's narrative monologue in the middle of the play.

If the distribution of segments is analyzed, it is revealed that in the utterances of the mystics, Blok groups together segments with a distal deixis. The following passage in which the mystics speculate about the arrival of death can serve as an example:

Третий мистик. Приближается дева из дальней страны.
Первый мистик. О, как мрамор—черты!
Второй мистик. О, в очах—пустота!
Третий мистик. О, какой чистоты и какой белизны!
Первый мистик. Подойдет—и мгновенно замрут голоса.
Второй мистик. Да. Молчание наступит.

Third mystic. A maiden from a distant land is drawing near.
First mystic. Oh, her features—like marble!
Second mystic. Oh, in her eyes—emptiness!
Third mystic. Oh, what cleanliness and what whiteness!
First mystic. She will approach and immediately voices will grow silent.
Second mystic. Yes. Silence will fall. (p. 7)

Distance Manipulation

However, in the statements made by Pierrot, Blok does what Zinaida Gippius did in *Holy Blood*. The playwright manipulates the distribution of the segments in such a way as to constantly interweave distal segments with proximal ones, especially those that function as expressives. Consider, for example, the protagonist's final monologue in which he remembers what happened, blames the abstract author, and expresses his feelings—all simultaneously:

Куда ты завел? Как угадать?	author
Ты предал меня коварной судьбе.	author
Бедняжка Пьеро, довольно лежать,	self, expressive
Пойди, поищи невесту себе.	self, appellative
(*Помолчав*)	
Ах, как светла—та, что ушла	absent bride
(Звенящий товарищ ее увел).	Harlequin
Упала она (из картона была).	absent bride
а я над ней смеяться пришел.	self in past
Она лежала ничком и бела.	absent bride
Ах, наша пляска была весела!	self, Harlequin in past
А встать она уж никак не могла.	absent bride
Она картонной невестой была.	absent bride
И вот, стою я, бледен лицом,	self in present
Но вам надо мною смеяться грешно.	recipient
Что делать! Она упала ничком ...	absent bride
Мне очень грустно? А вам смешно?	self, recipient
(p. 18)	

In the case of Zinaida Gippius, a certain ambiguity as to the emotiveness of the language arises at those times when her humor becomes biting. In *The Puppet Show*, it is the use of verse that may appear to add to the ambiguity. On one level, meter and rhyme always function emotively because they awaken the primal, protoaesthetic value of rhythm (see chapter 1). On another level, they are not as obviously and easily emotive as prosaic, colloquial language attempting to mimic spoken speech. However, if the verse is of high quality then it can stir recipients emotionally—for example, a passionate Shakespearean monologue. Blok is obviously a great poet who created some memorable and moving poems. In *The Puppet Show*, the eloquence of the poetry remains a matter of debate.

The Puppet Show will always remain a seminal work for Russian drama and especially theater. The measure of its influence may appear surprising considering how many major distancing elements it contains. To begin with, a metatheatrical discussion permeating every level of both form and content seems to be a distinctly distancing phenomenon. Yet Blok made metatheatrical questions the principal theme of his drama. The Author figure states these questions explicitly. Columbine actualizes them symbolically. Every recipient confronts them in the play-within-a-play. The decorations obviously destroy all realistic illusion. Blok, like Chekhov, juxtaposes comedic elements with a continuous undercutting of those very same elements. Theatrical, cultural, and ideological codes are sharply mixed and contrasted.

Part of the metatheatrical discussion includes the whole subject of masks. In *The Puppet Show,* the playwright uses masks in a distancing fashion. He masks every single character, and, because of the paucity of plot and character development, relies on the masks to carry the meaning of the work. By introducing masks, he also demands that the virtual recipient switch on his communal memory—which he hopes includes a knowledge of commedia dell'arte—and use this memory to interpret the play. Moreover, a stage direction like "Как все Пьеро," as well as the constant mixing of theatrical codes, forces every recipient to range over a broad area of Western dramatic tradition, and not just a small part of it. The effort required from the recipient is further increased by, as previously mentioned, a nontraditional plot. Once again, as in Chekhov, the lack of a causal, fast-moving plot—of intrigue, climax, and denouement—can only distance a twentieth-century recipient who in other respects has been set up to expect a comedy, even a farce. Furthermore, masks also substitute for character development. The absence of three-dimensional, believable figures precludes a personal and emotional identification with them. It is true that the character of Pierrot is created in such a way that he elicits the recipient's sympathy. He is multifaceted and lovable. However, the facets are not psychologically motivated. Therefore, the sympathy retains some of its distance because in the end Pierrot remains one more mask.

As if interpreting masks and theatrical codes was not enough, Blok saturates *The Puppet Show* with a myriad of themes. He tosses them around, mixes them up, and creates variations—all in the most laconic and compact fashion. Every recipient is forced to try to interpret this intellectual medley by putting together the briefest of scraps and hints, sometimes a few words. It is true that one of those themes, as well as the form of its presentation, elicits an emotive response. In the twentieth century, alienation is certainly an emotive topic. Moreover, the writer attempts to present it in such a way as to awaken sympathy, at least for the principal sufferer, namely, Pierrot. However, though the theme of alienation softens the distancing slightly, it cannot fully obliterate the difficulty of so many themes in so little space and time.

Yet, despite these strong distancing factors, *The Puppet Show* is quite successful dramatically. One might say that this is due to the general familiarity with *commedia,* clowns, and the eternal love triangle on the part of most recipients. Actually, it is two other elements that form the basis of the emotiveness of this work. The first of these is language usage. Once again, as if defying the modernists' devaluation of the word, this play underlines the importance of language in a dramatic text. Dramatic language can even have a nontraditional overall deixis, as it does here. However, if the distribution of segments is such as to increase emotiveness, alternating distal with proximal, especially proximal expressives, then the distancing effect of an abundance of distal segments is overcome. Equally significantly, Blok's language is "incomplete" in the sense that Keir Elam uses the term. Filled with indexical markers, it is constantly being "completed" through gestures, visual images, dance, song, color, and objects. Of course, consciously each recipient does not realize all of this when he experiences the play. However, a successful dramatic language functions at times as an almost invisible substratum that determines the emotiveness of a work.

Not only does *The Puppet Show* have that not quite definable language that drama needs, but equally importantly it captures that not quite definable spirit of the twentieth century by introducing the carnival-grotesque. Blok does not simply copy the historical genre of *commedia.* He does not clothe new themes in old garb. Rather, he takes from *commedia* a spirit, a worldview, that shocks, distances, and yet captivates the twentieth-century recipient. Actually, it captivates him more and more strongly as the century progresses. The jarring juxtapositions, the mésalliances, the profanation, the ludic tone in the presentation of deadly serious problems, the ambivalence, the violence, and the brittleness do not elicit traditional personal identification with a character. In fact, on the level of personal identification, the grotesque can only distance. However, as this century has proven—from high art to its most popular manifestations—the grotesque fascinates the modern recipient, resonates with him, makes sense. Therefore, he responds to such a work emotively. Overall, *The Puppet Show* is not a completely successful play. It remains somewhat overburdened with schematized masks, as well as philosophical and metatheatrical problems. However, it is a daring attempt to capture the mood of the modern era and to push the nature of aesthetic reception in a different direction. As later "theatricalizing" plays and performances have shown, though aesthetic reception must remain emotional at its core, perhaps the nature of that emotional foundation is transformed to some degree in this century of unprecedented changes.

Chapter Five

Viacheslav Ivanov's *Tantalus*

IN 1905, Viacheslav Ivanov, by then the recognized theoretician of the second generation of Russian symbolists, produced his first play, *Tantalus* (Тáнтал). It is a radical work that was inspired to a large degree by Friedrich Nietzsche's views on art and antiquity.[1] Ivanov sets himself the ambitious goal of substituting a new type of art for religious practices that he intends to use for transforming existence. Unfortunately, practice proved harder than theory and *Tantalus* is not a dramatic success. The playwright offers the recipient an intellectually challenging work and one in which the mythic story is internalized and psychologized, thus making it more appealing to a realistically oriented recipient. However, as in Sologub's *The Triumph of Death,* the emotiveness of the content is obliterated above all by the writer's usage of language. Ivanov's style is in many ways experimental and beautiful, far superior to the style that Sologub employs in his play. The language of *Tantalus* creates great poetry. Yet, as the language of a dramatic work, it becomes a hermetic, unbreakable barrier that can never be "completed" by nonverbal elements and that distances the recipient to the point of losing him.

Both Nietzsche and Ivanov emphasize the fact that tragedy developed from ritual and that it incorporates something of religious mystery rites. With such origins, there arises the possibility of interchangeability, of tragedy substituting for ritual and also functioning in a culture or life-producing mode (*kul'turotvorcheski, zhiznetvorcheski*). Furthermore, like Nietzsche, Ivanov is most interested in the highly emotional, orgiastic, and, therefore, emotive mysteries associated with the God Dionysus.[2] According to both thinkers, various elements, as well as the core spirit, of Dionysian ritual continue to exist after the coming of Christianity. They do so in rites and traditions that are part of carnivals and holidays. The concept of carnivals and holidays also illustrates how Nietzsche's ideas spread through many individuals and move from country to country. Each artist along the way adds something of his own, thus enriching the concept. In this case, the carnival/holiday notion catches the attention of the German theatrical director Georg Fuchs. From him, it is transferred around 1904–5 to Vsevolod Meierhold. This is an early period in the development of Meierhold's theatrical ideas, a time when he is working with the *Fakely* group, as well as with Komissarzhevskaia's Studio Theater. That era is also a period of closeness between Ivanov and Meierhold.[3]

However, Ivanov's ideas are not simply a copy of Nietzsche's mind-set, and there are some essential differences between the two systems of thought. In the end, despite writing of the religious origins of tragedy, Nietzsche approaches art in a more or less aesthetic fashion and subscribes to a rather elitist view of artistic production. This attitude is typical of the first generation of symbolists, especially Western ones such as Stéphane Mallarmé, Oscar Wilde, or Valerii Briusov. On the other hand, for Ivanov, the Dionysian is seen above all in religious-philosophical terms. For the playwright, drama (essentially tragedy) carries a heavy burden of social and moral responsibility. The artist has a duty to attempt the spiritual transformation of his own nation through the influence that his works of art can exert on their recipients.[4] Such serious transforming ambitions can be found among the second generation of symbolists even in western Europe; beginning, for example, with 1902 in the statements of William Butler Yeats. Overall, however, an emphasis on the moral, social, and national appears much more strongly in east European modernism, namely, in Poland and Russia. In Poland, it can be observed in the work of such diverse writers as Stanisław Wyspiański, Tadeusz Miciński, Jan Kasprowicz, and Stanisław Brzozowski. In Russia, it is to be seen in the works of the second generation of symbolists, in those of Aleksei Remizov, Zinaida Gippius, and Dmitrii Merezhkovskii, as well as in the discussions of the *Fakely* group.[5]

Thus, in keeping with these religious tendencies, Ivanov declares in his essays that art in general, and drama in particular, "служит познанию и что род познания представляемый искусством, в известном смысле превосходнее познания научного" (serves to acquire knowledge and that the type of knowledge represented by art is in some sense more wonderful than scientific knowledge [vol. 2, p. 641]).[6] With such aspirations for drama much is demanded of the artist. Ivanov writes that "в деле создания художественного произведения художник нисходит из сфер, куда он проникает восхождением, как духовный человек" (in the process of creating a work of art the artist descends from those spheres which he had penetrated through an ascent, as a spiritual man [vol. 2, p. 629]). At times this is stated even more strongly and the artist is perceived as a priest or healer: "мы требуем от художника в р а ч е в а н и я и о ч и щ е н и я в искупительном, разрешающем восторге" (we demand from the artist h e a l i n g and p u r i f y i n g in an expiatory, authorizing ecstasy [vol. 2, p. 78]).

Concurrently, artistic creation is presented as a kind of holy sacrifice with both aesthetic and ethic dimensions: "Один взгляд этой маски [that is, the mask of Melpomene]—и мы уже опоены дионисийским хмелом вечной жертвы" (One look from that mask [of Melpomene] and we are already intoxicated by the Dionysian drunkenness of eternal sacrifice [vol. 2, pp.

78–79]). Thus, it becomes understandable why drama, with its ties to religious rites, is the ideal form of art to fulfill these lofty goals. Theater for Ivanov moves beyond the limits of a single genre, and instead, "имеет своим художественным материалом целостный состав человека и стремится к произведению целостного события в некой совокупности душ" (with its artistic material encompasses the whole structure of man and tries to produce a whole event in a certain unity of souls [vol. 2, p. 213]). To this, the playwright adds a Neoplatonic vision of existence, speaking in terms not so much of the "real" versus the "ideal," as of the masculine principle opposing the feminine principle. Any work of art that is to present this dual essence of existence has to perforce include action: "искусство, посвященное раскрытию диады, необходимо будет искусством действия, 'действом'" (art devoted to the revealing of dualism will undoubtedly be an art of action, an "act" [vol. 2, p. 192]). Therefore, Ivanov calls his plays *deistviia,* though, as will be shown, in actual practice they contain little action, at least in the traditional sense.

Overall, in these statements one can see a blurring of boundaries between art and religion. This is very typical of Ivanov around the time that he wrote *Tantalus*. After 1910, his views on art will change. The playwright will advocate a more iconoclastic and individualistic form of art. He will also write of the need to add form to art, by combining Dionysian elements with Apollonian ones. In other words, Ivanov discovers that, like many modernists, in his search for an ecstatic art form, he has neglected aesthetic distance too much. When he writes of the Apollonian, he is really defending the existence of distance as a necessary part of aesthetic reception.[7]

A religious, or quasi-religious, approach to art often includes, as in Ivanov's case, one other important characteristic, namely, the use of myth. Many modernists turn to myths, either resurrecting classical ones or creating new ones.[8] Myths appear as one possible solution for modernist artists and intellectuals during a time of spiritual crisis that has led to a loss of faith. The use of myths can first be seen among romantics and such precursors of modernism as Charles Baudelaire or Richard Wagner. The permanent structure of myth allows artists to universalize their work, to take an archetypal approach to life, and to seek historical comparisons with earlier periods that might have experienced similar upheavals. In its own ahistorical, intuitive way, myth teaches people something about existence, as Ivanov writes:

> творится миф ясновидением веры и является вещим сном, непроизвольным видением, 'астральным' (как говорили древние тайновидцы бытия), иероглифом последней истины о вещи сущей воистину. Миф есть воспоминание о мистическом событии, о космическом таинстве.

a myth is created through the clairvoyance of faith and it appears as a prophetic dream, an involuntary vision, "astral" (as spoke the ancient soothsayers of existence), a hieroglyph of the ultimate truth indeed about the essential thing. A myth is a remembering of the mystical event, of the cosmic mystery. (vol. 2, p. 555)

For all of Ivanov's theoretical writing on drama and theater, his personal contacts with actual theater were of a limited nature. He was one of the organizer's of the *Fakely* group. Even if the group did not produce an actual theater, it included among its members the director Vsevolod Meierhold, who found the group's discussions about the theater significant even for the development of his own ideas. Later on, around 1910, Ivanov would again become one of the organizers of a theater in his own home, namely the *Bashennyi teatr*.[9] This second experimental theater came at a time when artists were trying to reintroduce more dynamic elements into drama and theater, as well as rethinking some of their ideas on the use of neomysteries.

Ivanov's efforts and ideas are acknowledged in the theoretical sphere by such contemporaries as Andrei Bely and Aleksandr Blok. On occasion his creative writing is received with sympathy, especially his poetry. Even his plays find temporary favor with such diverse figures as Valerii Briusov, Velimir Khlebnikov, and Vsevolod Meierhold. For a short time Meierhold even sees Ivanov the playwright as an equal of Anton Chekhov and Maurice Maeterlinck.[10] However, from the first, some of Ivanov's closest associates also express reservations about his work, finding in it an inaccessibility and level of difficulty that creates excessive opaqueness. Andrei Bely, for example, writes—in a highly esoteric style of his own—that reading Ivanov's work is like dealing with "обломочными комбинациями метафор, безумными тимпанами, словесным грохотом медоязычного гама" (fragmented combinations of metaphors, mad timbrels, a verbal crash of honey-tongued din).[11] Ivanov's drama *Tantalus* certainly grows out of a dramatic theory that emphasizes emotiveness to an inordinate degree. Yet the actualization of that theory turns out to be far from emotive.

The first obvious emotive element of *Tantalus* is the story itself. The figure of Tantalus is one of the best known in Greek mythology and familiar to a broad spectrum of recipients. Furthermore, the playwright makes the myth more intellectually challenging and interesting by combining different variants of the Tantalus myth, as well as attaching elements from the myths about Sisyphus and Ixion. As a genuine scholar who wrote a doctoral dissertation on the ancient world and later would produce a study of the Dionysian cult that is valuable to this day, he had the background to engage in such serious recombining. The story begins with King Tantalus expressing his dissatisfaction with life. Ivanov chooses to portray him as the half-mortal son of Zeus. He is a favorite with the gods and they continuously shower munificences upon him. However, Tantalus is irked by the fact that he is the one who is constantly receiving. He would prefer to give, to grant. He feels that the plenitude that surrounds him thwarts his creative powers and rights as an individual. Also, from his opening monologue he is depicted as struggling with his own mortality. The chorus of nymphs, which represents not only social norms but is also a *porte-parole* for the author, warns Tantalus that his rebellious behavior will lead to his downfall. Heedless of these admonitions, the King begins to plot his acts of rebellion. First, at a feast with the gods he serves them his son, Pelops, as a dish. If that weren't enough, he attempts, with the help of Sisyphus and Ixion, to steal the cup of ambrosia, the drink that would give immortality to mankind. The results are tragic. His younger son, Broteas, is killed when he drinks from the cup. The King and his two accomplices are given everlasting punishment. Of the extant versions of Tantalus's death, Ivanov chooses a lesser-known version in which the King is suspended in air holding up a sphere. This punishment is more ambiguous than the one depicting eternal thirst and hunger and can be applied to almost any crime. Furthermore, the undefined spatial amorphousness is in sharp contrast to the spatial symmetry of the rest of the play and emphasizes the disintegration of normal social hierarchies and moral codes. The play ends on a note, not of hope, but of an almost existential-like affirmation of the dignity of man's individualism. Adrasteia, Tantalus's divine wife, mother of his son, Pelops, speaks for the first time in the play and acknowledges her husband, despite the crimes that he has committed.

It should be noted that Ivanov's treatment of myth is quite typical of numerous modernists. Such an approach is brought about by the fact that many of them perceive the world in Neoplatonic terms, including the belief that the ideal sphere of existence is more or less closed to human beings. Thus the ideal becomes the mysterious with a capital M, and myth tends to move toward Mystery and toward religious mysteries. The mythical quest often becomes a mystical quest. And since mystical quests tend to be endless, infinite, and complex, what happens is that modernists "were not only attracted by the ambiguity of myth, but also toward myths so ambiguous that one is tempted to view them as symbols of ambiguity as such."[12] One of the ways that these beliefs manifest themselves artistically is by playing around with various combinations and variants. Ivanov, with his erudition, is better prepared than most to indulge in such exercises.

Perhaps even more importantly, the emotiveness of the story is increased because Ivanov imbues his myth with a modern content that resonates with the recipient. As Iu. K. Gerasimov writes: "Иванов усиливал его [мифа] многомерность и, не прибегая к открытой модернизации, наделял его современной проблематикой" (Ivanov strengthened its capacity and, while not employing an open modernization, filled it with contemporary problems).[13] This is partly due to Ivanov's particular interpretation of the Dionysian hero, which in this case coincides with the ideas of Nietzsche. For both, the transformation of the tragic hero is equivalent to the continuing transformation of Dionysus, with special emphasis on the Dionysian face of a blasphemer (*bogoborec*). Thus, a mystery play is also a tragedy, and therefore the mythical hero can become a tragic hero with all of the latter's internal struggle, hubris, and reflective soliloquies. In other words, the interpretation of the Dionysian allows Ivanov to introduce psychological material, to internalize the story. The myth of Tantalus becomes a modern-day biography of an individual tormented by death, making mistakes (even very serious ones) on his journey in search of self-development and self-affirmation. He emphasizes the self, the desire to do things himself, to be himself, and not just to exist as an object of compassion for the gods: "Я есмь; в себе я. Мне—мое; мое ж—я сам, / я, сущий" (I am; I am in myself. Mine to me; mine—I myself, / I am real [vol. 2, p. 28]). This self-examination is certainly the main focus of the first half of the play in which the chorus is the "character" who receives the protagonist's reflections. This is both an artistic device to break up the monologue and give it a pseudodialogic construction, but also a way of commenting on Tantalus's words and judging them by the norms of the community, as is done in ancient Greek theater. As the play shows, in his ascent and descent, Tantalus momentarily comes close to the elemental Dionysian force, such as when he announces that he will let others rule while he dances. In the end, however, Ivanov presents his protagonist as failing because in the author's weltanschauung it is unacceptable for the hero not to overcome his isolated individualism and become a part of the earth in whose name he is fighting. Ivanov's interpretation of this journey toward self-realization derives from two concepts. On the one hand, it refers to the Orthodox concept of *sobornost'* (unity of believers in the church through Christ). On the other, the interpretation coincides with a romantic vision of life in which the lonely hero, though often isolated, is obligated to fight for the good of his nation and in the end to resolve his conflict with the masses.

Formally, Ivanov presents his myth in *Tantalus* within a symmetrical structure. Symmetry is typical of traditional drama in general and tends to function emotively. Such a construction ties in well with mythological thought, which is often based on a "primordial fund" of opposites. Additionally, in Ivanov's case, it agrees with the writer's notion that a play must present the dyadic structure of existence.[14] The extreme symmetry of the structure of *Tantalus* has been well documented. All of the characters in this work are presented as contrasting pairs. There is the pair, Tantalus and Adrasteia: he the free-spirited, free-willed individual; she representing fate, necessity, the limitations of man's freedom, and thus mortality. Though invisible, she is a major force in the play and a part of Tantalus that he wishes to deny. Then there is the pair of brothers, Broteas and Pelops. The former is the earthly, dark, jealous, tormented, and active brother. The latter is the heavenly and passive one. As Tantalus says about the two: "Тот сам себя снедает; этот—снедь богам" (This one consumes himself; that one is food for the gods [vol. 2, p. 35]). There are the allies, Sisyphus and Ixion—opposites and in some sense projections of Tantalus's character. Furthermore, an internal opposition within Tantalus is constantly emphasized in the play. He is both "богоборец" (god-fighter) and "богоносец" (god-carrier), "жрец" (priest) and "жертва" (victim), "вечность" (eternity) and "миг" (moment).

The symmetry, besides being based on opposites, has a clear vertical construction as is typical of myth. The vertical spatial arrangement will be discussed later. The mythic cosmos is usually arranged vertically.[15] Thus, the characters are divided into three strata. Situated highest are the gods, then comes the earthly realm, and below it Hades. Earth itself is divided into levels, with Tantalus sitting at its pinnacle and a character like Broteas floundering at the bottom. Within this structure, the plot of the play proceeds as an ascent followed by a descent. In the first half, Tantalus tries to move up from his high point on earth into the even higher celestial sphere: he is invited to dine with the gods and offers his own son, Pelops, as a sacrifice to them. After his theft of the ambrosia, he begins his descent and he does not stop until he reaches Tartarus where he is punished for his blasphemy.

In *Tantalus* the opposites, constantly repeated, are in the end neutralized, as is typical of myth. Myth is intended as a means for overcoming contradictions so as to offer the continuing possibility of life, rather than destruction. During the course of Ivanov's play, the juxtaposition is so perfect that neither side of a contrasting pair comes across as dominant. The first moment of reconciliation "is accomplished in the ritual of sacrifice [of Pelops] which moves the world; this ritual is at the center of tragedy, and is its node and pivot."[16] And in the final scene, the protagonist is in some sense made whole again when Adrasteia recognizes him. She has been silent throughout the work because her other half, Tantalus, has been fighting with everything she represents. However, in the end the greatness of the hero's action, even if it fails, is recognized—for it stemmed from a genuine desire for self-transformation. This is not a very orthodox interpretation in the religious sense but a modernistic one with an emphasis on the individual. Nevertheless, artistically the opposites are, at least to some degree, neutralized.

V. I. Porfir'eva writes that such symmetry leads to the creation of "бесчисленных смысловых связей и выходов в новые смысловые пространства" (innumerable semantic connections and departures into new semantic spaces).[17] However, the symmetry accomplishes more than that. Being constantly reiterated on every level (including the smallest linguistic level, as will be shown later), the symmetry helps the recipient to orient himself and to understand the complex ideas of the work.

In keeping with myth's tendency to depict man as an integral part of nature, Ivanov, too, presents man within nature. Over and over, the abundance (*изобилье*) of Tantalus is complemented by the vision of a lush, moist landscape, as in the following:

Distance Manipulation

Завеса сквозит: в изумрудах лег
вертоград долин над змием-рекой.
И не облачный клуб
на лазурным излучинам млеет—
над глубью висит лебедей серебро
и к пучине серебряной реет . . .

It shines through the curtain: the garden of valleys lay down in emeralds
   above the snake-river.
And it is not a puff of clouds that is an ecstasy on the cerulean curves—
the silver of swans hangs over the depth and soars to the silver abyss. . . .
(vol. 2, p. 26)

    Additionally, the playwright tries to create the illusion of natural time. The events of the day, as fantastic as they may seem, follow the natural course of the sun, which organized primal man's existence. The appeal to the primal memory of every recipient, to the notion that man is part of nature—by the twentieth century a dream of some long-lost Arcadia—functions emotively, awakening fundamental communal feelings in every recipient.

    Later, the ritualizing elements of this play will be discussed. They function in a distancing manner. One aspect of the ritual is emotive and related to the internalization and psychologizing of the story. In some of Ivanov's theoretical writing, his attitude toward drama suggests some kind of *ostranenie*, a foregrounding of the textual world, to see the existence and oneself anew. In other words, a more anthropocentric goal is posited for theater. And in fact that is what happens in the play *Tantalus*. The ritualized atmosphere that is created (discussed below) is centered on a feeling of solidarity with mankind, with the individual who is faced by death and the terrors of existence, rather than on any Supreme Being. The gods are clearly secondary characters. The whole focus is on Tantalus who, for all of his pride, is portrayed as a tragic hero with whom the virtual recipient is expected to sympathize. In the end even the divine Adrasteia accepts Tantalus. This work is intended to elicit sympathy for the sufferings of the hero. Overall, Ivanov very skillfully adapts both myth and classical Greek drama to suit the sensibilities of the modern-day recipient.

    The usage of language will be discussed in detail as the major distancing element of this play. There are, however, two aspects of language that are emotive. Since the play is written in verse, there is a definite rhythm to the language. As was stated earlier, rhythm is a most fundamental value, one that lies at the basis of all aesthetic reception. It evokes in the recipient some kind of emotional response, even if an undefined one. Thus, in *Tantalus*, every recipient is moved along by the rhythm of the language, especially since this is a rich rhythm that ranges from the rhetorical, such as in the protagonist's pronouncements about himself, to the lyric, such as in the reflections found in the *stasimae* of the chorus, to the explosive rapid-fire exchanges between Tantalus and the chorus or Broteus.

Traditionally, perlocutionism is defined as the ability of discourse to elicit some kind of reaction from the speakers engaged in it. In traditional plays these reactions tend to be in the form of statements of intended action which may or may not be actually performed. The discourse of *Tantalus* shows a perlocutionism, but of a different kind. This is a play with very little action in the traditional sense. When clashes between characters occur, the result is not an exchange of intended actions that leads to concrete events. Instead, reaction is elicited—in the form of definitions. The opposing sides exchange contradictory points of view in rapid succession, and thus the hero is stimulated to take a closer look at himself. The protagonist also reveals more information about himself to every recipient. An example of this is the following discussion between Tantalus and the chorus concerning the king's desire to give and not just to take, to be godlike:

ПРЕДВОДИТЕЛЬНИЦА ХОРА
Дарить и щедрить, расточая без конца ...

ТАНТАЛ
Всех риз совлечься, нагу плыть в морях моих ...

ПРЕДВОДИТЕЛЬНИЦА ХОРА
Цвет выспренний ты волишь воли царственной!

ТАНТАЛ
К державству ж дольнему не нисходить.

ПРЕДВОДИТЕЛЬНИЦА ХОРА
Кто мужи, что наследят долу твой престол?

ТАНТАЛ
Иксион, царь Лапитов, и мой зять—Сизиф.

ПРЕДВОДИТЕЛЬНИЦА ХОРА
Мужей, надменных богоборством, ты назвал.

ТАНТАЛ
Богопокорных пусть ущедрит сам Кронид.

Chorus Leader. To give and to be bountiful, lavishing, endlessly ...

Tantalus. To discard all robes, to swim naked in my seas ...

Chorus Leader. You will the lofty color of imperial will!

Tantalus. One does not descend to the lower kingdom.

Chorus Leader. Who are the men, who will inherit in the depths your throne?

Tantalus. Ixion, car of the Lapiths, and my son-in-law—Sisyphus.

Chorus Leader. You name men arrogant with god-fighting.

Tantalus. The meek ones may the son of Cronus himself lavish. (vol. 2, p. 34)

Of this kind of perlocutionism there is actually much more in *Tantalus* than in the other plays that have been considered. It is a one-way form of exchange because the chorus is not a real partner in the dialogue and remains completely unaffected by it. Nevertheless, the device creates the suggestion of action and motion, a kind of illusory substitute that may heighten the work's emotiveness.

Certain aspects of language usage, a symmetrical composition, and above all, an appealing transformation of myth, all function emotively. Yet, as a dramatic work, *Tantalus* distances very strongly. A number of elements contribute to this distancing effect. There is little action in the traditional sense of conflict, intrigues, action, and reaction between characters. Instead, the story is really about the internal struggle of the protagonist. The two most dramatic events, the sacrifice of Pelops and the theft of the ambrosia, are not shown to the recipient but only recounted in a way that does not increase their emotive forcefulness. The greater part of the text consists of monologues or pseudodialogues that reveal the psyche of Tantalus. Pseudodialogue refers to an exchange of utterances between the hero and (usually) the chorus, where the role of the chorus is not that of an active participant in a conversation. Rather, it is present only in order to make interjections from time to time. These interjections serve to juxtapose the hero's statements with the norms and morals of society. The monologues are occasionally broken up by a character retelling action that has taken place offstage or is occurring onstage. In this respect, Ivanov is very much a modernist playwright creating a drama about the internal life of a character rather than presenting actual interaction between characters. It is true that the plot of this work is tightly constructed. However, every element of the plot simply feeds into the theme of an individual coming to grips with suffering, human limitations, and mortality. Pelops and Broteas represent two poles: infinity, immortality versus moment, mortality. Sisyphus and Ixion function as two refractions of Tantalus's character. Overall, then, the composition of this work is static in nature.

The static nature of the composition is further strengthened by the ritualizing elements introduced by Ivanov. The playwright's perception of a neomystery is that of a solemn, dignified, and elevated pseudoritual that awes the recipient and does not invite emotional identification. Ivanov employs a number of elements to achieve this effect. The first of these is his organization of dramatic space. As has been stated, it is clearly a vertical arrangement and one that pays scant attention to the practical possibilities of the stage. Actualizing the stage directions would require either extremely elaborate sets or some kind of simplified, symbolic presentation.[18] Mount Olympus, home of the gods, looms at the top in a shroud of clouds. Just below on the mountainside is the rough-hewn stone throne of Tantalus. Steps lead down the slope to the valley below which signifies earthly existence. At the end of the play, even further down, Hades becomes visible. At moments, there are bridges cast between the gods and earth along which communication occurs: Hermes steps out of a cloud, and Zeus and the other gods descend to a feast with Tantalus along a rainbow. Thus, all of the movement is that of ascending and descending. However, the visible focus of this pseudoritual is somewhat different. It is not a symbol of the divine that gathers attention, as, for example, the tabernacle or raised host do in a Catholic mass. Rather, the spatial arrangement is focused on the throne of Tantalus, which in a sense is like the altar around which the ritual takes place.

As in any ritual, there is a certain amount of pageantry here, though overall this is a stark and minimalistic rite. However, the chorus of nymphs moves about the throne, at times showering it with flowers, at times directing what might be termed songs at it (the *stasimae*). At other moments, the nymphs extend their arms in unison or together lament the sacrifice of Pelops. Often the actions and events are narrated even as they are occurring. For example, as Sisyphus and Ixion arrive on the scene, their progress is described by the chorus. This is again a typical element of ritual where words, often familiar and stereotypical formulae, reinforce the gestures and events. In an actual ritual, its leader—be it priest, rabbi, pastor, and so forth—appears as a nonpersonalized figure whose individualism is momentarily hidden by his symbolic function. Similarly, in *Tantalus,* characterization only strengthens the pseudoritual effect. For all of the focus on the internal struggle of Tantalus, he is not really a three-dimensional realistic character. Throughout the play, he is typified, generalized, and monumentalized. His private life is always played out in public. His inner struggle occurs before an audience and is a public event. He is never shown in an intimate setting, surrounded by everyday friends and/or family.[19] The generalized, monumentalized effect is achieved not only by situating him physically in an elevated, central position, but also by describing him with repeated formulaic epithets. Over and over, the chorus showers him with such phrases as "Солнце" (Sun), "Изобилья сын" (Son of bounty), "Обилья сын" (Son of plenty), "Тантал-царь" (Tantalus-tsar), "владыка" (lord), "человекобог" (Man-God), and "ты превыше долов, царь!" (you, o tsar, are higher than the dales!). Furthermore, his physical appearance is never described, leaving it up to either each individual recipient or the director to create his own image of this figure.

Moreover, as is expected of ritual, divine magical interventions take place in this play. In this pseudoritual, the gods come down from Olympus to take part in human affairs. The effect of their intervention is closer to magic than to the presence of the divine. For the modern-day recipient, even if a strong and clear connection is made in the text between the figure of Dionysus and Christ, Greek gods can only function as a fantastic, magical element and not as a true religious experience.

Distance Manipulation

Finally, of overwhelming importance for the ritualization of this play is the stylistic usage of language, the major distancing element in *Tantalus*. To begin with, the deixis is far from traditional. Approximately half of the segments are distally oriented and may recount the history of the characters:

От Зевса, девы, зачала меня Плуто́,
и—первенец—я на сосцах Обильной спал.

From Zeus, o maidens, Pluto conceived me, and—firstborn—I slept on the breasts of Plenty. (vol. 2, p. 27)

The distal orientation may also refer to narrated dreams:

Тогда затмились очи, будто Ночь сама
ко мне прильнула плотью; сила чресл ушла;
легла усталость влажная на мощь рамен
хитоном тяжким; и на выю сон налег.

Then the eyes went dark, as if Night herself had clung to me with her flesh; the strength of my limbs departed; like a heavy tunic a humid exhaustion lay on the power of my shoulders; and sleep came down on my neck. (vol. 2, p. 29)

The distal segments may describe offstage actions, such as when Broteas talks of his unfortunate hunting expedition during which Artemis misleads him and makes a laughing stock of him:

Всю ночь, водимый Артемидой лунною
медведицы бегущей призрак в злобе я
преследовал по кручам неприступных скал
бессильным дротом и стрелой бескрылою . . .

All night, led by the moonlit Artemis in anger I chased the ghost of a running she-bear, along the inclines of inaccessible rocks, with my helpless javelin and my wingless arrow. . . . (vol. 2, p. 44)

As in Gippius's *Holy Blood*, the segments may be general statements about the nature of gods and men, as when the nymphs say:

Щедр неисчерпно рог богов. Им говорят
желания сердца, духу сокровенные,
чреватой воли чада нерожденные.
С небес нисходит милость благодатная.

Infinitely bountiful is the horn of the gods. To them speak the desires of the heart, sacred to the spirit, the unborn offspring of a fertile will. From the heavens descends a beneficial grace. (vol. 2, p. 27)

As it happens in the *stasimae* of the chorus, the segments may be a commentary on the present situation, but expressed again in a generalized form that discusses the obligations and limitations of man in general, and not just the particular situation of Tantalus:

Неизменным быть—
незакатных богов удел;
а человеку суд—
солнцезарных достичь вершин
и нисходить в сумрак.

To be unchangeable is the fate of the never-setting gods; while man is fated to reach the dawn-lit heights and to descend into twilight. (vol. 2, p. 31)

Complementing the deixis, one finds a definite preponderance of referentials, followed by expressives. There appear very few appellatives.

The distancing effect is only strengthened by the lexicon of this work. A small number of church-slavonicisms appear repeatedly: "страстотерпец" (martyr), "дщер" (daughter), "перст" (finger), and "длань" (hand). Much more frequent are the archaisms, elevated, and bookish terms: "светоч" (light), "дебр" (thicket), "зачать" (conceive), "прядать" (jump), "алкать" (to be hungry), "червленеть" (to show red), "вертеп" (cave), "выя," (neck), "мнить" (to think), "зерцало" (mirror), and "тук" (flow). The list continues. Furthermore, in his desire to recreate Greek quantitative verse in Russian, Ivanov often resorts to a complicated and even convoluted syntax with numerous inversions, as in the following:

Не все ль сказали этим миром солнечным,
что я уведал и, познав, запечатлел
своим согласьем, в оный миг, когда
разверзлось это око и мой дух воззрел?

Have not they said everything with this sunny world, which I saw and, having discovered, imprinted with my agreement, in that moment when my eye opened and my spirit saw? (vol. 2, p. 28)

Запексиеся развевал, вод захлебнуть,
уста: уст мощных чьих-то дуновение
напухшей зыбью отдувало влаги стекло
от пещи рта.

I would open my scorched lips in order to swallow the waters; the powerful lips of somebody's breath blew back with a swelling ripple the glass of moisture from the sands of the mouth. (p. 30, vol. 2)

Затем что пременились жертвы тучные
моим веленьем по лицу земли с поры,
как в темь увел меня Аид,—и бог взалкал.

Because fat sacrifices have been made on the face of the earth by my order from the time that Aid lead me into the darkness, and the god began to cry. (vol. 2, p. 60)

Moreover, there is no differentiation of style among the various characters. The only change that occurs, reminiscent of Fedor Sologub's technique

Distance Manipulation

in *The Triumph of Death*, is a shift in sentence length to express shifting mood, and this happens equally with all of the characters. When a protagonist is angry or upset, the sentences become shorter, more broken, with more expressives and exclamations, and strings of nouns and adjectives, as in the following:

И царь! что вещает сон, гадать страшусь.

What your dream foretells, o tsar, I am afraid to say. (vol. 2, p. 30)

Ты темен! ты темен! Свет твой, свет угас!
Горе, Тантал! Твой свет угас!
Тантал, где твое солнце? где? . . .

You are dark! You are dark! Your light, light has gone out! O, misery, Tantalus! Your light has gone out! Tantalus, where is your sun? where? . . . (vol. 2, p. 73)

Мятежный, вольный, сильный, о хитрец—Сизиф,
неуловимый, тонкий, как подвижный ветр
священной соли, неистомный двигатель.

Rebellious, free, strong, clever—Sisyphus, uncatchable, subtle, as the moving wind of holy salt, inexhaustible mover. (vol. 2, p. 43)

The "rough" texture of a language with an elevated, esoteric lexicon and convoluted syntax is made rougher and more difficult to understand through the use of bound but static motifs at the level of syntax. Bound refers to the fact that these motifs (giving versus taking, momentary versus eternal, immortal versus mortal, passive versus active) all connect to the major theme of the play—Tantalus's process of self-realization. However, the motifs are static in nature because they do not move the plot forward in any way. They are usually expressed through a single root. The playwright then plays with this root, varying it by adding different prefixes and suffixes:

ПРЕДВОДИТЕЛЬНИЦА ХОРА
Твоих обилий *дань* и струй и веяний,
тебе *дар* утра, Тантал, от *даров* твоих.

ТАНТАЛ
Не *дань* мила: вы *дар* у *одаренного*
с отрадой *благодарности* отъемлете.

ПРЕДВОДИТЕЛЬНИЦА ХОРА
Ты полн, владыка! и тебя ль мне *одарить*?

Chorus Leader. A gift of your bounty and the flow and breath, for you a gift of the morning, from your gifts.

Tantalus. It is not the gift which is pleasing; with the pleasure of gratefulness you would take away the gift from the one on whom it has been bestowed.

Chorus Leader. You are full, o lord! how can I bestow upon you? (vol. 2, p. 26)

... Вечность я лобзал в уста,
лобзала *Вечность* в полные уста свой *Миг*,
безбрежный свой, свой неизбежный, Семя-*Миг*.

 . . . I kissed Eternity on the lips, Eternity kissed the full lips of her Moment, her boundless, unavoidable Seed-Moment. (vol. 2, p. 29)

ТАНТАЛ
Все, все—мое! Всю *вечность* каждый *миг* вместил;
один мой *миг* объемлет все *бессмертие*.
Не знаю *смерти* я; и что *бессмертие*,—
не знаю; и не знаю часа-времени . . .
Мгновенье—вечность; изобилье—теснота!

БРОТЕАС
Исполнен ты *бессмертья* каждый *смертный миг*;
я *смертен* был бы каждый *миг бессмертья*?

Tantalus. Everything, everything is mine! Each moment encompassed all of eternity; one of my moments will encompass all of immortality. I do not know death; and what is immortality,—I do not know; and I do not know hour-time.
. . . A moment—eternity; plenitude—tightness!

Broteas. You have filled every mortal moment of immortality; I would be mortal every moment of immortality? (vol. 2, p. 46)

Like the flickering of an impressionist's paintbrush, Ivanov dots the text with these tiny motifs that from a distance help create a subtle whole. However, when the recipient confronts them up close, the image disintegrates and each recipient loses himself in the little blobs of roots that dance before his eyes on the page.

As if this overwhelmingly rich and difficult language were not distancing enough, Ivanov contrasts it with another distancing element, namely, silence. On the one hand, the reliance on silence is a typically modernist way of emphasizing the ineffectiveness of language, its overconventionalization, and even deceptive character. On the other, in Ivanov's case, it is linked to his whole theory of poetry (vol. 3, p. 660). Silence signifies the achievement of Dionysian ecstasy, as well as the climactic moment in the creative process when the poet opens himself up completely and ingests the voices of a higher spiritual plane. For the playwright, clothing this ecstatic experience in words, giving it artistic shape is to some degree an impoverishment of the experience. Of course, the idea of impoverishing experience by verbalizing it is also found among many modernist writers, from Blok through Mallarmé to Miciński.

Furthermore, Ivanov makes the gods in this play silent both for ideological and formal reasons. Except for a brief moment when Hermes speaks and the break between the two worlds is bridged, the gods do not utter any words. Formally, divine silence focuses attention on the mortals, strengthening the work's anthropocentric orientation. More importantly, on the philosophical level, Adrasteia, the playwright's *porte-parole,* remains silent until the very end to signal disapproval of her double—Tantalus. The king is rebelling against values and concepts that are positive and absolutely necessary according to Ivanov's worldview. Adrasteia represents fate, necessity, and therefore man's mortality, which he must learn to accept. When she does speak in the end, she shows that, though Tantalus is being punished, he is also being forgiven for having come to terms with his mortality and having tried to eternalize the moment that was granted to him.

Despite its appeal to a common cultural basis, as well as to twentieth-century existential problems, *Tantalus* is a dramatic failure. Lack of a traditional type of action, a static nature, and abstracted, monumentalized characters are not the real problem. The single, most overwhelming distancing element in this work is its language usage. From the very first line the recipient is jarred and forced to fight his way through each line of verse in order to comprehend it. Unfortunately, this language deviates so much from both colloquial as well as literary norms that, great beauty notwithstanding, it becomes opaque. In a work of poetry it would be difficult, but much more acceptable. For a dramatic work it is too "complete," incapable of being complemented by nonverbal elements

As an experiment, *Tantalus* also reveals the fallacy of trying to equate drama with ritual. At the heart of both drama and ritual there must lie an emotional identification. In ritual the emotionalism is directed toward a higher being but only for the recipient who is also a genuine believer. Even if the rite is performed in a language incomprehensible to the recipient—the Latin, for example, of Catholic masses—the recipient comes to the "performance" having seen it numerous times. He knows beforehand what will happen and to what gestures and events the incomprehensible words correspond. Above all, the participant in a ritual knows about the spiritual significance of what he is about to witness even before the curtain rises. On the other hand, art, though requiring the acceptance of certain conventions, is not speaking to a recipient who is already a believer. In a sense the recipient must be "converted" during the course of the play, and that process requires tools other than those of ritual. The situation was different in the middle ages, when a community of believers, living in a religious world, experienced a mystery play that used familiar images, that served to reinforce their faith, and at the same time was a work of art. A religious genre with ritualistic aims cannot be transposed to the secularized world of the twentieth century without some significant adjustments. In practice, using art as a substitute for religion is more difficult than most thinkers, including Ivanov, envisioned.

Conclusion

FROM *THE CHERRY ORCHARD*'S supposed realism, through the fairy tale aura of *Holy Blood*, and the gloom and doom of the melodramatic *The Triumph of Death* to the playfulness of *The Puppet Show* and the hieratic Neoclassicism of *Tantalus*, the modernist search for a new drama presents a motley but invigorating scene. Each playwright develops his or her own way of dealing with distance in order to give the recipient a fresh perspective on some topic.

Distance is manipulated through a broad range of elements, both traditional and nontraditional in nature. The traditional techniques are taken from a variety of sources. For example, in *The Cherry Orchard,* Anton Chekhov employs the traditional comedic distancing element of incongruity between the situation and the protagonists' methods of dealing with it. Both Ranevskaia's and Gaev's responses to the loss of the estate are those of ineffectual wastrels. Another comedic distancing technique used is that of parodying the major characters through the secondary ones—Duniasha becomes a caricature of a lady, Jasha of the arrogant fop. In a somewhat different fashion, Aleksandr Blok in *The Puppet Show* adopts elements of commedia dell'arte in order to distance the recipient. These elements include the use of masklike effects that reify such dramatis personae as the mystics, as well as reliance on the "noncoincidental" characterization typical of *commedia*. With the tragic as the overriding mode in *Holy Blood,* Zinaida Gippius only very sporadically introduces a biting humor, another comedic technique that lessens sympathy for the protagonists. However, she quite definitely increases distance through such traditional means as a fairy tale-like setting and a nonhuman heroine. Fedor Sologub employs traditional methods of distancing in *The Triumph of Death* with less-than-human characters reminiscent of medieval allegory, accompanied by an elevated style of language. Viacheslav Ivanov in *Tantalus* distances by having a chorus, as in Greek drama, that comments on the events of the play, thus introducing a mediating figure (collective in nature) between the micro- and macrolevels of his work.

At the same time, all of the playwrights manipulate distance through nontraditional means in order both to increase and decrease it. For example, Anton Chekhov and Aleksandr Blok undercut recipient expectations through a constant and intricate interweaving of different theatrical codes and genres.

Additionally, Chekhov relies on a finely tuned and very complex orchestration of rhythm to carry the meaning of his play, while simultaneously evoking a new kind of emotive response from the recipient. Blok and especially Zinaida Gippius introduce innovative deictic and communicative constructions. In their texts a large number of distally oriented and nonperlocutionary referential segments are alternated with proximal expressive segments. Such a distribution substitutes for the drama's traditional highly perlocutionary and proximally oriented discourse, while continuing to present abstract, distal material. Viacheslav Ivanov achieves distance by carrying his stylistic experiment with language to an extreme that is as radical in its own way as any of the poetic innovations of Velimir Khlebnikov or Aleksei Kruchenykh. He attempts to balance the distancing effect by internalizing and psychologizing ritual in order to create a feeling of an anthropomorphically oriented *sobornost'*. In its own way, more or less successfully, each of these works strives for a balance between distancing and emotiveness.

Through the collective effect of these various elements, all of the works in some fashion or another disturb the relationship between genre and distance, a relationship that traditionally has been clearly defined and has supported recipient expectations. Some of the plays revive old genres such as the commedia dell'arte (*The Puppet Show*) or the Greek choric drama (*Tantalus*). Others employ popular "low forms" like melodrama (*The Triumph of Death*), whereas still others (*The Cherry Orchard, Holy Blood*) experiment with current mainstream genres such as comedy and tragedy. However, in each case what occurs is not a clear-cut, straightforward use of the given genre but an adaptation of some sort designed to better fit the demands of the modern period. For example, Aleksandr Blok dips into the entire wealth of an international centuries old *commedia* tradition in order to create a complex character, one that would be more appealing to a psychologically oriented modern recipient. A similar awareness of recipient needs lies behind Viacheslav Ivanov's internalizing and psychologizing of a neomystery, a quasi-religious ritual traditionally oriented toward a supreme being. Zinaida Gippius in her work turns the benign lightheartedness of the fairy tale genre into a tragedy with an intriguing, nonhuman heroine. In his finely wrought play, Anton Chekhov seems to be continuously either breaking the work's comedic "energy" or trivializing its tragic pathos, either collecting realistic details that particularize the story and characters or destroying realistic illusion.

The result of such strategies is that these particular works—like the majority of innovative plays written during modernism and throughout the twentieth century—manipulate distance in one of two ways. Either they greatly increase the distance to a fixed point where the recipient becomes estranged because the emotive elements are considerably weaker, or they create a constantly shifting distance. *The Triumph of Death* and *Tantalus* fall in the first group. *The Puppet Show* very visibly keeps shifting distance and pushing the recipient from one theatrical code to another, from one set of rules suggesting a specific genre to another. In *The Cherry Orchard* and *Holy Blood*, shifting occurs mostly underneath the surface, while leaving a surface that is seemingly smooth and quite traditional.

All of the analyzed plays reveal the viability of drama. At times disparaged for its ambiguity, for its uncertain status in relation to the other major literary forms, drama in the twentieth century has shown its great potential. It is ideally suited for the presentation of a plurality of voices. In prose and poetry, the possibilities of distance manipulation are circumscribed to some degree by the single voice of the narrator. Drama does not have that problem precisely because it is not a strictly literary form.

Yet for all of its "nonliterary" qualities, this analysis has also demonstrated the overwhelming importance of language in drama, as well as the specificity of that language's nature. In order to succeed, dramatic language must be characterized by "incompleteness." Only then will the connotative and denotative dynamism of the sign be fully realized in all of its richness. Thus, a language such as Fedor Sologub's in *The Triumph of Death* or Viacheslav Ivanov's in *Tantalus* is in some sense too complete. On the other hand, Zinaida Gippius's *Holy Blood* shows what an important emotive function language can have. When its colloquial style is combined with an innovative distribution of deictic segments, it humanizes an estranging story and increases the strength of the protagonist's passion. Of course, emotiveness in language is not only achieved through a more widespread use of colloquialisms or deictic combinations. The effect can also be created in a traditional fashion through great poetry that stirs the recipient's emotions, as happens to some degree in Aleksandr Blok's *The Puppet Show*.

Furthermore, the use of language in these plays reveals that when dealing with distance manipulation not all elements are of equal importance and strength. If a major element such as language style is employed in a distancing fashion, then it must be balanced by elements of equal strength, for balance is always needed in order to create a masterpiece. Anton Chekhov's *The Cherry Orchard* can serve as an example. Balance, however, should not be mistaken for moderation or timidity. The enormous potential of distance manipulation in producing a work that both breaks and fulfills expectations can be employed in radical, wildly innovative ways. The one condition for success is that in the end the balance of distancing and emotive forces, whether traditional or nontraditional, must be equal. Great drama is an art of balanced extremes and thus perfectly suited for the existential extremes of the twentieth century.

Of importance is the fact that in all of these works, as in modern drama in general, the relationship between distance and genre continues to exist. However, the nature and character of this relationship is redefined. In the cases where a shifting distance is created, genres usually do not appear as a

Distance Manipulation

whole or in their entirety; they do not define the work. Instead, bits and pieces of different genres are offered to the recipient. These pieces continue, just as in traditional works, to "whet his appetite," and, above all, to channel his expectations—even if only momentarily and not throughout the duration of the work.

Such alternation of genres, and consequently of distances, might conceivably bring to mind tragicomedy. This would be an incorrect conclusion, for these works cannot be put into one group with such traditional tragicomedy as that of Giovanni Guarini or Lope de Vega. Though they certainly borrow something from Shakespeare and German romantic plays such as Kleist's *The Prince of Homburg*, they differ from these works in some essential ways. Perhaps a more useful attempt at a definition is Albert Bermel's theory of "comic agony." Bermel writes of comic agony as being an offshoot of tragicomedy, with roots that go back to Euripides and Shakespeare. He sees tragicomedy as *alternating* genres, whereas comic agony *interweaves* the tragic and the comic. Bermel writes that in comic agony "the tragic and comic are interwoven 'simultaneously, each heightening the other'; they are threads of contrasting colors in a fabric that is iridescent, neither of the colors and yet derived from both."[1] Bermel states that this approach to creating drama allows for a "playful" method of dealing with wrenching subjects—an idea reminiscent of the carnivalization theory of Mikhail Bakhtin and Martin Green. According to Bermel the end result of such a method is greater realism, a greater approximation of what real life is like.

Bermel's distinction between alternation and interweaving is a valuable one for describing what occurs in the plays analyzed in this study. He is also correct in saying that the latter approach to distance has a long tradition. However, his conclusion that such a presentation leads to greater "realism" does not allow one to effectively distinguish between a *King Lear* and a *Cherry Orchard*, or, perhaps even more remarkably, a play like *The Puppet Show*. First, all of these plays contain elements that might be called "unrealistic." Second, no one would easily group the three plays together, and everyone would automatically know which plays were written three hundred years later.

Instead, the conclusion that can be reached is that distance is manipulated and genres are interwoven for a new purpose in modern drama. Traditionally, distance is tied to genre and clearly defined because its goal is to help satisfy recipient expectations of greater or lesser identification with and sympathy for the protagonist(s)—depending on the genre. Thus, the reception of a work of art is aimed at fulfilling expectations, though, if the work is a great one, this is accomplished with a good dose of surprise, suspense, and "openness" in the presentation. Maurice Descotes concludes something similar in his historical study of theatrical audiences. He writes: "C'est qui retient le public, c'est la manière, plus ou moins nouvelle, plus ou moins

Conclusion

frappante, par laquelle est provoquée l'émotion qu'il attend d'éprouver" (What captures the audience is the more or less new, more or less striking, way in which is evoked the emotion that it [the audience] expects to experience).[2]

It is the existential situation of earlier historical eras that allows for the kind of distance manipulation and genre interweaving that leads to a greater "realism," whatever the term may mean for any given period. As stated in the introduction to this study, as different as the historical periods are, as much as the playwrights vary by temperament and method, there is an underlying coherence to their existential universe. Thus, Shakespeare's distance manipulation is aimed at creating a sense of greater "realism" (verisimilitude, believability), therefore making his works more attractive to a larger cross section of Elizabethan society.

By the time modernism arrives, the existential situation has changed radically. The playwrights discussed here, as well as many of their contemporaries, for the most part write from a position that recognizes little or no underlying orthodox philosophical foundations. On occasion, a highly personal system of ideas is constructed by the author and thus would be unfamiliar to the recipient. As a result, in practice the modernist and twentieth-century existential situation leads to a more frenetic manipulation of distance, and with it of genres, to the openness of perspective and lack of heroes observed in modern drama. In all cases the relationship between distance and genre continues. Nevertheless, its aim is no longer a greater "realism" in order to fulfill recipient expectations with some surprising twists. The primary purpose of manipulating distance is now to wrench the recipient out of his expectations, out of his passivity, and to force him to become an active participant along with the playwright in a desperate search for answers.

However, every audience has its limitations. And a truly great playwright does not despise them, but respects them. As Maurice Descotes writes (though with his own francophile bias): "Les deux plus grands ècrivains de théâtre de tous le temps, Shakespeare et Molière, avaient pour le public, sans réserves ni distinctions de classe ou de la culture, un sentiment qui ressemble beaucoup à l'estime" (The two greatest playwrights of all time, Shakespeare and Molière, had for the audience, without any reservations or distinctions of class or culture, a feeling which greatly resembles esteem).[3] Thus, among the modern plays, those that are dramatically successful fulfill both functions. They simultaneously manipulate distance so as to elicit emotive responses—often in new and unexpected ways (*dulce*), and destroy them so as to break the recipient's passivity (a new *utile*). Anton Chekhov's *The Cherry Orchard* is a case in point.

If this new function of reception is understood, then it becomes clear that the best of modern drama does not relinquish its ethical role. It is true that this new interpretation of *dulce et utile* radically changes the nature of reception by making it more intellectual and by forcing the recipient to become consciously involved in answering the questions posed by the given work. Albeit, by concurrently retaining art's original function of awakening emotive reactions, the emotional aspect of identification is also preserved and safeguarded. Thus, by continuing to engage the emotions of the recipient, the playwright is still able to fulfill an ethical role when, along with the recipient, he seeks solutions to existential problems. Simply put, the author does not offer answers—he treats the recipient more as a partner, whether the latter likes this relationship or not. However, the very fact that he poses these questions—then manipulates distance both in order to force from the recipient an intellectual response and to engage his emotions—reveals a deep ethical concern.

Overall, the plays in this study fall into several categories. They could have directly influenced later dramatic works and theatrical performances and styles. They could also represent the beginning of currents and trends that would keep reappearing with numerous variations throughout the twentieth century. The only one of these works that actually entered into the canon of world repertoire is, of course, Chekhov's *The Cherry Orchard.* Though in many ways inimitable, his plays influenced a diverse group of artists, from the Russian symbolists and the Oberiuty through Eugene O'Neill, Harold Pinter, and Tennessee Williams. The mixing of theatrical codes and the use of the grotesque in Blok's *The Puppet Show* clearly influenced Vsevolod Meierhold's work in the theater. Moreover, this kind of grotesque fantasy satire continues to appear more and more frequently throughout the twentieth century in the most diverse range of examples, from the works of Friedrich Dürrenmatt and Sławomir Mrożek to those of Peter Brooks and Federico Fellini. Elements of this form will also be clearly visible in popular, commercial art. Blok may not have exerted a direct influence on world drama, but his play certainly captures one of the dominant tendencies of the twentieth century. Ivanov's dramatic work brought an immediate and positive response from contemporaries such as Innokentii Annenskii, Aleksei Remizov, Velimir Khlebnikov, and Meierhold, even though one cannot speak of any direct imitation. Furthermore, it inspired a short-lived postrevolutionary proletarian theatrical group. More importantly, however, Ivanov's minimalistic approach to the presentation of quasi rituals echoes in the work of his contemporary Georg Fuchs, and later reappears in yet another important trend of the twentieth century, including the theatrical work of Jacques Copeau and the early performances of Jerzy Grotowski. Concurrently, both Ivanov's and Sologub's desire to create neomysteries that would serve as rites will reappear—long after the symbolists—in the theatrical "happenings" of the 1960s and 1970s. Most of these happenings do not have openly religious ambitions, though the work of Grotowski in the second phase of his Teatr Laboratorium leans in that direction. Finally, although Gippius's *Holy Blood* was never published and remained completely unknown, her presentation of serious drama as a fairy tale can be seen in the works of such modernists as Aleksei Remizov, Evgenii Shvarc, William Butler Yeats, and Bolesław Leśmian.

In the end, what remains is the question of why so many modernist plays have not been assimilated by the average recipient to this day; Chekhov, of course, being the exception. No clear-cut answer exists, but some suggestions can be put forth. First of all, acceptance and popularity are not merely the result of merit, for historical factors always play an important role in the aesthetic reception of any work. It is a historical factor that in the second half of the twentieth century the recipients of serious art, especially in the theater, encompass a much larger percentage of the general population. This is a result of economic prosperity rather than of cultural development, and the average recipient still favors traditional forms of drama. Another historical factor is the decision of an author not to publish a work, as happened with Gippius's *Holy Blood.* One can only speculate what recipient reactions would have been if the playwright allowed her work to see the light of day. Yet another historical factor that always plays a role in the creation of canons is how successfully a work is sold and marketed. Chekhov is a case in point. For all of his innovativeness, it is the seeming realism of his plays that Stanislavsky seized upon and sold to the Russian recipient. That same realism later would be disseminated throughout the West by Stanislavsky's disciples. To this day, Chekhov's popularity among the general audience is primarily due to the perception of the writer as a nostalgic painter of a bygone era, rather than to the radically new elements of his plays.

Second and more importantly, the nature of the aesthetic reception required in all of these plays needs to be considered. The nature of this reception does not give a definitive answer, but it does lead us closer to the heart of the matter. If one considers all of the distancing and emotive elements of the works discussed here, one must conclude that, in general, modernist playwrights posited a much more intellectually subtle and emotionally developed virtual recipient than the average recipient of the entire twentieth century. Modernists often wrote of creating a new art form for a new epoch, and in a sense that is what they did. On the one hand, these playwrights often filled their works with an intellectual content that was not familiar to the average twentieth-century recipient. These dramas were not medieval morality plays whose Christian beliefs were familiar throughout the community. Rather, modernist ideas were taken from elite philosophies and systems of thought prevalent at the time, and often, as in Sologub's *The Triumph of Death,* made even more difficult by the addition of highly individualized elements. On the other hand, it must be noted that, though each writer balanced his distancing elements with emotive ones, more often than not the emotive elements employed were *not* traditional. Such devices as rhythm that carries meaning, the weaving of deictic segments of different orientation, or the psychologizing of a mythological figure were meant to function emotively—and to do so gradually. However, because they are so new to the recipient and so nontraditional they do not act as easily in an emotive fashion. The recipient must become comfortable with them and be trained, and only then can he respond emotionally. Sometimes, if a play is a true masterpiece, this education can happen in the course of a single performance. More often than not, however, the duration of a single play is not enough to overturn expectations that have existed for centuries, if not for a thousand years. In other words, possibly because the very fabric of life changed in the twentieth century faster than at any other time in the history of mankind, the dramatic works produced by the modernists affected the nature of reception more radically than anything seen before. And Chekhov is no exception. His innovativeness is as equally radical as that of the symbolists except that it is covered by the seeming familiarity of realism. Perhaps the measure of whether recipients will ever come to assimilate modernist plays is really a test of whether human beings will ever emotionally come to terms with the existential changes that have occurred in our century.

Notes

INTRODUCTION

1. See Elam 1980; Goffman 1974; Worth and Gross 1974; Mukařovsky 1979; Iser 1974; Gombrich 1960, 373; Jauss 1978, 137–47; Jauss 1982b: 152–88; Jauss 1973; Ben Chaim 1984; Koestler 1964, 345; Bullough 1912; Sartre 1948; Brecht 1964, 194–95; Holland 1968, 102.

2. Beginning with some of Bertolt Brecht's writing (Brecht 1964, 15, 25, 32, 47, 50, 58, 71, 78) and throughout the twentieth century, theories have been put forth for a new, intellectual, and rational type of identification. This author agrees with such diverse writers as Sartre and Jauss, who posit the idea that even if intellectual identification occurs it is always preceded, followed, or accompanied by some emotional response to the work. At times the emotion may simply be pleasure at the presented intellectual challenge or a very rudimentary emotion more akin to a sensation (Bullough 1912; Sartre 1948; Jauss 1982a, 152–88; Ben Chaim 1984, 74). However, without that emotional core there is no identification. Furthermore, as some critics have pointed out, in Brecht's best plays emotional identification also occurs, despite the author's intentions (Demarcy 1973, 357–63).

3. "Alienation" and "alienating" are very loaded terms with long and complex histories (for a good discussion of the term, see Schacht 1984). Therefore, this study will employ the terms "distance" and "distancing" in reference to the phenomenon as a whole and to the techniques employed to achieve this effect. It will use the terms "estrangement" and "estranging" in reference to the effect that the nontraditional manipulation of distance has on the recipient.

4. For discussion of alienation as a theme, see Hallman 1961; Lukacs 1950; Porter 1981; Bloch 1971; Nielsen 1982; Konrad 1986; Stoianov 1988; Sypher 1962; Williams 1966.

5. See also Ben Chaim 1984, 80.

6. See Jarvis 1961, 415, 422.

7. See also Ratajczakowa 1993, 374, 379; Karnick 1988, 73.

8. See also Steiner 1971; Cantor 1988; Silverman 1989; Shattuck 1968.

9. Naturalism grew out of the same spiritual crisis as modernism, but the works that it produced, in general, did not experiment with form, except

for the shock value of introducing topics that had been taboo up till then in literature.

10. For examples, see Brecht 1964; Sartre 1948; Artaud 1971–74; Styan 1960, 1975; Bentley 1964; Eco 1977; Elam 1980; Goffman 1974.

11. See Grotowski 1968. Ironically, drama as a religious ritual is what many modernists desire (Ivanov 1971–87, 629–31). Unfortunately, often they do not seem to realize that ritual and art are not identical, that art requires certain conventions; otherwise it will not work successfully with the audience. It is for this reason that one often finds in modernism a large discrepancy between the playwright's theory and practice, with artistic intuition often prevailing over theory in the actual plays. In other instances the plays produced are simply dramatic failures, albeit ambitious ones.

12. See Ben Chaim 1984, 73–74; Elam 1980; Goffman 1974; Worth and Gross 1974; Mukařovsky 1979; Iser 1974; Gombrich 1960, 373; Jauss 1978, 137–47.

13. However, the significance of the familiar should not be overemphasized, as happens with Stanley Fish's concept of interpretative communities (Fish 1980).

14. Grygar 1985, 103.

15. See Koestler 1964, 345; Ben Chaim 1984, 74; Bullough 1912; Sartre 1948; Brecht 1964, 194–95; Holland 1968, 102.

16. See Pearse 1980, 74–75; Iser 1974, xiv; Iser 1978, 111; Jarvis 1961, 425; Eco 1984, 49.

17. See, for example, such diverse works as Cornford 1914; Sławińska and Kruk 1966; Glatzer-Rosenthal 1986.

18. See Bab 1928; Braun 1984; Shattuck 1968; Szondi 1973; Brockett and Findlay 1991, 29, 114–21, 202–3, 130–32, 179–85.

19. See Köhler 1982.

20. See Gasparov 1984, 276–77.

21. See Ben Chaim 1984; Bennett 1990; Eco 1984; Jauss 1982b.

22. See Eco 1979, 7–10.

23. For sociological discussions, see, for example, Burns 1972; Goffman 1974; Goodlad 1972; Pavis 1992.

24. See Xolodov 1982; Descotes 1964.

25. See, for example, Eco 1977; Hess-Lutich 1979; Jansen 1991; Melrose 1994; Pavis 1982; Kobernick 1989; Hartmann 1964; Grosse 1972. Furthermore, there exists the eternal debate over which is more stable an element of theater: the text or the actor. Both certainly form the basis of theater, though both in rare situations have been dispensable. There certainly can be a theater of improvisation without a text. However, there have also been experimental theaters of light, sound, and abstract images, without an actor. The question does not seem to destroy the validity of the proffered definition of drama.

26. For similar definitions, see Elam 1980, 2, 158–59, 209; Steen 1991, 220; Filipowicz 1991, 27; Issacharoff 1989; Pfister 1988; Ubersfeld 1977; Stelleman 1992; Tonnelli and Hubert 1978.

27. The term is borrowed from Ratajczakowa 1990, 84.

28. See Elam 1980, 140–41.

29. See Abel 1963; Frow 1986; Snyder 1991; Cohen 1986; Miller 1984; Cranny-Francis 1990, 16–17.

30. See Brustein 1964, 4; Goldman and Traschen 1968, 303; Driver 1970: 219–20; Esslin 1969, 6.

31. It should be noted that there are sporadic cases in earlier historical periods of, if not an "absolute collapse" of values, then at least of very strong doubts. Such, for example, is Adam Mickiewicz's *Forefathers' Eve, Part III*.

32. See Snyder 1991, 205, 212.

33. See Elam 1980, 95; Pfister 1988, 26–27, 34–36.

34. See Grubber 1980, 168; Norris 1993; Wellmer 1991.

35. For the influence of Chekhov on the symbolists and absurdists, see Bicilli 1983; Meierkhol'd 1967; Schmid 1984; Dlugosch 1977; Kesting 1959; Belyi 1968; Merezhkovskii 1968; Cymborska-Leboda 1989; Straszkowa 1989.

36. See Baran 1986.

CHAPTER ONE

1. See, for example, Chekhov 1974–83, 4: 465; Mirsky 1958; Mikhailovskii 1957; Shestov 1978; Grigorovich 1974–82; Pervukhina 1993.

2. They were also greatly admired by such members of the second generation of symbolists as Andrei Belyi and Aleksandr Blok and were made part of their canon of literary culture—though this opinion would not have influenced mainstream reaction. See Cymborska-Leboda 1989; Straszkowa 1989; *Literaturnoe nasledstvo* 1960; Remizov 1981. However, a primarily aesthetically oriented symbolist such as Briusov had only negative remarks to make about Chekhov (Briusov 1927).

3. See Stanislavskii 1988 1: 305, 568; Stanislavskii 1993 5 (1): 104; Chekhov 1973: 459–60.

4. See Stelleman 1992, 105; Turner 1994, 87; Styan 1989, 199; Styan 1972; Rokem 1986, 32, 35; Skaftymov 1967, 87; Schmid 1984, 32; Tulloch 1980, 186; Sobennikov 1984, 194.

5. See Skaftymov 1972; Skaftymov 1967, 75, 81, and Pitcher 1973, 172–73; Fergusson 1967, 148.

6. This topic is analyzed in greater detail in the section on genre.

7. See Cymborska-Leboda 1989; Straszkowa 1989; Meierhold 1967; Maiakovskii 1955.

8. Chekhov 1944–51, 11: 584; Chekhov 1974–83, 2: 281.

9. Annenkov 1966, 64.

10. Maiakovskii 1955, 294–301.

11. See Brownstein 1991; Fisher 1985; Jackson 1967; Gerould 1958; Pitcher 1973; Cantor 1988; Orr 1991; Pierrot 1981; Silverman 1989; Steiner 1971.

12. Grubber 1980, 144.

13. Styan 1972, 181.

14. Some critics disagree with this and insist that the play is divided into traditional parts. See, for example, Fergusson 1967. However, this author feels that the seeming division into parts is yet another Chekhovian illusion and that what the recipient really receives is something quite different.

15. Balukhaty 1967, 139; also Esslin 1985, 137.

16. Lopakhin's opening speech also contains information that could be seen as expository. However, there are certain aspects of the presentation that undercut the expository effect. The monologue will be analyzed in greater detail in conjunction with the discussion on genre. All page numbers after quotations from and references to the primary text refer to the Chekhov 1970 edition listed in the References.

17. Balukhaty 1967, 139.

18. Yarrison 1988, 154; Fergusson 1967, 151.

19. Stelleman 1992, 12.

20. See Brémond 1973, 201. Such a tripartite definition of action is quite typical for structuralists. Similar definitions have been proposed by Tsvetan Todorov, A. Hübler, and Jurii Lotman (Pfister 1988, 199).

21. Styan 1989, 196; Styan 1985b, 110–11, 10; Brownstein 1991, 157; Balukhaty 1967, 140.

22. The abstractness is also influenced by other aspects of characterization, which are discussed later.

23. See Pavis 1988; Senelick 1982, 244; Cymborska-Leboda 1989, 118; Holland 1982, 238; Esslin 1985, 139.

24. Pavis 1988.

25. Fergusson 1967, 149. Francis Fergusson compares Chekhov's use of the social occasion to that of Henry James (Fergusson 1967). This may be a valid conclusion in some respects. However, a comparison with the Russian symbolists seems more appropriate here because it is closer to home and direct influences are more probable. See Ivanov and Gershenzon 1921, 54; Lavrov 1978, 137; Belyi 1966, 366.

26. See Rokem 1986, 11–12.

27. See Esslin 1985, 143–44.

28. See also Rokem 1986, 35.

29. See also Tulloch 1980, 185–87.

30. See Skaftymov 1967, 73–81; Esslin 1985, 139.

31. See also Pitcher 1973, 178–85; Styan 1985b, 129.
32. See Hristić 1985, 281–82.
33. See ibid., 282.
34. See also Grubber 1980, 139–40.
35. The term "language" is here used in a broad sense. It includes verbal utterances, sounds, nonsense words, as well as the gestures and movements that accompany them. It also embraces those moments of silence that function as a means of communication, which happens quite often in this work.
36. Issacharoff 1989, 93–126; Gerould 1958.
37. Elam 1980, 138–39; Serpieri 1981.
38. Jakobson 1960; Pfister 1988, 105–18.
39. Elam 1980, 159–69.
40. Stelleman 1992, 19.
41. For more details, see Kot 1995, 111–26.
42. Grubber 1980, 131, 140; Fergusson 1967, 149; Yarrison 1988; Styan 1985b, 118; Nilsson 1960.
43. It should, however, also be noted, as Francis Fergusson shows, that at times the rhythm, and especially the pauses, increase the work's lyricism (Fergusson 1967, 149).
44. See also Grubber 1980, 132.
45. Grubber 1980, 128; also Brustein 1964.
46. Gerould 1958, 113–14; also Bentley 1965; Esslin 1970.
47. Schmid 1984, 27–31; Gerould 1958, 116; Senelick 1982, 249; Tulloch 1980, 192; Esslin 1985, 138; Brownstein 1991, 160.
48. Clayton 1993, 163–64.
49. Schmid 1984, 28.
50. Grubber 1980, 131–34.
51. See also Pitcher 1973, 181–83, 208–10; Holland 1982, 239; Grubber 1980, 131, 142; and Stanislavskii 1988, 1: 351.
52. See Chekhov 1973, 461.
53. It should be made clear that traditional comedy elicits sympathy for some of the characters, but at a distance. In traditional tragedy, the sympathy, or more precisely the compassion, would most often be based on a sense of identification with a character. In typical farce and satire, the distance is even greater than in comedy. In farce the recipient looks down on the characters. In satire the recipient may be frightened by the characters, if the work clearly aims to attack him. In neither genre is sympathy particularly active. In melodrama, tragedy's compassion turns to pity—for a number of reasons.
54. Here is a situation where virtual, modernist, and contemporary recipients come together in their expectations because of the patterns of historical development. In earlier periods, before the nineteenth century, there have been complex comedic characters who evoked great sympathy, such as

Falstaff or Don Quixote, and even in the twentieth century, Charlie Chaplin can be classified as such. However, for the most part, the expectations of Chekhov's contemporaries, of today's recipient, and in this case, of the virtual recipient, develop out of nineteenth-century conventions typical of popular dramatic fare. As a result, depth of feeling, complexity, and, above all, juxtaposition of stock and three-dimensional types within a comic character is, in general, a surprise to all three kinds of recipients. The nineteenth century is not a high point of theatrical development, and staple fair means simple plays that cater to the tastes of the bourgeoisie, including melodrama, undemanding comedies, and farce of the lightest sort. (See also Gerould 1958, 115–20.) Simultaneously, it must be kept in mind that Russia had an exceptional tradition of comedy in the nineteenth century, what with the plays of Nikolai Gogol', whose works had both great depth and a very modern sense of absurdity. Such a legacy had to affect all later attempts at comedy by playwrights in Russia, whether they were conscious of it or not.

55. Schmid 1984, 32–40.

56. See Styan 1985b, 121; Pitcher 1973, 208; Gerould 1958, 122; Brownstein 1991, 162.

57. See also Grubber 1980, 142–43.

58. See also Gerould 1958, 119; Deer 1959; Senelick 1982; Esslin 1970.

59. See Styan 1972, 1989; Esslin 1970, 1980; Brownstein 1991.

60. See Grubber 1980, 65; Bentley 1965, 296–97.

CHAPTER TWO

1. There seems to be some uncertainty as to the dating of the play with both 1901 and 1900 being given (Schuler 1995, 138; Segel 1993, 59; Gippius 1972a, vii; Smith 1994, 191). It seems that the latter was the date of composition and the former that of publication in the journal *Severnye Cvety*.

2. See Gippius 1972a, xi; Gippius 1972b, xi, xvii; Matich 1972, 53–99; Kelly 1994, 152–53; Schuler 1995, 133–38; Taubman 1994, 174–75; Segal 1993, 60; Donchin 1958, 58.

3. See also Schuler 1995, 140–41; Gilbert 1989, 102.

4. For more information on Gippius's religious views, see Matich 1972, 54, 60–63, 71–72, 74.

5. See Weststeijn 1989, 113–14.

6. See Kalbouss 1982, 46; Xolodov 1982, 6: 276.

7. See Moyle 1986; Ivanits 1989, 75–81; Xolodov 1982, 6: 440–561; 7, 447–560; Markov 1968, 13; Schuler 1995, 137, 140.

8. All quotations from Gippius will be followed by a page number referring to the edition listed in the References.

9. See Matich 1993, 237–50; Schuler 1995, 141, 143, 146–47.

10. This absence of reaction to utterances is not just a question of the innate nature of water nymphs, who supposedly neither love nor hate but are rather lukewarm in their reactions to everything. The lack of a perlocutionary effect is visible both in the utterances of the old monk and the central protagonist, both of whom are very passionate and loving creatures.

11. As late as the seventeenth century, unity of time was not rigorously observed and was seen as part of the secondary attributes of a play. However, it became emphasized in neoclassical works and codified into a rigid rule that continued to be a requirement and expectation throughout most of the nineteenth century (Ratajczak 1985, 88).

12. See Kalbouss 1982, 43.

13. See Abel 1964, 2–38; Goldman and Traschen 1968, 2–5; Bentley 1965, 276–81.

14. See Pfister 1988, 205.

15. Bentley 1965, 121.

16. Henn 1966, 262.

17. Lorca quoted in Bentley 1965, 278.

CHAPTER THREE

1. The Western medieval tradition is employed in *The Triumph of Death,* but in *Van'ka the Steward* the author actually turns to native Russian folklore.

2. See Meyerhold 1978, 56; *Russian Symbolist Theatre* 1986, 147.

3. Śliwowski 1976, 243.

4. *The Russian Symbolist Theatre* 1986, 149.

5. Ibid., 158, 159.

6. Ibid., 113–20, 135–41.

7. Sologub 1908, 23. All future references to the text of the play will be followed by page numbers referring to the 1908 edition of Sologub's work listed in the bibliography.

8. See Greene 1986, 99.

9. See also Bentley 1965, 102–17.

10. The notion of rhythm has a double meaning and function. On the one hand, it is perceived to be one of the most primal aesthetic principles that lie at the basis of reception and, therefore, are emotive in nature for recipients of all historical periods (Grygar 1985, 103). On the other hand, rhythms can vary in tempo and character, and, therefore, depending on the context within which they are placed, they can affect recipients in different ways. Thus, a slow ponderous rhythm, like the one in *The Triumph of Death,* simultaneously supports an elevated and distancing style, and, on some very basic, instinctive level affects the recipient emotively. This is discussed more in the section on the emotive elements of this play.

Notes to Pages 72–86

11. See Kalbouss 1968, 67. There is also one moment where the stage directions do not support the general solemn mood. This is discussed in the section on juxtapositions and inconsistencies.

12. See Kotow 1982, 31; Meyerhold 1978, 49–58; *Russian Symbolist Theatre* 1986, 159.

13. Dzhonson 1983, 135.

14. George Kalbouss tries to make a case for comparing her to Henrik Ibsen's Nora and the latter's search for self-definition. That seems to be somewhat of an overstatement (Kalbouss 1982, 49).

15. Ibid., 86.
16. See, for example, Śliwowski 1976, 243.
17. See Kalbouss 1968, 72–73.
18. Elam 1980, 187; see also Kalbouss 1968, 170.
19. Kalbouss 1968, 181.
20. Ibid., 156.
21. Bentley 1965, 207.
22. In actuality this may not be true, but that is how the Middle Ages were perceived.
23. Elam 1980, 10–13, 140–41.

CHAPTER FOUR

1. Kalbouss 1982, 86.
2. Jones 1993, 186; see also Porfir'eva 1988, 40–42.
3. See Bennett 1982, 144; Douglas 1993, 140; Westphalen 1992, 435; Jones 1993, 185, 193; *Istoriia russkogo dramaticheskogo teatra* 1987, 7, 326, 327; West 1970, 132–34.
4. See Zarovnaia 1972, 127–29, 132; Bennett 1982, 158; Banjanin 1990, 6; Jones 1993, 191, 192; Minc 1986, 45; Rodina 1972; Gromov 1981, 9, 10; Gerasimov 1987, 572; Mochulskii 1948, 123, 129–33, 141–43; Kipnis 1984, 45; Köhler 1982, 413.
5. Blok 1960, 8: 212 and 7: 301.
6. Chulkov 1930, 221.
7. See Zarovnaia 1972, 131, 141; Westphalen 1992, 435; Jones 1993, 187; Bennett 1982, 158; Blok 1960, 106, 190, 199, 212.
8. Zarovnaia 1972, 132.
9. Westphalen 1992, 436.
10. Rudnitskii 1969, 114; see also Douglas 1993, 80.
11. Minc 1986, 49.
12. Douglas 1993, 10, 11.
13. See ibid., 16–43; Jones 1993, 186.
14. Douglas 1993, 21; Westphalen 1993, 56; Jones 1993, 193, 194.
15. See Zarovnaia 1972, 135.

16. See Smith 1984, 3, 126–28; Hogendoorn 1989, 100–4.

17. Malraux cited in Smith 1984, 4, 5.

18. Douglas 1993, 49; see also Meyerhold 1978, 56, 125 and Douglas 1993, 55, 56.

19. See Douglas 1993, 35; Bennett 1982, 153; Ritter 1989, 1–8.

20. Douglas 1993, 11, 12.

21. See Meyerhold 1978, 139, 142; Green 1986, XIV–XVIII, 267–69.

22. Smith 1984, 88 and 25.

23. All quotations from and references to *The Puppet Show* will be followed by page numbers referring to the 1971 six volume edition of Blok's work listed in the bibliography.

24. Stelleman 1989, 294, 302.

25. See Stelleman 1989, 303; Westphalen 1993, 57; Zarovnaia 1972, 143; Bennett 1982, 166, 167.

26. Westphalen 1993, 66 and 59.

27. Verigina as quoted in Douglas 1993, 78.

28. Hogendoorn 1989, 106 and 95, 96.

29. See Ritter 1989, 194.

30. Zarovnaia 1972, 136.

31. See Douglas 1993, 36; Bennett 1982, 155; Ritter 1989, 5.

32. Douglas 1993, 36, 37.

33. See Zarovnaia 1972, 138, 139.

34. See Banjanin 1990, 5; Westphalen 1993, 58.

35. See Bakhtin 1973, 100–7; Green 1986, XIII–XVIII.

36. See Banjanin 1990; Westphalen 1993, 59–62; Kipnis 1984, 49, 50; Zarovnaia 1972, 138, 139.

37. *The American Heritage College Dictionary* 1993, 177.

38. Ibid., 517.

39. Stelleman 1989, 294 and 297; also Westphalen 1993, 62 and Kipnis 1984, 50.

40. Westphalen 1993, 64.

41. The question of an individual country's tradition and dramatic history and how these influence reception is certainly of great interest. If one even briefly considers two neighboring countries such as Russia and Poland and the very different dramatic traditions of each in the nineteenth century, it becomes obvious that reception would differ. Russia saw the creation of some brilliant comedies, at a time when that genre was in decline. During Romanticism Poland witnessed a period of unprecedented dramatic achievements, of plays so experimental that no other country produced anything similar until the beginning of the twentieth century. However, this historical problem is beyond the scope of the present study.

42. Smith 1984, 183.

43. See Eco 1984, 39, 40, 49.

Notes to Pages 100–27

44. See Zarovnaia 1972, 135–37; Banjanin 1990; Jones 1993, 192; Bennett 1982, 168; Minc 1964, 20.

45. Jones 1993, 192.

CHAPTER FIVE

1. See Cymborska-Leboda 1987, 153; Kot 1991, 7, 8, 35.

2. See ibid., 153, 154; Kot 1991, 35, 36.

3. See ibid., 154; Braun 1984, 110–14; Kot 1991, 212; Williams 1977; Porfir'eva 1988, 40.

4. See Cymborska-Leboda 1987, 154; Kot 1991, 25.

5. See Williams 1961, 213; Kot 1991, 24, 25; Ortwin 1966, 173–91; Brzozowski 1966, 199–206.

6. All quotations from and references to the works of Ivanov will be followed by volume and page numbers referring to the *Sobranie sochinenii* listed in the bibliography.

7. See Cymborska-Leboda 1987, 155; Kot 1991, 35, 36.

8. See Kot 1991, 8–15; Brunel 1982; Eliade 1967; Filipkowska 1972; Forsyth 1977; Foster 1981; West 1970.

9. See *Istoriia russkogo dramaticheskogo teatra* 1987, 7, 326, 327, 387.

10. See Blok 1962, 7; Belyi 1922; Kot 1991, 23, 24; Meierhol'd 1908, 150, 151.

11. Bely as quoted in Porfir'eva 1988, 38.

12. Brunel 1982, 405, 406.

13. Gerasimov 1987, 656, and 565; see also Cymborska-Leboda 1987, 157; Venclova 1984, 91.

14. See Venclova 1984, 93; Stephan 1980, 84–98.

15. See Cymborska-Leboda 1987, 156, 157; Venclova 1984, 93.

16. Venclova 1984, 93 and 95.

17. Porfir'eva 1988, 45.

18. See Kot 1991, 153, 154; Cymborska-Leboda 1987, 156; Venclova 1984, 93, 94.

19. See Kot 1991, 140, 141, 143; Cymborska-Leboda 1987, 157.

CONCLUSION

1. Bermel 1993, 4, and also 11, 195, 196.

2. Descotes 1964, 348.

3. Ibid., 352.

Works Cited

Abel, Lionel. 1963. *Metatheatre: A New View of Dramatic Form.* New York: Hill and Wang.

Abramowska, Janina. 1988. Literatura—dramat—teatr. In *Problemy teorii dramatu,* ed. Janusz Degler, 195–200. Wrocław, Poland: Wydawnictwo Uniwersytetu Wrocławskiego.

Al'tshuler, A. Ia., ed. 1988. *Russkii teatr i dramaturgiia 1907–1917.* Leningrad: Leningradskii Gosudarstvennyi Intitut Teatra, Muzyki i Kinemotografii imeni N. K. Cherkasova.

Amossy, Ruth. 1981. Semiotics and Theater: By Way of an Introduction. *Poetics Today* 2, no. 3: 5–10.

Annenkov, Iurii. 1966. *Dnevnik moikh vstrech. Cikl tragedii.* Vol. 2. New York: Inter Language Literary Associates.

Artaud, Antonin. 1971–74. *Collected Works.* Trans. V. Corti. Vols. 1–4. London: Calder and Boyars.

Auchard, John. 1986. *Silence in Henry James: The Heritage of Symbolism and Decadence.* University Park: Pennsylvania State University Press.

Auconturier, Michel. 1984. Theatricality as a Category of Early Twentieth-Century Russian Culture. In *Theater and Literature in Russia 1900–1930,* ed. Lars Kleberg and Nils Åke Nilsson, 9–22. Stockholm: Almqvist and Wiksell.

Austin, J. L. 1973. *Sense and Sensibilia.* Ed. B. J. Wamock. Oxford: Oxford University Press.

Azov, Vladimir. 1983. Pobeda smerti. Tragediia Fedora Sologuba. In *O Fedore Sologube. Stat'i i zametki,* ed. Anastasiia Chebotarevskaia, 325–29. Ann Arbor, Mich.: Ardis.

Bab, Julius. 1928. *Das Theater der Gegenwart. Geschichte der dramatische Bühne seit 1870.* Leipzig: Verlag von J. J. Weber.

Balukhaty, D. S. 1967. *The Cherry Orchard.* In *Chekhov: A Collection of Critical Essays,* ed. Robert Louis Jackson, 136–46. Englewood Cliffs, N.J.: Prentice-Hall.

Banjanin, Milica. 1990. Echoes of the "Commedia dell'Arte" in the Works of Blok: Transformations of an Image. *Australian Slavonic and East European Studies* 4, no. 1/2: 1–20.

Works Cited

Baran, Henryk. 1986. Towards a Typology of Russian Modernism: Ivanov, Remizov, Xlebnikov. In *Aleksej Remizov: Approaches to a Protean Writer*, ed. Greta N. Slobin, 175–93. Columbus: Slavica.

Barker, Muriel. 1970. "The Novels of Fedor Sologub." Ph.D. diss. abstract, University of Michigan.

Bartels, Emily C. 1993. *Spectacles of Strangeness: Imperialism, Alienation and Marlowe*. Philadelphia: University of Pennsylvania Press.

Bartha, Peter, ed. 1991. *The European Foundations of Russian Modernism*. Studies in Slavic Languages and Literatures, vol. 7. Studies in Russian and German, no. 4. Lewiston, N.Y.: Edwin Mellon Press.

Beckson, Karl, and Arthur Ganz. 1975. *Literary Terms: A Dictionary*. New York: Farrar, Straus and Giroux.

Belsey, Catherine. 1980. *Critical Practice*. London and New York: Methuen.

Belyi, Andrei. 1922. *Sirin uchenogo varvarstva (po povodu knigi V. Ivanova "Rodnoe i vselenskoe")*. Berlin: Skify.

———. 1966. *Na rubezhe dvukh stoletii*. Moskau: Nachdruck der Ausgabe, 1930. Reprint, Letchworth, Engl.: Bradda Books.

———. 1968. A. Chekhov. *Vesy* 8. 1904. Reprint, Liechtenstein: Kraus.

Ben Chaim, Daphna. 1984. *Distance in the Theatre: The Aesthetics of Audience Response*. Ann Arbor, Mich.: UMI Research Press.

Bennett, Robert B. 1991. The Golden Age in the Cycles of History: Analogous Visions of Shakespeare and Chekhov. *Comparative Literature Studies* 28, no. 2: 156–77.

Bennett, Susan. 1990. *Theatre Audiences*. London and New York: Routledge.

Bennett, Virginia. 1982. Russian *Pagliaci:* Symbols of Profaned Love in *The Puppet Show*. In *Drama and Symbolism: Themes in Drama*, ed. James Redmond, 141–78. Vol. 4. Cambridge: Cambridge University Press.

Bentley, Eric. 1964. *The Life of the Drama*. New York: Atheneum.

———. 1965. *The Playwright as Thinker: A Study of Drama in Modern Times*. New York: Meridian Books.

Bermel, Albert. 1993. *Comic Agony: Mixed Impressions in the Modern Theatre*. Evanston, Ill.: Northwestern University Press.

Bicilli, P. M. 1983. *Chekhov's Art: A Stylistic Analysis*. Ann Arbor, Mich.: Ardis.

Billington, James H. 1966. *The Icon and the Axe: An Interpretative History of Russian Culture*. New York: Alfred A. Knopf.

Bloch, Ernst. 1971. Alienation, Estrangement. *Drama Review* 15, no. 1: 120–25.

Blok, Aleksandr. 1962a. O sovremennom sostoianii russkogo simvolizma. In *Aleksandr Blok. Sobranie sochinenii,* 425–36. Vol. 5. Leningrad and Moscow: Khudozhestvennaia Literatura.

Works Cited

———. 1960. *Sobranie Sochinenii.* Moscow: Gosudarstvennoe Izdatel'stvo Khudozhestvennoi Literatury. Vols. 1–8.

———. 1962b. Tvorchestvo Viacheslava Ivanova. In *Aleksandr Blok: Sobranie sochinenii,* 7–18. Vol. 5. Leningrad and Moscow: Khudozhestvennaia Literatura.

———. 1971. *Sobranie sochinenii v shesti tomakh.* In *Dramaticheskie proizvedeniia.* Vol. 4. Moscow: Biblioteka Ogoniok, Izdatel'stvo Pravda.

Booth, Wayne C. 1983. *The Rhetoric of Fiction.* 2nd ed. Chicago: University of Chicago Press.

Bowie, Malcolm. 1978. *Mallarmé and the Art of Being Difficult.* Cambridge: Cambridge University Press.

Brach-Czaina, Jolanta. 1975. *Na drogach dwudziestowiecznej myśli teatralnej.* Wrocław, Poland: Ossolineum.

Braun, Kazimierz. 1984. *Wielka reforma teatru w Europie. Ludzie—idee-zdarzenia.* Wrocław, Poland: Ossolineum.

Brecht, Bertolt. 1964. *Brecht on Theatre: The Development of an Aesthetic.* Ed. and trans. J. Willet. New York: Hill and Wang.

Brémond, C. 1973. *Die Erzählnachricht.* In *Literaturwissenschaft und Linguistik,* ed. J. Ihwe, 177–217. Vol. 3. Frankfurt am Main: Atheneum.

Briusov, Valerii. 1927. *Dnevniki 1891–1910.* Moskva: M. i S. Sabashnikovy.

Brockett, Oscar J., and Robert F. Findlay. 1991. *Century of Innovation: A History of European and American Theatre and Drama since the Late Nineteenth Century.* 2nd ed. Boston: Allyn and Bacon.

Brook, Peter. 1984. *The Empty Space.* New York: Atheneum.

Brownstein, Oscar Lee. 1991. *Strategies of Drama: The Experience of Form.* New York: Greenwood Press.

Brunel, Pierre. 1982. The Beyond and the Within: The Place and Function of Myths in Symbolist Literature. In *The Symbolist Movement in the Literature of European Languages,* ed. Anna Balakian, 399–412. Budapest: Akademiai Kiodó.

Brustein, Robert. 1964. *The Theatre of Revolt.* Boston: Little, Brown.

Büdel, Oscar. 1961. Contemporary Theater and Aesthetic Distance. *Publication of the Modern Language Association* 77, no. 3: 277–91.

Bullough, Edward. 1912. "Psychical Distance" as a Factor in Art and as an Aesthetic Principle. *British Journal of Psychology* 5 (June): 87–118.

Burdowicz-Nowicka, Maria. 1971. *Rozprawy z socjologii teatru.* Wrocław, Poland: Ossolineum.

Burns, Elizabeth. 1972. *Theatricality: A Study of Convention in the Theatre and in Social Life.* London: Longman Group.

Cantor, Norman F. 1988. *Twentieth-Century Culture: Modernism to Deconstruction.* New York: Peter Lang.

Carden, Patricia. 1985. The Aesthetics of Performance in the Russian Avant-garde. *Canadian-American Slavic Studies* 19, no. 4: 375–83.

Centola, Steven R. 1984. Confrontation with the Other: Alienation in the Works of Arthur Miller and Jean-Paul Sartre. *Journal of Evolutionary Psychology* 5, no. 1/2 (March): 1–11.

Chekhov, Anton. 1944–51. *Polnoe sobranie sochinenii v dvadcati tomakh.* Moskva: Gosudarstvennoe Izdatel'stvo Khudozhestvennaia Literatura.

———. 1970. *Sobranie sochinenii v vos'mi tomakh.* Moscow: Pravda.

———. 1973. *Letters of Anton Chekhov.* Trans. Michael Heim. Intro. Simon Karlinsky. New York: Harper and Row.

———. 1974–83. *Polnoe sobranie sochinenii i pisem v tridcati tomakh.* 30 vols. Moscow: Nauka.

Chulkov, Georgii. 1930. *Gody stranstvii.* Moscow: Federaciia.

Clayton, Douglas J. 1993. *Pierrot in Petrograd: "Commedia dell'Arte"/"Balagan" in Twentieth-Century Russian Theatre and Drama.* Montreal: McGill Queen's University Press.

Cohen, Ralph. 1986. History and Genre. *New Literary History* 17, no. 2 (Fall–Winter): 241–57.

Coleridge, Samuel Taylor. 1960. *Shakespearian Criticism.* Ed. T. Rayson. Vol. 2. New York: E. P. Dutton.

Cornford, F. M. 1914. *The Origin of Attic Comedy.* London: E. Arnold.

Cranny-Francis, Anne. 1990. *Feminist Fiction: Feminist Uses of Generic Fiction.* Oxford: Polity Press.

Cymborska-Leboda, Maria. 1987. O koncepcji tragedii dionyzyjskiej. "Tantal" Wiachesława Iwanowa. *Slavia* 56, no. 2: 153–61.

———. 1989. Czechow a estetyka symbolizmu. In *Antoni Czechow,* ed. René Śliwowski, 113–24. Warsaw: Wydawnictwo Uniwersytetu Warszawskiego.

Dambska, Izydora. 1975. *O konwencjach i konwencjonaliźmie.* Wrocław, Poland: Ossolineum.

Danek, Danuta. 1972. *O polemice literackiej w powieści.* Warsaw: Państwowy Instytut Wydawniczy.

Deer, Irving. 1959. Speech Association in Chekhov's *The Cherry Orchard. Educational Theatre Journal* 10: 30–34.

Demarcy, Richard. 1973. *Éléments d'une sociologie du spectacle.* Paris: Union Generale d'Editions.

Descotes, Maurice. 1964. *Le public de théâtre et son histoire.* Paris: Presses Universitaires de France.

D'Haen, Theo, Rainer Grübel, and Helmut Lethen. 1989. Introduction to *Convention and Innovation in Literature,* viii–xxii. Amsterdam and Philadelphia: John Benjamins.

Dickinson, Hugh. 1969. *Myth on the Modern Stage.* Urbana: University of Illinois Press.

Dlugosch, I. 1977. *Anton Pavlovič Čechov und das Theater des Absurden.* Munich: Wilhelm Fink Verlag.

Dolinin, A. S. 1986. Estranged: Toward a Psychology of Sologub's Work. In *The Noise of Change: Russian Literature and the Critics (1891–1917),* ed. and trans. Stanley Rabinowitz, 123–48. Ann Arbor, Mich.: Ardis.

Draper, R. P. 1980. *Tragedy: Developments in Criticism.* London: Macmillan Press.

Drews, Peter. 1983. *Die slawische Avantgarde und der Westen.* Munich: Wilhelm Fink Verlag.

Driver, Tom F. 1970. *Romantic Quest and Modern Query: A History of the Modern Theatre.* New York: Delacorte Press.

Dzhonson, I. 1983. Sologub i ego p'esy. In *O Fedore Sologube. Stat'i i zametki,* ed. Anastasiia Chebotarevskaia, 129–41. Ann Arbor, Mich.: Ardis.

Eco, Umberto. 1977. Semiotics of Theatrical Performance. *Drama Review* 21, no. 1: 107–17.

———. 1984. *The Role of the Reader: Exploration in the Semiotics of Texts.* Bloomington: Indiana University Press.

Eekman, Thomas, ed. 1989. *Critical Essays on Anton Chekhov.* Boston: G. K. Hall.

Elam, Keir. 1977. *Language in the Theater: Sub-Stance* 18/19: 139–61.

———. 1980. *The Semiotics of Theatre and Drama.* London and New York: Methuen.

Eliade, Mircea. 1967. *Myths, Dreams and Mysteries: The Encounter between Contemporary Faiths and Archaic Realities.* Trans. Philip Mairet. New York: Harper and Row.

Eng, Jan van der, Jan M. Meijer, and Herta Schmid. 1978. *On the Theory of Descriptive Poetics: Anton P. Chekhov as Story-teller and Playwright.* Lisse, Netherlands: Peter de Ridder Press.

Erlich, Victor. 1963. Chekhov and West European Drama. *Yearbook of Comparative and General Literature* 12: 56–60.

———. 1964. *The Double Image: Concept of the Poet in Slavic Literatures.* Baltimore: Johns Hopkins University Press.

Esslin, Martin. 1969. *Reflections: Essays on Modern Theatre.* New York: Doubleday.

———. 1970. *Brief Chronicles: Essays on Modern Theatre.* London: Maurice Temple Smith, Ltd.

———. 1977. *An Anatomy of Drama.* 1st American ed. New York: Hill and Wang.

———. 1980. *The Theatre of the Absurd.* 3rd ed. Middlesex and New York: Penguin Books.

———. 1985. Chekhov and the Modern Drama. In *A Chekhov Companion,* ed. Toby W. Clyman, 135–45. Westport, Conn.: Greenwood Press.

Works Cited

———. 1987. *The Field of Drama.* London: Methuen.
Evreinov, Nikolai. 1958. Vsegdashni shashni. Pamiati Fedora Sologuba. Parts 1 and 2. *Russkaia Mysl'*, 1194 (3 April): 4–5; 1196 (8 April): 4–5.
Fedorov, A. V. 1972. *Teatr A. Bloka i dramaturgiia ego vremeni.* Leningrad: Izdatel'stvo Leningradskogo Universiteta.
Fergusson, Francis. 1949. *The Idea of Theater: The Art of Drama in Changing Perspective.* Princeton, N.J.: Princeton University Press.
———. 1967. The Cherry Orchard. In *Chekhov: A Collection of Critical Essays,* ed. Robert Louis Jackson, 147–60. Englewood Cliffs, N.J.: Prentice-Hall.
Field, Andrew. 1961. The Created Legend: Sologub's Symbolic Universe. *Slavic and East European Journal* 5, no. 4 (Winter): 341–49.
Filipkowska, Hanna. 1972. Z problematyki mitu w literaturze Młodej Polski. In *Problemy literatury polskiej 1890–1939,* 221–52. Vol. 2. Wrocław, Poland: Ossolineum.
Filipowicz, Halina. 1991. *A Laboratory of Impure Forms: The Plays of Tadeusz Różewicz.* Westport, Conn.: Greenwood Press.
Finke, Michael. 1994. The Hero's Descent to the Underworld in Chekhov. *Russian Review* 53, no. 1 (January): 67–80.
Fischer-Lichte, Erika. 1992. *The Semiotics of Theater.* Trans. J. Gaines and D. L. Jones. Bloomington: Indiana University Press.
Fish, Stanley. 1980. *Is There a Text in This Class? The Authority of Interpretative Communities.* London: Harvard University Press.
Fisher, Ralph T. 1985. Chekhov's Russia: A Historian's View. In *A Chekhov Companion,* ed. Toby W. Clyman, 3–16. Westport, Conn.: Greenwood Press.
Fludas, John. 1973. Chekhovian Comedy: A Review Essay. *Genre* 6, no. 3: 333–45.
Fokkema, Douwe. 1989. The Concept of Convention in Literary Theory and Empirical Research. In *Convention and Innovation in Literature,* ed. Theo D'Haen, Rainer Grübel, and Helmut Lethen, 1–16. Amsterdam and Philadelphia: John Benjamins.
Forsyth, John. 1977. Prophets and Superman: German Ideological Influence on Aleksandr Blok's Poetry. *Forum for Modern Language Study* 13: 33–46.
Foster, John Burt. 1988. *Heirs to Dionysus. A Nietzschean Current in Literary Modernism.* Princeton, N.J.: Princeton University Press.
Frost, Edgar B. 1976. Characterization through Time in the Works of Chekhov with an Emphasis on *The Cherry Orchard.* In *Studies in Language and Literature: Proceedings of the 23rd Mountain Interstate Foreign Language Conference,* ed. C. Nelson, 169–73. Richmond: Eastern Kentucky University Press.
Frow, John. 1986. *Marxism and Literary History.* Cambridge: Harvard University Press.

Ganz, Arthur. 1980. *Realms of the Self: Variations on a Theme in Modern Drama.* New York: New York University Press.

Gasparov, Boris. 1984. Posleslovie. Struktura teksta i kul'turnyi kontekst. In *Literaturnye leitmotivy: Ocherki russkoi literatury XX veka,* 274–303. Moscow: Nauka/Izdatel'skaia firma "Vostochnaia literatura."

———. 1984. Tema sviatochnogo karnavala v poeme A. Bloka "Dvenadcat'." In *Literaturnye leitmotivy: Ocherki russkoi literatury XX veka,* 4–27. Moscow: Nauka/Izdatel'skaia firma "Vostochnaia literatura."

Gerasimov, Iu. K. 1987. Dramaturgiia simvolizma. In *Istoriia russkoi dramaturgii: Vtoraia polovina XIX—nachalo XX veka, do 1917g,* 552–605. Leningrad: Nauka.

Gerould, Daniel. 1958. *The Cherry Orchard* as a Comedy: *The Journal of General Education* 11: 109–22.

———. 1985. The Art of Symbolist Drama: A Re-Assessment. In *Doubles, Demons and Dreamers,* 7–33. New York: Performing Arts Journal Publications.

Geyer, R. F., and D. Schweitzer, eds. 1981. *Alienation: Problems of Meaning, Theory and Method.* London: Routledge.

Gibian, G., and H. W. Tjalsma, eds. 1976. *Russian Modernist Culture and the Avant-garde, 1900–1930.* Ithaca, N.Y.: Cornell University Press.

Gibson, A. Boyce. 1973. *The Religion of Dostoevski.* London: SCM Press.

Gippius, Z. N. 1972. *P'esy* // Hippius, Z. N. *Collected Dramatical Works.* Intro. Temira Pachmuss. Centrifuga Russian Reprintings and Printings, vol. 19. Munich: Wilhelm Fink Verlag.

———. 1973. *Novye ljudi/pobediteli* // Hippius, Z. N. *People of Today/The Victors.* Intro. Temira Pachmuss. Centrifuga Russian Reprintings and Printings, vol. 17. Munich: Wilhelm Fink Verlag.

Glatzer-Rosenthal, Berenice, ed. 1986. *Nietzsche in Russia.* Princeton, N.J.: Princeton University Press.

Goffman, Erving. 1974. *Frame Analysis: An Essay on the Organization of Experience.* Cambridge: Harvard University Press.

Goldman, Lucien. 1980. *Essays on Method in the Sociology of Literature.* Ed. and trans. W. Boelhauer. St. Louis: Telos Press.

Goldman, Mark, and Isadore Traschen, eds. 1968. *The Drama: Traditional and Modern.* Boston: Allyn and Bacon.

Gombrich, E. H. 1960. *Art and Illusion: A Study in the Psychology of Pictorial Representation.* Princeton, N.J.: Princeton University Press.

Goodlad, J. S. R. 1972. *A Sociology of Popular Drama.* Totowa, N.J.: Rowman and Littlefield.

Green, Martin, and John Swan. 1986. *The Triumph of Pierrot, the "Commedia Dell'Arte" and the Modern Imagination.* New York: Macmillan Publishing.

Greene, Diana. 1986. Images of Women in Fedor Sologub. *Proceedings of the Kentucky Foreign Language Conference, Slavic Section* 4, no. 3: 90–103.

Works Cited

Grigorovich, D. 1974–82. Pis'mo ot 25 marta, 1886. In Chekhov 1974–83, 4: 519.

Gromov, P. P. 1981. Poèticheskii teatr Aleksandra Bloka. In *Teatr,* by Aleksandr Blok, 5–56. Leningrad: Sovetskii Pisatel'.

Grosse, S. 1972. *Literarischer Dialog und gesprochene Sprache.* Ed. H. Eggers. Tübingen, Germany: NA.

Grotowski, Jerzy. 1968. *Towards a Poor Theatre.* New York: Simon and Schuster.

Grubber, William. 1980. *Comic Theaters.* Athens: University of Georgia Press.

———. 1994. *Missing Persons: Character and Characterization in Modern Drama.* Athens: University of Georgia Press.

Grygar, Mojmír. 1985. On a Structural Analysis of the Literary Process. In *Proceedings of the Xth Congress of the International Comparative Literature Association,* ed. Anna Balakian, 99–105. New York: Garland Publishing.

Hallman, Ralph. 1961. *Psychology of Literature: A Study of Alienation and Tragedy.* New York: Philosophical Library.

Hamburger, H. 1986. "Aktionsart" as a Textual Category. *Russian Literature* 20, no. 3: 239–65.

Hartmann, P. 1964. Text, Texte, Klassen von Texten. *Bogwus* 1/2: 15–25.

Hassan, Ihab. 1967. *The Literature of Silence: Henry Miller and Samuel Beckett.* New York: Alfred A. Knopf.

Hawthorn, Jeremy. 1994. *A Glossary of Contemporary Literary Terms.* 2nd ed. London: Edward Arnold.

Henn, Thomas R. 1966. *The Harvest of Tragedy.* New York: Barnes and Noble.

Herman, Vimala. 1991. Dramatic Dialogue and the Systematics of Turn-Taking. *Semiotica* 83, no. 1/2: 97–121.

Hess-Lutich, Ernst W. B. 1979. Drama, Silence and Semiotics. *Kodikas/Code* 1, no. 2: 105–20.

———. 1991. Towards a Semiotics of Discourse in Drama. In *Drama und Theater: (Theorie—Methode—Geschichte),* ed. Herta Schmid and Hedwig Kral, 282–303. Munich: Verlag Otto Sagner.

Hogendoorn, W. 1989. A Question on Pirandello's "Six Characters": Semiotics of the Mask. In *Festschrift für Herta Schmid,* ed. Jenny Stelleman and Jan van der Meer, 95–110. Amsterdam: Universität von Amsterdam.

Holland, Norman. 1968. *The Dynamics of Literary Response.* New York: Oxford University Press.

Holland, Peter. 1982. Chekhov and the Resistant Symbol. In *Drama and Symbolism: Themes in Drama,* ed. James Redmond, 227–42. Vol. 4. Cambridge: Cambridge University Press.

House, Clarence Louis. 1984. Fedor Sologub's Philosophy of Reality as Reflected in His Works from 1884–1912. In "Quest of a Quixotic Miracle," Ph.D diss., Georgetown University.

Howard, Jean E. 1984. *Shakespeare's Art of Orchestration.* Urbana: University of Illinois at Urbana Press.

Hristić, Jovan. 1985. Time in Chekhov: The Inexorable and the Ironic. *New Theatre Quarterly* 1: 271–82.

Hubbs, Joanna. 1982. The Goddess of Love and the Tree of Knowledge: Some Elements of Myth and Folklore in Chekhov's *The Cherry Orchard*. *South Carolina Review* 14, no. 2: 66–77.

Hübner, Friedrich. 1971. *Die Personendarstellung in der Dramen Anton P. Čechovs.* Amsterdam: Verlag Adolf M. Hakkert.

Hutnikiewicz, Artur. 1988. Czy dramat jest dziełem literackim? In *Problemy teorii dramatu,* ed. Janusz Degler, 125–31. Wrocław, Poland: Wydawnictwo Uniwersytetu Wrocławskiego.

Ingarden, Roman. 1973. *The Literary Work of Art: An Investigation on the Borderlines of Ontology, Logic, and Theory of Literature.* Trans. and intro. George G. Grabowicz. Evanston, Ill.: Northwestern University Press.

Iser, Wolfgang. 1974. *The Implied Reader: Patterns of Communication in Prose Fiction from Bunyan to Beckett.* Baltimore: Johns Hopkins University Press.

———. 1978. *The Act of Reading: A Theory of Aesthetic Response.* Baltimore: Johns Hopkins University Press.

Issacharoff, Michael. 1989. *Discourse as Performance.* Stanford, Calif.: Stanford University Press.

Ivanits, Linda J. 1989. *Russian Folk Belief.* Intro. Felix J. Oinas. Amonck: M. E. Sharpe, 75–82.

Ivanov, Viacheslav. 1971–87. *Sobranie sochinenii.* Ed. Ol'ga Deshart and Dmitrii Ivanov. Vols. 2, 3. Bruxelles: Foyer Oriental Chrétien.

Ivanov, Viacheslav, and Mikhail Gershenzon. 1921. *Perepiska iz dvukh uglov.* St. Petersburg: Alkonost'.

Jackson, Robert Louis, ed. 1967. *Chekhov: A Collection of Critical Essays.* Englewood Cliffs, N.J.: Prentice-Hall.

———. ed. 1993. *Reading Chekhov's Text.* Evanston, Ill.: Northwestern University Press.

Jakobson, Roman. 1960. Linguistics and Poetics. In *Style in Language,* ed. Tomas Sebeok, 350–77. Cambridge: Harvard University Press.

Jansen, Steen. 1991. Texte dramatique et spectacle théâtrale. In *Drama und Theater: (Theorie—Methode—Geschichte),* ed. Herta Schmid and Hedwig Kral, 217–37. Munich: Verlag Otto Sagner.

Jarvis, Ursula Liebrecht. 1961. *Theories of Illusion and Distance in the Drama: From Lessing to Brecht.* Ann Arbor, Mich.: University Microfilms.

Jauss, Hans Robert. 1973. Levels of Identification of Hero and Audience. *New Literary History* 5 (Autumn): 283–317.

———. 1978. Thesis on the Transition from the Aesthetics of Literary Works to a Theory of Aesthetic Experience. In *Interpretation of Narrative,* ed. M. Valdes and O. Miller, 137–47. Buffalo: University of Toronto Press.

Works Cited

———. 1979. The Alterity and Modernity of Medieval Literature. *New Literary History* 10, no. 2: 181–227.

———. 1982a. *Aesthetic Experience and Literary Hermeneutics.* Trans. Michael Shaw, intro. Wlad Godzich. Theory and History of Literature, vol. 3. Minneapolis: University of Minnesota Press.

———. 1982b. *Toward an Aesthetic of Reception.* Trans. Timothy Bahti, intro. Paul de Man. Theory and History of Literature, vol. 2. Minneapolis: University of Minnesota Press.

Jay, Martin. 1988. *"Fin-de-siècle" Socialism and Other Essays.* New York: Routledge.

Jones, W. Gareth. 1993. "Commedia dell'Arte": Blok and Meyerhold, 1905–1917. In *Studies in the "Commedia dell'Arte,"* ed. David J. George and Christopher J. Gossip, 185–97. Cardiff: University of Wales Press.

Kalbouss, George. 1968. *The Plays of Fedor Sologub.* Ann Arbor, Mich.: Dissertation Abstracts.

———. 1982. *The Plays of the Russian Symbolists.* East Lansing, Mich.: Russian Language Press.

Karnick, Manfred. 1988. Strindberg and the Tradition of Modernity: Structure of Drama and Experience. In *Strindberg's Dramaturgy,* ed. Göran Stockenström, 54–74. Minneapolis: University of Minnesota Press.

Kaufmann, Walter. 1969. *Tragedy and Philosophy.* Garden City, New York: Doubleday.

Kesting, Marianne. 1959. *Das epische Theater.* Berlin: W. Kohlhammer Verlag.

Kim, Ji-won. 1992. Aura and Mass Culture: Walter Benjamin's Theory of Art. *English Language and Literature* 38, no. 4: 733–50.

Kipnis, L. M. 1984. O liricheskom geroe dramaticheskoi trilogii Aleksandra Bloka. In *Russkii teatr i dramaturgiia nachala XX veka,* ed. A. Al'tshuler, 45–65. Leningrad: Leningradskii Gosudarstvennyi Institut Teatra, Muzyki i Kinematografii.

Kleberg, Lars. 1984. Vjačeslav Ivanov and the Idea of Theater. In *Theater and Literature in Russia 1900–1930,* ed. Lars Kleberg and Nils Åke Nilsson, 57–70. Stockholm: Almqvist and Wiksell.

Klinger, Helmut. 1986. "Tragedy" 1660–1737: Terminology and Genre. In *A Yearbook of Studies in English Language and Literature 1985/86,* ed. Otto Rauchbauer, 79–92. Vienna: Wilhelm Braumüller.

Knowles, Dorothy. 1934. *La réaction idéaliste au théâtre (depuis 1890).* Paris: Librairie E. Droz.

Kobernick, Mark. 1989. *Semiotics of the Drama and the Style of Eugene O'Neill.* Amsterdam and Atlanta: John Benjamins.

———. 1991. Linguistic Matrices and the Semiotics of Dramatic Texts. In *Drama und Theater: (Theorie—Methode—Geschichte),* ed. Herta Schmid and Hedwig Kral, 304–19. Munich: Verlag Otto Sagner.

Koestler, Arthur. 1964. *The Act of Creation.* New York: Macmillan.

Works Cited

Köhler, Hartmut. 1982. Symbolist Theater. In *The Symbolist Movement in the Literature of European Languages*, ed. Anna Balakian, 413–24. Budapest: Akademiai Kiodó.

Kot, Joanna. 1991. The Dramas of Tadeusz Miciński and Vjačeslav Ivanov: Two Experiments in Modern Mystery Plays. Ph.D. diss., University of Chicago.

———. 1995. Alienation as Expressed through Silence in Anton Čechov's Drama *Three Sisters: Slavica Gandensia* 22: 111–26.

Kotow, Helena. 1982. Tradycje teatru ludowo-jarmarcznego w dramacie F. Sołoguba "Wańka klucznik i paź Jean". Zeszyty Naukowe Wydziału Humanistycznego Uniwersytetu Gdańskiego. *Filologia rosyjska* 10: 31–41.

Krajewska, Anna. 1988. Milczenie w dramacie. In *Problemy teorii dramatu*, ed. Janusz Degler, 93–103. Wrocław, Poland: Wydawnictwco Uniwersytetu Wrocławskiego.

Lakshin, V. Ia., ed. 1990. *Chekhoviana. Stat'i, publikacii, èsse*. Moscow: Nauka.

Lambert, Carole. 1990. *The Empty Cross: Medieval Hopes, Modern Futility in the Theater of Maurice Maeterlinck, Paul Claudel, August Strindberg, Georg Kaiser.* New York: Garland Publishing.

Lauer, Bernhard. 1986. *Das lyrische Frühwerk von Fedor Sologub. Weltgefühl, Motivik, Sprache und Versform.* Gessen, Germany: Wilhelm Schmidt.

Leitch, Vincent B. 1992. *Cultural Criticism, Literary Theory, Poststructuralism.* New York: Columbia University Press.

Lewis, Peter. A Note on Audience Participation and "Psychical Distance." 1985. *British Journal of Aesthetics* 25, no. 3 (Summer): 273–87.

Liberman, Anatoly. 1984. Between Myth and the Wondertale. In *Myth in Literature*, ed. Andrej Kodjak, Krystyna Pomorska, and Stephan Rudy, 9–18. Columbus: Slavica.

Literaturnoe nasledstvo. 1960. Vol. 68. Moscow: Akademiia Nauk SSSR.

Liubimova, Iu. 1984. Dramaturgiia Fedora Sologuba i krizis simvolistskogo teatra. In *Russkii teatr i dramaturgiia nachala veka,* ed. A. Al'tshuler, 66–91. Leningrad: Leningradskii Gosudarstvennyi Institut Teatra, Muzyki i Kinematografii.

Lotman, Jurii. 1979. *Struktura khudozhestvennogo teksta: Semioticheskie issledovaniia po teorii iskusstva.* Moscow: Iskusstvo, 1979.

———. 1980. Semiotika sceny. *Teatr* 43: 89–99.

Love, H. W. 1984. Audience Perspective and Dramatic Character: The Dynamics of a Monologue. *AUMLA* 62: 179–91.

Lukacs, Georgy. 1950. *Studies in European Realism.* London: Hillway.

Maiakovski, Vladimir. 1955. Dva Chekhova. In *Polnoe Sobranie Sochinenii*, 294–301. Vol. 1. Moscow: Khudozhestvennaia Literatura.

Markov, Vladimir. 1968. *Russian Futurism.* Berkeley: University of California Press.

Works Cited

Matejka, L., and I. Titunik. 1976. *Semiotics of Art: Prague School Contributions*. Cambridge: Massachusetts Institute of Technology Press.

Matich, Olga. 1972. *The Religious Poetry of Zinaida Gippius*. Centrifuga Russian Reprintings and Printings, vol. 7. Munich: Wilhelm Fink.

———. 1993. Zinaida Gippius: Theory and Praxis of Love. In *Readings in Russian Modernism*, ed. Ronald Vroon and John Malmstaad, 237–50. Moscow: Nauka.

Maxwell-Mahon, W. D., ed. 1981. *Critical Theory and Literary Texts: The Application of Critical Theories or Approaches in the Understanding of Specific Literary Texts*. Pretoria: University of South Africa Press.

May, Keith M. 1990. *Nietzsche and the Spirit of Tragedy*. New York: St. Martin's Press.

McCormack, Kathryn Louise. 1982. *Images of Women in the Poetry of Zinaida Gippius*. Ann Arbor, Mich.: Dissertation Abstracts.

Meierkhol'd, Vsevolod. 1908. Teatr (K istorii i tekhnike). In *Teatr: Kniga o novom teatre*, 148ff. St. Peterburg: Shipovnik.

Meister, C., ed. 1985. *Chekhov Bibliography: Works in English by and about Anton Chekhov; American, British and Canadian Performances*. Jefferson, N.C.: McFarland.

———, ed. 1988. *Chekhov Criticism, 1880 through 1986*. Jefferson, N.C.: McFarland.

Melrose, Susan. 1994. *A Semiotics of the Dramatic Text*. New York: St. Martin's Press.

Merezhkovskii, Dmitrii. 1968. O Chekhove. *Vesy* 11. Reprint, vol. 2. Liechtenstein: Krauss.

Meyerhold, Vsevolod. 1967. Naturalist Theatre and Theatre of Mood. In *Chekhov: A Collection of Critical Essays*, ed. Robert Louis Jackson, 62–68. Englewood Cliffs, N.J.: Prentice-Hall.

———. 1978. *Meyerhold on Theatre*. Trans. and ed. Edward Braun. London: Methuen.

Mikhailov, A., and S. Lesnevskii. 1981. *V mire Bloka*. Moscow: Sovetskii Pisatel'.

Mikhailovskii, N. K. 1957. Ob otcakh i detiakh i o Chekhove. In *Literaturokriticheskie stat'i*, 594. Moscow: Khudozhestvennaia Literatura.

Miller, Christine. 1984. *The Rhetoric of "the Rhetoric of . . ." A Conceptual Analysis of Genre Theory and Criticism*. Carbondale: Southern Illinois University Press.

Minc, Z. G. 1986. V smyslovom prostranstve "Balaganchika." In *Semiotika prostranstva i prostranstvo semiotiki. Trudy po znakovym sistemam*. Vol. 19. *Uchenye Zapiski Tartuskogo Gosudarstvennogo Universiteta* 720: 44–53.

———. 1988. V "khudozhestvennom pole" "Balaganchika." In *Semiotics and the History of Culture: In Honor of Jurii Lotman*, ed. Morris Halle, Krystyna Pomorska, Elena Seneka-Pankratow, and Boris Uspenskii, 400–7.

Studies in Russian. University of California at Los Angeles Slavic Studies, vol. 17. Columbus: Slavica.

Mirsky, Dmitry. 1958. *A History of Russian Literature: Compromising a History of Russian Literature and Contemporary Russian Literature.* Rev. ed. New York: Alfred A. Knopf.

Mochulskii, Konstantin. 1948. *Aleksandr Blok.* Paris: YMCA Press.

Moyle, Natalie, K. 1986. Mermaids (*Rusalki*) and Russian Beliefs about Women. In *New Studies in Russian Language and Literature,* ed. Anna Lisa Crone and Catherine V. Chvany, 221–38. Columbus: Slavica.

Mukařovsky, Jan. 1979. *Aesthetic Function, Norm and Value as Social Facts.* Trans. M. Swino. Michigan Slavic Contributions, no. 3. Ann Arbor: University of Michigan Press.

Nakhimovsky, A. D., and A. Stone Nakhimovsky, eds. 1985. *The Semiotics of Russian Cultural History.* Intro. Boris Gasparov. Ithaca, N.Y.: Cornell University Press.

Nemirovich-Danchenko, Vladimir. 1960. Chekhov. In *A. P. Chekhov v vospominaniiakh sovremennikov,* 419–38. Moscow: Sovetskii Pisatel'.

Nielsen, E., ed. 1982. *Focus on Vienna 1900: Change and Continuity in Literature, Music, Art and Intellectual History.* Houston German Studies, vol. 4. Munich: Wilhelm Fink Verlag.

Nilsson, Nils A. 1986. *The Slavic Literatures and Modernism.* Stockholm: Almqvist and Wiksell International.

Nilsson, Nils Åke. 1960. Intonation and Rhythm in Chekhov's Plays. In *Anton Čexov 1860–1960: Some Essays,* ed. Thomas Eekman, 168–80. Leiden: E. J. Brill.

Norris, Christopher. 1993. *The Truth about Postmodernism.* Oxford: Blackwell.

Olsson, Barbara. 1986. Alienation in Storey and Chekhov: A Reassessment of *In Celebration* and *The Farm.* In *A Yearbook of Studies in English Language and Literature 1985/86,* ed. Otto Rauchbauer, 119–33. Vienna: Wilhelm Braumüller.

Orr, John. 1991. *Tragic Drama and Modern Society: Studies in the Social and Literary Theory of Drama from 1870 to the Present.* Totowa, N.J.: Barnes and Noble Books.

Orwin, Donna Tussing. 1993. *Tolstoy's Art and Thought, 1847–1880.* Princeton, N.J.: Princeton University Press.

Osiński, Zbigniew. 1977. Przekład tekstu literackiego na język teatru. In *Dramat i teatr: Konferencja teoretyczno literacka w Świętej Katarzynie,* ed. Jan Trzynadlowski, 119–56. Wrocław, Poland: Ossolineum.

Pachmuss, Temira. 1971. *Zinaida Hippius, an Intellectual Profile.* Carbondale: Southern Illinois University Press.

Pahomov, George S. 1993. Essential Perception: Čechov and Modern Art. *Russian Literature* 35, no. 2: 195–202.

Pavis, Patrice. 1982. *Languages of the Stage: Essays in the Semiology of the Theatre*. New York: Performing Arts Journal Publications.

———. 1985. *Voix et images de la scène: Pour une sémiologie de la réception: (Nouvelle édition revue et augmentée)*. Lille, France: Presses Universitaires de Lille.

———. 1988. Textual Mechanisms in *The Cherry Orchard: Assaph*, Section C. *Studies in the Theatre* 4: 1–18.

———. 1992. *Theatre at the Crossroads of Culture*. Trans. L. Kruger. London: Routledge.

Pearse, James A. 1980. Beyond the Narrational Frame: Interpretation and Metafiction. *Quarterly Journal of Speech* 66 (February): 73–84.

Pervukhina, Natalia. 1993. *Anton Chekhov: The Sense and the Nonsense*. Ottawa, Toronto, and New York: Legas.

Peterson, Ronald, E. 1993. *A History of Russian Symbolism*. Amsterdam and Philadelphia: John Benjamins.

Pfister, Manfred. 1988. *The Theory and Analysis of Drama*. Trans. J. Halliday. Cambridge: Cambridge University Press.

Pierrot, Jean. 1981. *The Decadent Imagination 1880–1900*. Trans. D. Coltman. Chicago: University of Chicago Press.

Pitcher, Harvey. 1973. *The Chekhov Play: A New Interpretation*. London: Chatto and Windus.

Polanyi, Michael. 1966. *The Tacit Dimension*. Garden City, New York: Doubleday.

Porfir'eva, A. L. 1988. Viacheslav Ivanov i nekotorye tendencii razvitiia uslovnogo teatra v 1905–1915 godakh. In *Russkii teatr i dramaturgiia 1907–1917 godov*, ed. A. Al'tshuler, 37–53. Leningrad: Leningradskii Gosudarstvennyi Institut Teatra, Muzyki i Kinematografii imeni N. K. Cherkasova.

Porter, Carolyn. 1981. *Seeing and Being*. Middletown, Conn.: Wesleyan University Press.

Przybylski, Ryszard. 1985a. Don Juan jako gaduła. "Płatonow" A. Czechowa. In *Wtajemniczenie w los. Szkice o dramatach*, 141–53. Warsaw: Państwowy Instytut Wydawniczy.

———. 1985b. Dramat teatru. "Czajka" A. Czechowa. In *Wtajemniczenie w los: Szkice o dramatach*, 154–69. Warsaw: Państwowy Instytut Wydawniczy.

———. 1985c. Grzech niemożności. "Trzy siostry" A. Czechowa. In *Wtajemniczenie w los: Szkice o dramatach*, 170–82. Warsaw: Państwowy Instytut Wydawniczy.

Raszewski, Stefan. 1988. Partytura teatralna. In *Problemy teorii dramatu*, ed. Janusz Degler, 133–62. Wrocław, Poland: Wydawnictwo Uniwersytetu Wrocławskiego.

Ratajczak, Dobrochna. 1979. *Teatr artystyczny Bolesława Leśmiana: Z problemów przełomu teatralnego w Polsce (1893–1913)*. Wrocław, Poland: Ossolineum.

———. 1985. *Przestrzeń w dramacie i dramat w przestrzeni.* Poznań, Poland: Wydawnictwo Naukowe Uniwersytetu imenia Adama Mickiewicza w Poznaniu.

———. 1988. Teatralność i sceniczność. In *Problemy teorii dramatu,* ed. Janusz Degler, 261–73. Wrocław, Poland: Wydawnictwo Uniwersytetu Wrocławskiego.

Ratajczakowa, Dobrochna. 1990. Sługa dwóch panów: dwoisty żywot dramatu. *Teksty Drugie* 5/6: 80–92.

———. 1993. *Komedia oświeconych, 1752–1795.* Warsaw: Państwowe Wydawnictwo Naukowe.

Revzina, O. G., and I. I. Revzin. 1975. A Semiotic Experiment on Stage: The Violation of the Postulate of Normal Communication as a Dramatic Device. *Semiotica* 14: 245–68.

Ritter, Naomi. 1989. *Art as Spectacle: Images of the Entertainer since Romanticism.* Columbia: University of Missouri Press.

Rodina, T. M. 1972. *A. Blok a russkii teatr nachala XX veka.* Moscow: Nauka.

———. 1977. Russkii teatr v konce XIX—nachale XXv. In *Khudozhestvennye processy v russkom i pol'skom iskusstve XIX—nachala XX veka,* ed. E. A. Borisova, A. B. Sterligov, and G. Iu. Sternin, 159–89. Moscow: Nauka.

Rokem, Freddie. 1986. *Theatrical Space in Ibsen, Chekhov and Strindberg: Public Forms of Privacy.* Ann Arbor, Mich.: UMI Research Press.

———. 1988. The Camera and the Aesthetics of Repetition: Strindberg's Use of Space and Scenography in *Miss Julie, A Dream Play, The Ghost Sonata.* In *Strindberg's Dramaturgy,* ed. Göran Stockenström, 107–28. Minneapolis: University of Minnesota Press.

Rozik, Eli. 1991. Theatrical Conventions—A Semiotic Approach. In *Drama und Theater: (Theorie—Methode—Geschichte),* ed. Herta Schmid and Hedwig Kral, 127–43. Munich: Verlag Otto Sagner.

Rudnitskii, Konstantin. 1969. *Rezhisser Meierkhol'd.* Moskva: Nauka.

Russell, R. and A. Barratt, eds. 1990. *Russian Theatre in the Age of Modernism.* New York: St. Martin's Press.

Sartre, Jean-Paul. 1948. *The Emotions: Outline of a Theory.* Trans. B. Frechtman. New York: Philosophical Library.

Scanlon, James, James Edie, and Mary-Barbara Zeldin, eds. *Russian Philosophy.* Chicago: Quadrangle Books, 1969.

Schacht, Richard. 1984. *Alienation.* Intro. Walter Kaufman. Lanham, Md.: University Press of America.

———. 1992. Hegel, Marx, Nietzsche, and the Future of Self-alienation. In *Alienation, Society and the Individual,* ed. F. Geyer and W. R. Heinz, 1–16. New Brunswick, N.J.: Transaction Publishers.

Schaffer, David Royal. 1979. The Short Stories of Zinaida Gippius: Decadent or Symbolist? M.A. thesis, University of Wisconsin–Madison.

Works Cited

Schmid, Herta. 1978. Text—und Bedeuntungsaufban in Čechovs "Tri sestry." In *On the Theory of Descriptive Poetics: Anton P. Chekhov as Storyteller and Playwright,* ed. Jan van der Eng, 179–209. Lisse, Netherlands: Peter de Ridder, 1978.

———. 1984. Chekhov's Drama and Stanislavsky's and Mejerxol'd's Theories of Theater. In *Theater and Literature in Russia 1900–1930,* ed. Lars Kleberg and Nils Åke Nilsson, 23–41. Stockholm: Almqvist and Wiksell International.

Schmid, Herta, and Aloysius van Kesteren, eds. 1984. *Semiotics of Drama and Theater.* Linguistic and Literary Studies in Eastern Europe, vol. 10. Amsterdam and Philadelphia: John Benjamins.

Schmid, W., ed. 1987. *Mythos in der slawischen Moderne.* Vienna: Wiener Slawistischer Almanach.

Schuler, Catherine. 1995. Zinaida Gippius: An Unwitting and Unwilling Feminist. In *Theatre and Feminist Aesthetics,* ed. Karen Laughlin and Catherine Schuler, 131–47. London: Associated University Presses.

Schwalbe, M. L. 1992. Alienation as the Denial of Aesthetic Experience. In *Alienation, Society and the Individual,* ed. F. Geyer and W. R. Heinz, 91–106. New Brunswick, N.J.: Transaction Publishers.

Segel, Harold. 1993. *Twentieth-Century Russian Drama from Gorky to the Present.* Rev. ed. Baltimore: Johns Hopkins University Press.

Senderovich, Savely. 1993. *The Cherry Orchard:* Čechov's Last Testament. *Russian Literature* 35, no. 2: 223–41.

Senderovich, S., and M. Sendich, eds. 1987. *Anton Chekhov Rediscovered: A Collection of New Studies with a Comprehensive Bibliography.* East Lansing, Mich.: Russian Language Journal.

Senelick, Lawrence. 1982. Chekhov and the Irresistible Symbol: A Response to Peter Holland. In *Drama and Symbolism: Themes in Drama,* ed. James Redmond, 243–51. Vol. 4. Cambridge: Cambridge University Press.

———. 1985. Chekhov on Stage. In *A Chekhov Companion,* ed. Toby W. Clyman, 209–32. Westport, Conn.: Greenwood Press.

Serpieri, Alessandro et al. 1981. Toward a Segmentation of the Dramatic Text. *Poetics Today* 2, no. 3: 163–200.

Sewall, Richard, B. 1980. *The Vision of Tragedy.* New Haven, Conn.: Yale University Press.

Shattuck, Roger. 1968. *The Banquet Years.* New York: Vintage Books.

Shcheglov, Iurii. 1988. O khudozhestvennom iazyke Chekhova. *Novyi Zhurnal* 172/173: 294–322.

Shestov, Lev. 1978. Tvorchestvo iz nichego. In *Nachala i koncy,* 1–68. Ann Arbor, Mich.: Ardis.

Silverman, Debora L. 1989. *"Art Nouveau" in "Fin-de-siècle" France: Politics, Psychology and Style.* Berkeley: University of California Press.

Sinko, Grzegorz. 1988. *Postać sceniczna i jej przemiany w teatrze XX wieku.* Wrocław, Poland: Ossolineum.

Works Cited

Skaftymov, A. 1967. Principles of Structure. In *Chekhov: A Collection of Critical Essays,* ed. Robert Louis Jackson, 69–87. Englewood Cliffs, N.J.: Prentice-Hall.

———. 1972a. K voprosu o principakh postroeniia p'es A. P. Chekhova. In *Nravstvennye iskaniia russkikh pisatelei,* 404–35. Moscow: Khudozhestvennaia Literatura.

———. 1972b. O edinstve formy i soderzhaniia v "Vishnevom sade" A. P. Chekhova. In *Nravstvennye iskaniia russkikh pisatelei,* 339–80. Moscow: Khudozhestvennaia Literatura.

Skwarczyńska, Stefania. 1988s. Dramat—literatura czy teatr. In *Problemy teorii dramatu,* ed. Janusz Degler, 187–94. Wrocław, Poland: Wydawnictwo Uniwersytetu Wrocławskiego.

———. 1988b. Zagadnienie dramatu. In *Problemy teorii dramatu,* ed. Janusz Degler, 105–23. Wrocław, Poland: Wydawnictwo Uniwersytetu Wrocławskiego.

Slater, Ann Pasternak. 1982. *Shakespeare the Director.* Brighton, Sussex, Engl., and Totowa, N.J.: Harvester Press.

Sławińska, Irena. 1988a. Główne problemy struktury dramatu. In *Problemy teorii dramatu,* ed. Janusz Degler, 21–37. Wrocław, Poland: Wydawnictwo Uniwersytetu Wrocławskiego.

———. 1988b. Odczytanie dramatu. In *Problemy teorii dramatu,* ed. Janusz Degler, 63–80. Wrocław, Poland: Wydawnictwo Uniwersytetu Wrocławskiego.

Sławińska, Irena, and Stefan Kruk, eds. 1966. *Myśl teatralna Młodej Polski.* Warsaw: Państwowy Instytut Wydawniczy.

Sławiński, Janusz. 1976. *Słownik terminów literackich.* Wrocław, Poland: Ossolineum.

Śliwowski, René. 1976. Fiodora Sołoguba wizja teatru i próby wcielenia jej w życie. *Studia Rossica* 1: 239–58.

Smith, Melissa T. 1994. Waiting in the Wings: Russian Women Playwrights in the Twentieth Century. In *Women Writers in Russian Literature,* ed. Toby W. Clyman and Diana Greene, 188–203. Westport, Conn.: Greenwood Press.

Smith, Susan Valeria Harris. 1984. *Masks in Modern Drama.* Berkeley: University of California Press.

Snyder, John. 1991. *Prospects of Power: Tragedy, Satire, the Essay, and the Theory of Genre.* Lexington: University Press of Kentucky.

Sobennikov, A. S. 1984. *Khudozhestvennyi simvol v dramaturgii A. P. Chekhova: Tipologicheskoe sopostavlenie s zapadno-evropeiskoi dramoi.* Irkutsk, Russia: Izdatel'stvo Irkutskogo Universiteta.

Sologub, Fedor. 1908. *Pobeda smerti: Tragediia v trekh deistviiakh s prologom.* St. Peterburg: Fakely.

Stanislavski, Constantin. 1956. *My Life In Art.* New York: Meridian Books.

Works Cited

Stanislavskii, Konstantin. 1960. A. P. Chekhov v Khudozhestvennom Teatre ("Vishnevyi sad"). In *A. P. Chekhov v vospominaniiakh sovremennikov*, 407–18. Moscow: Khodozhestvennaia Literatura.

Stapele, Peter van. 1989. The Segmentation of the Dramatic Text through the Analysis of Deixis. In *Festschrift fur Herta Schmid*, ed. Jenny Stelleman and Jan van der Meer. Amsterdam: Universität von Amsterdam.

Steiner, George. 1963. *The Death of Tragedy*. New York: Alfred A. Knopf.

———. 1970. *Language and Silence. Essays on Language, Literature and the Inhuman*. New York: Atheneum.

———. 1971. In *Bluebeard's Castle: Some Notes Towards the Redefinition of Culture*. New Haven, Conn.: Yale University Press.

Stelleman, Jenny. 1989. Innovative Use of "Commedia dell'Arte" Elements in A. Blok's *The Fairground Booth*. In *Convention and Innovation in Literature*, ed. Theo D'Haen, Rainer Grübel, and Helmut Lethen, 293–304. Amsterdam and Philadelphia: John Benjamins.

———. 1991. The Role of Metalanguage in Action and Discourse in Chekhov's *Ivanov* and *Three Sisters*. In *Drama und Theater: (Theorie—Methode—Geschichte)*, ed. Herta Schmid and Hedwig Kral, 587–600. Munich: Verlag Otto Sagner.

———. 1992. *Aspects of Dramatic Communication: Action, Non-action, Interaction (A. P. Čechov, A. Blok, D. Charms)*. Amsterdam and Atlanta: Rodopi.

Stephan, Viola. 1980. *Studien zum Drama des Russischen Symbolismus*. Frankfurt am Main: Peter D. Lang.

Straszkowa, Olga. 1989. Chekhov, simvolisty i novaia drama. In *Antoni Czechow*, ed. René Śliwowski, 125–37. Warsaw: Wydawnictwo Uniwersytetu Warszawskiego.

Styan, J. L. 1960. *The Elements of Drama*. London: Cambridge University Press.

———. 1968. *The Dark Comedy: The Development of Modern Comic Tragedy*. 2nd ed. Cambridge: Cambridge University Press.

———. 1971. *Chekhov in Performance*. Cambridge: Cambridge University Press.

———. 1972. Delicate Balance: Audience Ambivalence in the Comedy of Shakespeare and Chekhov. *Costerus* 7, no. 2: 159–84.

———. 1975. *Drama, Stage and Audience*. London: Cambridge University Press.

———. 1981. *Modern Drama in Theory and Practice: Realism and Naturalism*. Vol. 1. Cambridge: Cambridge University Press.

———. 1985a. Chekhov on Stage. In *A Chekhov Companion*, ed. Toby W. Clyman, 209–32. Westport, Conn.: Greenwood Press.

———. 1985b. Chekhov's Dramatic Technique. In *A Chekhov Companion*, ed. Toby W. Clyman, 107–22. Westport, Conn.: Greenwood Press.

———. 1989. *The Cherry Orchard.* In *Critical Essays on Anton Chekhov,* ed. Thomas Eekman, 192–200. Boston: G. K. Hall.

Stykowa, Maria. 1983. Wiera Komissarzewska a teatr polski. *Slavia Orientalis* 32: 65–75.

Świontek, Sławomir. 1988. O strukturalnych związkach i zależnościach tworzyw dzieła dramatycznego. In *Problemy teorii dramatu,* ed. Janusz Degler, 47–54. Wrocław, Poland: Wydawnictwo Uniwersytetu Wrocławskiego.

Sypher, Wylie. 1962. *Loss of the Self in Modern Literature.* New York: Random House.

Szondi, Peter. 1987. *Theory of the Modern Drama.* Ed. and trans. Michael Hays, intro. Jochen Schulte-Sasse. Theory and History of Literature, vol. 29. Minneapolis: University of Minnesota Press.

Taubman, Jane A. 1994. Women Poets of the Silver Age. In *Women Writers in Russian Literature,* ed. Toby W. Clyman and Diana Greene, 171–88. Westport, Conn.: Greenwood Press.

Teffi. 1905. Fedor Sologub. "Pobeda smerti." *Rech'* 2 (2 January): 5.

Tompkins, Jane P. 1980. The Reader in History: The Changing Shape of Literary Response. In *Reader-Response Criticism from Formalism to Post-Structuralism,* 201–32. Baltimore: John Hopkins University Press.

Tonnelli, Franco, and Judd Hubert. 1978. Theatricality: The Burden of the Text. *Sub-Stance* 21: 79–102.

Trojanowska, Tamara, and Krzysztof Pleśniarowicz. 1988. *Poszukiwania nowego teatru, w kręgu teorii 1887–1939.* Wrocław, Poland: Ossolineum.

Tulloch, John. 1980. *Chekhov: A Structuralist Study.* New York: Barnes and Noble Books.

Turner, C. J. G. 1994. *Time and Temporal Structure in Chekhov.* Birmingham Slavonic Monographs, no. 22. Birmingham: University of Birmingham Press.

Ubersfeld, Anne. 1977. *Lire le théâtre.* Paris: Editions Sociales.

Veltrusky, Jarmila. 1991. Composite Dramatic Character. The Conjunction of Heterogeneous Images in Some Dramatic Characters from the Middle Ages to the Seventeenth Century. In *Drama und Theater: (Theorie—Methode—Geschichte),* ed. Herta Schmid and Hedwig Kral, 267–81. Munich: Verlag Otto Sagner.

Veltrusky, Jiři. 1976. Dramatic Text as a Component of Theater. In *Semiotics of Art: Prague School Contributions,* ed. L. Matejka and I. Titunik, 94–117. Cambridge: Massachusetts Institute of Technology Press.

———. 1977. *Drama as Literature.* Lisse, Netherlands: Peter de Ridder Press.

Venclova, Tomas. 1984. On Russian Mythological Tragedy: Vjačeslav Ivanov and Marina Cvetaeva. In *Myth in Literature,* ed. Andrej Kodjak, Krystyna Pomorska, and Stephan Rudy, 89–109. Columbus: Slavica.

———. 1994. Shade and Statue: A Comparative Analysis of Fedor Sologub and Innokentii Annenskii. *Russian Review* 53, no. 1 (January): 9–21.

Works Cited

Vickery, W., ed. 1982. *Aleksandr Blok Centennial Conference*. Columbus: Slavica.
Vogel, Lucy. 1990. Illusions Unmasked in Blok's *Puppet Show: Canadian-American Slavic Studies* 24, no. 2 (Summer): 169–98.
Ward, Dana Derrick. 1987. *Dramas of Defamiliarization and Distanciation: A Comparative Study of the Selected Works of Eugene Ionesco, Tom Stoppard and Antonio Vallejon*. Ann Arbor, Mich.: Dissertation Abstracts.
Wellmer, Albrecht. 1991. *The Persistence of Modernity: Essays on Aesthetics, Ethics and Postmodernism*. Trans. D. Midgley. Cambridge: Massachusetts Institute of Technology Press.
West, James. 1970. *Russian Symbolism: A Study of Vyacheslav Ivanov and the Russian Symbolist Aesthetic*. London: Methuen.
Westphalen, Timothy C. 1992. The Ongoing Influence of V. S. Solov'ev on A. A. Blok: The Particular Case of "Belaja lilija" and "Balagančik." *Slavic and East European Journal* 36, no. 4: 435–51.
———. 1993. The Carnival Grotesque and Blok's *The Puppet Show. Slavic Review* 52, no. 1: 49–66.
Weststeijn, Willem G. 1989. "Svjataja krov'," Love, God and Death in the Work of Zinaida Gippius. In *Festschrift für Herta Schmid*, ed. Jenny Stelleman and Jan van der Meer, 111–21. Amsterdam: Universität von Amsterdam.
———. 1993. Sologub and the Poetry of the Eighties. In *Readings in Russian Modernism*, ed. Ronald Vroon and John E. Malmstaad, 365–77. Moscow: Nauka/Vostochnaia Literatura.
Williams, Raymond. 1961. *Drama from Ibsen to Eliot*. London: Chatto and Windus.
———. 1966. *Modern Tragedy*. London: Chatto and Windus.
Williams, Robert C. 1977. *Artists in Revolution: Portraits of the Russian Avant-Garde 1905–1925*. Bloomington: Indiana University Press.
Wilshire, Bruce. 1982. *Role Playing and Identity: The Limits of Theatre as Metaphor*. Bloomington: Indiana University Press.
Wilson, Edmund. 1984. *Axel's Castle: A Study in the Imaginative Literature of 1870–1930*. New York: W. W. Norton.
Woods, Leigh. 1982. Chekhov and the Evolving Symbol: Cues and Cautions for the Plays in Performance. In *Drama and Symbolism: Themes in Drama*, ed. James Redmond, 253–58. Vol. 4. Cambridge: Cambridge University Press.
Worth, Sol, and Larry Gross. 1974. Symbolic Strategies. *Journal of Communication* 24 (Autumn): 27–39.
Xolodov, G., ed. 1987. *Istoriia russkogo dramaticheskogo teatra*. Vols. 6, 7. Moscow: Iskusstvo.
Yarrison, Betsy G. 1982. The Future in an Instant. In *To Hold a Mirror to Nature. Dramatic Images and Reflections*, ed. Karelisa V. Hartigan, 137–58. Vol. 1. Washington, D.C.: University Press of America.

Works Cited

Zarovnaia, V. P. 1972. Liricheskaia drama A. Bloka "Balaganchik." *Voprosy Russkoi Sovetskoi i Zarubezhnoi Literatury* 1: 125–46.

Zlobin, Vladimir. 1980. *A Difficult Soul: Zinaida Gippius*. Ed. and intro. Simon Karlinsky. Berkeley: University of California Press.

Znosko-Borovskii, E. A. 1966. *Russkii teatr nachala XX veka*. Praga: Plamia, 1925. Reprint, Ann Arbor, Mich.: University Microfilms.

Index

Action, definition of, 30
Aesthetic reception of the plays, 129
Alienation, 131n3. *See also* Estrangement
    Chekhov, Anton, and, 26
    in *The Cherry Orchard,* 26, 47
    in *The Puppet Show,* 96, 100–1, 105
Ambuiguity, 125
    in *The Cherry Orchard,* 46, 47
    in *The Puppet Show,* 104
    in *The Triumph of Death,* 74–75, 80
Andreev, Leonid, 20
    Life of Man, The, 72
Annenkov, Iurii, on Anton Chekhov, 25–26
Annenskii, Innokentii, 128
    demonic eternal feminine image of, 52
    Laodamia, 20
    Thamyras the Cythara Player, 20
Anouilh, Jean, 93, 101
Antoine, André, Théâtre Libre, 19
Appia, Adolphe, 19
    on drama, 10
Aristophanes, 100
Audiences, 127–28

Bakhtin, Mikhail, 97, 98, 126
Bashennyi teatr, 110
Baudelaire, Charles, 109
Beardsley, Aubrey, 86
Beaumarchais, Pierre, *The Marriage of Figaro,* 4
Beckett, Samuel, 3, 88, 101
    Waiting for Godot, 3
Belyi, Andrei, 65, 110
    Puppet Show, The, reaction to by, 84
    on Viacheslav Ivanov, 110
Bentley, Eric, 11, 15, 61
Bermel, Albert, on alternating genres, 126
Blok, Aleksandr, 1, 5, 72, 73, 110, 121, 128. *See also* Puppet Show, The

    autobiographical elements in *The Puppet Show,* 101
    characters and distance of, 73
    City, The, 67
    demonic eternal feminine image of, 52
    physical devices used by, 74
    Puppet Show, The, 1, 11, 18, 22, 43, 63, 72, 83–106
    religious theater and, 83
    Rose and the Cross, The, 19, 63
    Sologub, Fedor, prologue inspired by, 74
    state of mind while writing *The Puppet Show,* 83–84
    Zarovnaia, V. P., on, 84
Bowie, David, 88
Boy George, 88
Brecht, Bertolt, 3, 15, 131n2
    on alienation, 8
    ethics and aesthetics, relationship of for, 18
    Good Woman of Setzuan, The, 17
    Mother Courage, 3
    techniques of alienation, 3
    "theater of alienation" theory, 5
Brémond, C., on action, 30, 99
Briusov, Valerii, 65, 108, 110
    on Anton Chekhov, 133n2
    Earth, The, 19, 72
    religious theater and, 83
Brooks, Peter, 88, 128
Brzozowski, Stanisław, 108
Büchner, Georg, *Woyzeck,* 4
Bulgakov, Mikhail, 93
Bullough, Edward, 6, 7

Cabarets, 20
Calderón de la Barca, Pedro, *Devotion to the Cross,* 20, 61
Cervantes, Miguel de, *Don Quixote,* 70, 72

163

Index

Characterization
  in *The Cherry Orchard*, 44–45
  in *Holy Blood*, 54
  in *The Puppet Show*, 93, 100
  in *Tantalus*, 119, 122
  in *The Triumph of Death*, 72–73, 76
Chekhov, Anton, 1, 15, 16, 19, 20–21, 105, 110, 130. *See also Cherry Orchard, The*
  alienation in writing of, 26
  Annenkov, Iurii, on, 25–26
  balance between distancing and emotive elements, 34
  Bear, The, 23
  Briusov, Valerii, on, 133n2
  characters of, 21, 40
  The Cherry Orchard, 1, 11, 17, 20, 21, 23–48
  expressives used in works of, 39
  first success of, 23
  genres of plays of, 21
  holiday approach by, 33
  Holy Blood comparison to rhythm of, 56
  influence on others, 128
  Ivanov, 23
  marketing of plays of, 129
  Mayakovsky, Vladimir, on, 26
  Notebooks, 25, 26
  Platonov, 48
  plots of, 105
  public versus private sphere in plays of, 35
  rhythm in works of, 41
  Schmid, Herta, on styles of staging plays of, 45
  Sea Gull, The, 23, 33
  Skaftymov, A., on, 24–25
  Stanislavsky, Konstantin, and, 24
  Stelleman, Jenny, on characters of, 40
  symbolism and, 6
  Three Sisters, The, 23, 33, 36, 39, 48
  Uncle Vanya, 23
  vague moralistic subtext in writing of, 18–19
  Wedding, The, 23
  writings of, 23
Cherry Orchard, The, 1, 11, 17, 20, 21, 23–48, 123, 124, 128. *See also Chekhov, Anton*
  action and, 30, 34, 43
  alienation in, 26, 47
  ambivalence of, 46, 47
  as defining approach to genre in, 47
  balance between distancing and emotive elements in, 34, 127
  broadening of horizons in, 36
  characters in, 25, 31, 34–35, 47
  continuity versus discontinuity in, 37
  critics and, 24
  discontinuity in, 34–35, 37
  distance increase in, 43–44
  emotions in, 31–32, 34, 44, 45, 48, 102, 124
  ending of, 45–46
  endurance of, 128
  as farce, 41–42, 43–44
  fourth act of, 28
  future time used in, 36–37
  genre expectations in, 41, 123, 124, 125
  Grubber, William, on, 27
  holiday approach used in, 33, 34
  humor in, 38
  incongruity in, 41, 42, 47, 123
  language
    role in, 37–40, 41, 47–48, 125
    and rhythm in, 40–41
  moods in, 31, 34
  movement in, 30–31
  opening of, 29
  parodying of characters in, 42–43, 123
  Pavis, Patrice, on symbolism of orchard in, 32–33
  plot and lack of in, 30, 34
  Puppet Show, The, comparison to, 90, 96
  reasons for distance manipulation in, 23, 28
  recurring images used in, 32
  rhythm of, 37, 40–41, 124
  shifting of distance in, 27
  stage business in, 42
  Stanislavsky, Konstantin, and, 24
  start of, 29
  subtitle of, 41
  thematic threads of, 29–30
  themes of the acts in, summary of, 28
  time frame of, 35
  Triumph of Death, The, versus, 77
  unseen characters in, 36
Chulkov, Georgii, 83, 84
Claudel, Paul, 5
  Annunciation, 63
Coleridge, Samuel Taylor, 6

Index

Comedy
　traditional, ambivalence of, 46
　versus tragedy, 2, 8–9, 14–15, 46,
　　135n53
Commedia dell'arte, 85–89
　ambiguous aspect of, 88
　dangers of, 89
　grotesque and carnivalistic nature of, 88
　improvisational aspect of, 87
　metatheatricalism in, 87–88
　in *The Puppet Show*, 83, 85, 89
　violence in, 98
Complexity of distance, 11, 12
"Context of utterance," 39
Continuity
　versus discontinuity, 34, 37
　in *Holy Blood*, 54–55
Copeau, Jacques, 19, 128
Craig, Gordon, 19
　on drama, 10
　Hamlet staging in Moscow by, 20
Crooked Mirror, 20
Cvetaeva, Marina, *Casanova's End,* 20

D'Annunzio, Gabriele, 5
　Francesca da Rimini, 63
Deburau, Charles, 86
Descotes, Maurice, on theatrical
　　audiences, 126–27
Distance
　awareness of, 6
　changing attitudes about, 3–4
　comedy versus tragedy and, 2, 8–9,
　　14–15
　complexity of, 11, 12
　description of, 2
　examples of, 12
　expectations and, 7, 12, 18
　importance of, 3
　manipulation and historical significance
　　in drama, 10
　modern changes in, 8
　practical application of, 6
　purpose of manipulating, 127
　questions arising about, 3
　relationship to genre of, 16–17, 124,
　　125–27, 135n53
　shifting of, 9
　traditional drama and, 14
　types of, 2
Dostoevski, Fedor, 50, 73

Drama
　defining, 13, 132n25
　elements of, 14
　historical significance of distance
　　manipulation in, 10
　openness versus closure and, 17–18
　reason valued by modernists, 10
　three unities in, avoidance of, 15
　traditional
　　definition, 16
　　Western, 12
　versus other literary texts, 14
Dürrenmatt, Friedrich, 88, 93, 128

Elam, Keir, 38, 39, 106
　on emotionalism, 31–32, 76
　on "perlocutionary act," 39
Emotiveness, 124, 129–30
　in *The Cherry Orchard,* 31–32, 34, 44,
　　45, 48, 102, 124
　in *Holy Blood,* 54–55, 56–57, 58, 75,
　　102
　in *The Puppet Show,* 95, 105, 106
　in *Tantalus,* 107, 110, 111, 114, 116
　in *The Triumph of Death,* 76–77, 78–79,
　　81, 107
Esslin, Martin, 11, 15
Estrangement, 3–4, 5
　Brecht, Bertolt, on, 8
　characters of Anton Chekhov and, 26
　nature of identification and, 8
Ethics, 18–19
Euripedes, 126
Evreinov, Nikolai, 5, 87
　Happy Death, 20
Expectations
　established patterns and tendencies of,
　　12
　first, 7, 18
　twentieth-century art and, 8

Fakely group, 83, 107, 108, 110
Farce, 89, 135n53
　versus tragedy, 12–13
Fellini, Federico, 88, 128
Fictionality
　accepting, 7
　becoming aware of, 6–7
Foreign works staged in Moscow, 20
Fuchs, Georg, 19, 107, 128
Fuentes, Carlos, 93

165

Index

Genre(s), 15, 125–27
  Bermel, Albert, on, 126
  Cherry Orchard, The, and, 41, 47, 123, 124, 125
  commedia dell'arte, 85–89
  definition of, 14
  distance manipulation and usage of, 17, 124, 125–26, 135n53
  expectations of, 41
  farce, 89
  medieval mystery, 81
  melodrama, 81, 135n53
  mixing of, 15–16
  plays by Anton Chekhov and, 21
  Puppet Show, The, and parody of conventions of, 92, 94, 99, 105, 123
  reason for using, 17
  relationship to distance of, 1, 16–17
  Shakespeare, William, and mixing of, 15–16
  tragedy, 81
  tragicomedy, 126
  Triumph of Death, The, and melodrama, 21, 79–80, 124
Gerasimov, Iu. K., 111
Gerould, Daniel
  on language, 37
  on traditional comedy endings, 46
Gippius, Zinaida, 1, 108. *See also Holy Blood*
  ambiguity as to emotiveness of language by, 104
  Holy Blood, 1, 11, 18, 21, 49–62, 63, 128, 129
  ideas of others borrowed by, 50
  love, definition of by, 50
  spreading religious ideas in writing, 18
  tragedy, essence of for, 61–62
Gogol, Nikolai, 135–36n54
  Inspector General, The, 100
Goldoni, Carlo, 85
Gorky, Maksim, 19, 83
Gozzi, Carlo, 85
Grass, Günter, 93
Green, Martin, 97, 98, 126
Griboedov, Aleksandr, 85
  Woe from Wit, 100
Grotesque, examples of, 93, 128
Grotowski, Jerzy, 6, 128
Grubber, William, on *The Cherry Orchard,* 27

Guarini, Giovanni, 126
Gumilev, Nikolai, *Don Juan in Egypt,* 20

Habimah Theater, 20
Hauptmann, Gerhart, 20
Hegel, Georg, World Spirit, 16
Hoffman, E. T. A., 85
Hofmannsthal, Hugo von, 5
Holidays in plays, 33, 34, 107
Holy Blood, 1, 11, 18, 21, 49–62, 123, 128–29. *See also* Gippius, Zinaida
  characters in, 54
  Christianity, treatment of in, 56, 60
  composition of, 53
  continuity in, 54–55
  distancing examples in, 49, 54, 60, 61
  emotive strategies of, 54–55, 56–57, 58, 75, 102
  eternal feminine concept of, 52
  experimentation in, 53
  fairy-tale aspect of, 50, 51, 52, 55, 61, 123, 128–29
  females, treatment of in, 49, 52
  folkloric style of, 21, 49, 51, 55
  humor used in, 55–56, 123
  language in, 55, 56–57, 81, 101, 124, 125
  narration in, 100
  never published, 128, 129
  pantheism in, 50–51
  parallelisms in, 56
  plot and story of, 49–50
  Puppet Show, The, comparison to, 101, 104
  religious devotion as seeming fanaticism in, 50
  rhythm of Anton Chekhov in comparison to, 56
  slow pace of, 61
  Tantalus, comparison to, 118
  time treatment in, 54, 58, 59, 137n11
  Triumph of Death, The, versus, 67, 68
Hugo, Victor
  Hernani, 15, 21
  lofty and moving rhetoric of, 79–80

Ibsen, Henrik, 16, 20, 35
  Pretenders, The, 63
International movement of Russian modernism, 20
Ionesco, Eugène, 3, 93, 101
Issacharoff, Michael, on comedy, 37

Index

Ivanov, Viacheslav, 1, 20, 65, 128. *See also* Tantalus
  Bashennyi teatr and, 110
  Fakely group and, 83, 110
  on myths, 109–10, 111
  neomystery element in writing of, 128
  Neoplatonic vision of existence of, 109
  Nietzsche, Friedrich, versus, 108, 111
  religious tendencies of, 108–9
  religious theater and, 83
  spiritual experience in writing of, 18
  Tantalus, 1, 11, 18, 22, 66, 107–22

Jakobson, Roman, model of communication, 39, 69
Jarry, Alfred, 5
Johnson, Samuel, 6
Jonson, I., on *The Triumph of Death*, 73

Kalbouss, George, 74, 78
Kant, Immanuel, 6
Kasprowicz, Jan, 108
Khlebnikov, Velimir, 110, 124, 128
Kleist, Heinrich von, *The Prince of Homburg*, 126
Komissarzhevskaia, Vera, Studio Theater, 84, 107–8
Krasiński, Zygmunt, *Un-Divine Comedy*, 4, 15
Kruchenykh, Aleksei, 124
Kuz'min, Mixail
  Alexis Man of God, 19
  Venetian Madcaps, The, 19

Laforgue, Jules, 86, 94, 95
Language, 125
  balance in, 125
  in *The Cherry Orchard*, 37–41, 47–48
  definition of, 135n35
  of drama, 14
  emotiveness in, 125
  Gerould, Daniel, on, 37
  in *Holy Blood*, 55, 56–57, 81, 101, 125
  in *The Puppet Show*, 92, 97, 101, 105–6, 125
  stylistic use of, 1, 13
  in *Tantalus*, 107, 114–16, 118, 119–21, 122, 125
  in *The Triumph of Death*, 63, 68–70, 71–72, 74, 76, 78, 79, 81–82, 107, 125
  usage, 13

Lermontov, Mikhail, 85
Lesmian, Bolesław, 129
Lessing, Gotthold, 6
  Mirra von Barnhelm, 4
Loneliness. *See* Estrangement
Lope de Vega, 100, 126
Lorca, Federico García, 62

Madonna, 88
Maeterlinck, Maurice, 5, 20, 30, 51, 61, 92, 110
  approach to holiday, 33
  characters of, 34
  Pelleas and Melisande, 63
Mallarmé, Stéphane, 108, 121
Marlowe, Christopher
  lofty and moving rhetoric of, 79–80
  Tamburlaine, 79
Márquez, Gabriel García, 93
Mayakovsky, Vladimir, 93
  on Anton Chekhov, 26
Medieval neomysteries, 19, 81
Meierhold, Vsevolod, 19, 63, 87, 107, 128
  Blok, Aleksandr, influence on, 128
  comparisons between Fedor Sologub and, 63–64, 65, 72, 73, 74
  on drama, 10
  Fakely group and, 83, 110
  on the grotesque, 88
  Ivanov, Viacheslav, and, 108, 110
  on "plasticity," 87
  Puppet Show, The, staging by, 83, 84, 85, 90, 93
  religious theater and, 83
  Sologub, Fedor, and, 21
  staging of Anton Chekhov by, 45
  symmetry used by, 72
Melodrama, 81, 135n53
  Triumph of Death, The, as, 21, 79–80, 124
Merezhkovskii, Dmitrii, 49, 108
  Return to Nature, 21
Miciński, Tadeusz, 5, 108, 121
Mickiewicz, Adam
  Forefathers' Eve, Part III, 4, 27, 101
  Messianism, 16
Minskii, Nikolai, *The Sun*, 21
Modernism as turning point, 5–6
Molière, 100, 127
Monty Python, 88
Moscow Art Theater, 19, 20
  Sea Gull, The, at, 23

167

Index

Mrozek, Sławomir, 128
Musset, Alfred de, *Lorenzaccio*, 4, 15
Mystical anarchism, 83
Myths and use of, 109, 111

Narration
  in *Holy Blood*, 100
  in *The Puppet Show*, 99–100, 103
  in *Tantalus*, 117
  in *The Triumph of Death*, 75
Nemirovich-Danchenko, Vladimir, Moscow Art Theater, 19
Neoclassic plays, 19–20
Neoplatonism, 111
  Triumph of Death, The, and, 67, 68
Nietzsche, Friedrich, 9, 22, 50, 65, 87
  as influence for *Tantalus*, 107, 111
Norwid, Cypriot Kamil, 4

O'Neill, Eugene, 128
Open plays, 17–18

Pavis, Patrice, on *The Cherry Orchard*, 32–33
Petrushevskaia, Liudmila, 93
Pierrot, figure of, 86, 87
  in *The Puppet Show*, 89, 90, 91, 92, 93, 94–96, 97, 98, 99, 101, 102, 103, 104, 105
Pinter, Harold, 128
Pirandello, Luigi, *Six Characters in Search of an Author*, 94
Plato, 50
Porfir'eva, V. I., on symmetry, 113
Przybyszewski, Stanisław, 20
Puppet Show, The, 1, 11, 18, 22, 43, 63, 72, 83–106, 123. *See also* Blok, Aleksandr
  action of, 99–100
  alienation in, 96, 100–1, 105
  ambiguity in, 104
  autobiographical elements in, 101
  Belyi, Andrei, reaction to, 84
  caricature in, 91
  carnivalization of, 97, 98, 99, 106
  characterization in, 93, 100
  Cherry Orchard, The, comparison to, 90, 96
  Chulkov, Georgii, on, 84
  commedia dell'arte used in, 83, 85, 89, 90, 92, 93, 94, 95, 98, 105, 106, 123, 124

  complexity of, 100
  crowning-discrowning ritual in, 98
  decadence in, 98
  emotionalism in, 95, 105, 106
  flamboyance of, 98–99
  grotesque quality of, 88, 91–93, 94, 106, 128
  Holy Blood comparisons to, 101, 104
  language usage in, 92, 97, 101, 105–6, 124, 125
  love triangle in, 96, 100
  masks in, 93–94, 96, 100, 105, 106
  Meierhold, Vsevolod
    on grotesqueness of, 88
    staging of, 83, 84, 85, 90, 93
  metatheatricalism of, 89, 90–91, 94, 104–5, 106
  narration in, 99–100, 103
  parody
    of genre conventions in, 92, 94, 99, 105, 123
    of Neoplatonic idealism in, 97
  Pierrot in, 89, 90, 91, 92, 93, 94–96, 97, 98, 99, 101, 102, 103, 104, 105
    versus Hamlet in, 95
  poetry usage in, 104
  prologue of *The Triumph of Death* and, 74
  referential treatment in, 101–2
  Rudnitskii, Konstantin, on staging of, 85
  stage sets of, 90
  stylization in, 97
  themes in, 100–1, 105
  violence in, 98, 106
  Westphalen, Timothy C., on, 91
  writing of, 83
  Zarovnaia, V. P., on, 84, 95
Pushkin, Aleksandr, 85
  Little Tragedies, 27

Racine, Jean, 16
Recipient, definition of, 11
Reinhardt, Max, 19
Religious theater, 83
Remizov, Aleksei, 51, 108, 128, 129
  demonic eternal feminine image of, 52
  Devil Play, The, 19
  Prince of Iscariot, 66
  Tragedy of Judas, The, 66
Rhythm, 137n10
  in *The Cherry Orchard*, 37, 40–41, 124
  in works of Anton Chekhov, 41

Index

"Romantic escapist" current, 20
Romanticism, 4
Rudnitskii, Konstantin, on *The Puppet Show*, 85

Scenic space, 13
Schiller, Friedrich, 4, 6
   Don Carlos, 101
   Maria Stuart, 4
Schlegel, August, 4, 6
Schlegel, Friedrich, 4, 6
Schmid, Herta, on styles of staging of Chekhov's plays, 45
Schulz, Bruno, 93
Serpieri, Alessandro, 38, 39
Shakespeare, William, 3, 46, 81–82, 89, 100, 104, 126
   distance manipulation of, 127
   feeling for audiences by, 127
   King Lear, 126
   lofty and moving rhetoric of, 79–80
   mixing of genres, 15–16
   Much Ado about Nothing, 3
   Richard III versus *The Triumph of Death*, 79, 80
   three unities in drama, 15
   Troilus and Cressida, 46
   Twelfth Night, 46
Shaw, George Bernard, 19
Shelley, Percy Bysshe, *Cenci*, 21, 63
Shvarc, Evgenii, 129
Skaftymov, A., on Anton Chekhov, 24–25
Słowacki, Juliusz
   Kordian, 101
   Salomea's Silver Dream, 4
Sologub, Fedor, 1, 63–82. *See also Triumph of Death, The*
   on audience for his work, 65
   demonic eternal feminine image of, 52
   on director's role, 65
   foregrounding by, 64
   Gift of the Wise Bees, The, 66
   Meierhold, Vsevolod, and, 21, 63–64, 65, 72
   mystery play creation by, 65
   neomystery element in writing of, 128
   social commentary in writing of, 67
   Theater of a Single Will, 65, 66
   Triumph of Death, The, 1, 11, 21
   Vanka the Steward and the Page Jehan, 63, 66, 137n1

Solov'ev, Vladimir, 50
   Blok, Aleksandr, and, 84
   White Lily, 84
Sophocles, 16
Stanislavsky, Konstantin, 19, 32, 87
   Chekhov, Anton, and, 24
   Cherry Orchard, The, production by, 41, 44, 45
   Moscow Art Theater of, 19
Stelleman, Jenny, on Chekhov's characters, 40
Stoppard, Tom, *Jumpers*, 17
Strindberg, August, 5
   Dream Play, A, 35
Structure, study of, 12–13
Styan, J. L., on "dark comedies," 46
Symmetry
   in *Tantalus*, 112–13, 116
   in *The Triumph of Death*, 72, 76
Synge, John, 5
Szondi, Peter, *Theory of the Modern Drama*, 9

Tantalus, 1, 11, 18, 22, 66, 107–22, 123. *See also* Ivanov, Viacheslav
   action lacking between characters in, 116, 122
   carnival/holiday aspect of, 107
   characters in, 119, 122
   classical Greek drama and myth, combination of in, 114, 124
   emotiveness of, 107, 110, 111, 114, 116
   Gerasimov, Iu. K., on, 111
   Holy Blood comparison to, 118
   journey toward self-realization in, 112
   lack of intimate setting for, 117
   language usage in, 107, 114–16, 118, 119–21, 122, 124, 125
   man as integral part of nature in, 113–14
   myth treated in, 111, 112–13
   narration in, 117, 123
   Nietzsche, Friedrich, as influence for, 107
   Porfir'eva, V. I., on symmetry of, 113
   religious aspect of, 22, 117, 122
   rhythm of, 114–15
   ritualization of, 116–18, 122, 124
   silence used in, 121
   static nature of, 116, 122
   story line of, 110–11
   symmetry of, 112–13, 116

Index

Triumph of Death, The, comparison to, 119
vertical spatial construction in, 113, 116–17
"Theater of alienation" theory, 5
Theater of the Absurd, 34
Théâtre de Funambules, 86, 87
Tieck, Ludwick, 86, 90
Tolstoy, Lev, and "superfluous detail," 36, 64
Tower Theater, 20
Tragedy, 81
    versus comedy, 2, 8–9, 14–15, 46, 135n53
    versus farce, 12–13
Triumph of Death, The, 1, 11, 21, 22, 63–82, 123, 129. *See also* Sologub, Fedor
    ambiguity in, 74–75, 80
    characterization in, 72–73, 76
    Cherry Orchard, The, versus, 77, 78
    compositional elements employed in distancing fashion in, 75
    crowds used in, 76
    deception in, 77–78, 80
    emotiveness in, 76–77, 78–79, 81, 107
    expressives used in, 77
    Holy Blood versus, 67, 68
    Jonson, I., on characters in, 73
    Kalbouss, George, on Al'gista in, 78, 138n14
    language
        versus physical devices used in, 74
        style of, 63, 68–70, 71–72, 76, 78, 79, 81–82, 107, 123, 125
    lighting of, 79
    melodrama of, 21, 79–80, 124
    mystery play aspect of, 65, 66, 71, 81, 128
    neomedieval aspect of, 63, 66, 81, 123
    Neoplatonic world of, 67, 68
    neoromantic aspect of, 21, 63, 66
    plot of, 66–67, 74, 76

prologue of, 66, 74
referential usage in, 69–70
religion and, 65
repetition in, 77, 79
rhetoric of, 79–80
rhythm of, 77, 79, 137n10
Richard III versus, 79, 80
social commentary aspect of, 67–68
songs in, 75
stage directions of, 71–72
symbolism in, 70–71
symmetry usage in, 72, 76
Tantalus comparison to, 119
tragedy and, 80
voice-over narration in, 75

Verlaine, Paul, 86
Vigny, Alfred de, 4
    Chatterton, 101

Wagner, Richard, 10, 109
Wandering Dog, 20
Waugh, Evelyn, 99
Wedekind, Franz, 5, 15, 19
    on drama, 10
Westphalen, Timothy C., on *The Puppet Show,* 91
Wilde, Oscar, 108
Williams, Tennessee, 128
    Glass Menagerie, The, 3
Witkiewicz, Stanisław Ignacy, 93
Wyspiański, Stanisław, 5, 15, 19, 108
    Bolesław the Brave, 63
    on drama, 10

Yeats, William Butler, 5, 19, 108, 129
    King's Threshold, The, 63

Zapolska, Gabriela, 19
Zarovnaia, V. P., on *The Puppet Show,* 84, 95
Znanie group, 83